New Hampshire Patriot and State Gazette

1835

Deaths, Marriages and Miscellaneous

Compiled by
Elaine Morrison Fitch

HERITAGE BOOKS
2007

HERITAGE BOOKS
AN IMPRINT OF HERITAGE BOOKS, INC.

Books, CDs, and more—Worldwide

For our listing of thousands of titles see our website
at
www.HeritageBooks.com

Published 2007 by
HERITAGE BOOKS, INC.
Publishing Division
65 East Main Street
Westminster, Maryland 21157-5026

Copyright © 2007 Elaine Morrison Fitch

Other books by the author:

Independent Chronicle and Boston Patriot *1839: News Summary and Marine Disasters, Marriages and Deaths*

New Hampshire Patriot and State Gazette *1824*

Newspaper Abstracts from the Philadelphia Repository, 1803

Portland Advertiser and Gazette of Maine*: Marriages, Deaths and News, from November 1838-May 1839*

The *1848* Boston Cultivator*: Marriages, Deaths and Miscellaneous Readings*

The Boston Recorder and Telegraph, *1825*

The Portland [Maine] Transcript, *1869-1870, News and Summary, Marriages and Deaths*

All rights reserved. No part of this book may be reproduced or transmitted in any form or by any means, electronic or mechanical, including photocopying, recording or by any information storage and retrieval system without written permission from the author, except for the inclusion of brief quotations in a review.

International Standard Book Number: 978-0-7884-3846-8

Dedicated to Dick, faithfully

FOREWORD

While New Hampshire was ninth of the original thirteen states, it was the first state to adopt its own constitution. It has also been the birthplace of some important people of the 1800s. They include Franklin Pierce, Daniel Webster, Soloman P. Chase and Horace Greely. These people made a difference, but the people written about in the *New Hampshire Patriot and State Gazette* were also important. Patriots, farmers, ministers or ordinary people; whether they were noted for their good or evil, they are all part of the history of New Hampshire.

People elsewhere in the United States and overseas are also recorded here; and no matter what they did, their stories show that we are still all alike in many ways.

NEW HAMPSHIRE PATRIOT & STATE GAZETTE
Concord, Monday, March 2, 1835

MELANCHOLY OCCURANCE. On Tuesday the 20th ult., Mrs. Martha Hunt, wife of Mr. Hiram K. Hunt, of Sharon in this county, his sister Harriet Gilbert, daughter of T. Gilbert, Esq., of Westhaven, Vt., aged 18 years, and an infant daughter and niece of Mrs. Hunt, also of the name Gilbert, ten years of age, left Sharon in a sleigh on a journey to Westhaven. They were accompanied by a brother-in-law of Mrs. Hunt, Edward W. Andrews, Esq. of Cornwall, (late a resident of this village,) and a young man from Vermont. They arrived at Williamstown, Mass., on Wednesday evening, as the snow was nearly all gone, they left their sleigh and took a wagon. About two miles north of Williams College the road enters Pownall in Vermont, and runs on the northeast bank of the Hoosic River, which at that time was very deep and rapid—having been much swollen by the recent rains. As they were passing this place, by the breaking of some part of the wagon, they were all precipitated down a precipice of 15 feet into the river and though by the greatest exertion Mr. Andrews and the driver were able to rescue Mrs. Hunt and the little girl, Miss Gilbert and the infant were drowned. The body of Miss Gilbert was taken from the water in a short time about 80 rods below where she fell in, but resuscitation was found impossible. The body of the child had not been found by the last advices. *Litchfield Enquirer.*

Loss of the packet ship Sovereign. The Sovereign, Capt. Griswold, from London for New York, left England, Jan. 8, and made the land off Long Island on Monday last, at 4 o'clock on Tuesday morning during a storm of sleet, the ship went head on the Jersey shore at Squam beach, 30 miles below Sandy Hook; she was not discovered by the inhabitants on shore until Wednesday morning, soon after she struck the mast were cut away. During Tuesday and Wednesday, the crew and passengers got onshore, except one passenger, who putting some money in his pocket, attempted to swim, but perished in the breakers. A messenger with the news arrived in the city yesterday by the Philadelphia Railroad Line; he left Squam on Wednesday evening, at which time the ship lay on the outer beach, 100 yards from the shore, bilged and apparently "hogged" and full of water to the top of the tide. She will be an entire wreck, but if the weather should continue mild, a large portion of the goods will be saved. The Sovereign cleared with a full cargo of wines, brandy, dry goods, &c. worth probably from two to three hundred thousand dollars, besides from one to two hundred thousand dollars in gold. The freight list is longer than any ship of this line has brought out for some months—the loss will be heavy upon the underwriters in Wall Street and in London. A steamboat was dispatched last night by the insurance companies with supplies.

The Senate of New York, on Thursday last, passed a bill to prohibit the circulation of bank notes of a less denomination that $5, by a vote of 25 to 2.

$200,000 Borrowed! In the Massachusetts House of Representatives on Thursday last, a "resolve authorizing the Treasurer to borrow a sum of money not exceeding $200,000 to meet the expenses of the Commonwealth for the ensuing year, passed to a second reading. This is *federal economy*, a touch of which we had in this state in 1828, when Jacob B. Moore got THREE THOUSAND DOLLARS of the people's money for printing.

Melancholy Accident. Death of Lieutenant W. S. Chandler, of the U. S. Army. On the 26th ult., Lieutenant Walter S. Chandler, an estimable and intelligent officer of the United States Army, left Mobile in a small boat, with a sergeant and four soldiers for Fort Morgan, where he was stationed. The boat was capsized in a gale, about two miles below the Choctaw Point light house, and all on board perished except one soldier who clung to the bottom of the boat, and was taken off the following morning by Capt. Prior, of the steamboat Watchman, from New Orleans. The name of the soldier saved is Clarke. Those in the boat were Sergeant Grant, and soldiers Wise, Finn and Stevens. Clarke states that Lieut. Chandler, as each man relaxed his hold was swept off the from the boat by the current, swam immediately to his relief, and with encouraging words and actions, endeavored to sustain him. As Lieutenant Chandler was a tall and athletic young man, and an expert swimmer, it is more than probable that he would have escaped with his life had not his strength been exhausted by these humane efforts. It is also said by Clarke that Lieut. Chandler, who was the last to sink, a few moments before he descended in the struggle of death told Clarke to exert every nerve to preserve his own life—that he himself could not endure it much longer, but if they must *die* they would *die* like *men.* These were his last words, and soon after they were uttered his lips were forever sealed. Lieutenant Chandler was a native of the District of Columbia and graduated at West Point in 1830.

Murder. An atrocious murder, (says the Augusta Constitutionalist, of the 11th inst.) was committed at a place called Florenceville, in Augusta, on Monday evening last, with a large knife, on a man named Richardson, from Vermont. An inquest was held over the body yesterday, and from evidence adduced to the jury they came to the conclusion that he had been murdered by a man by the name of John Grey, from Lincoln County, Georgia, who has fled from the state, but officers are in pursuit of him—he was traced as far as Hamburg, and is supposed to have fled to South Carolina. On the body of the deceased was found several counterfeit 25 and 12 ½ pieces well executed. Charleston *Cour.Marvin*

Marvin Marcy, Jr., was yesterday brought before the Supreme Court, at East Cambridge, and sentenced to three days solitary confinement, and imprisonment at hard labor for life in the state prison. The trial of Pond and others, indicted as participators in the destruction of the Convent, was continued to April next, at Concord. A motion to admit H. Buck, state's evidence, to bail, was rejected by the court, and he was remanded to prison, to await the final termination of the trials.

We learn from Mr. Briggs the following: Yesterday afternoon about three o'clock, Marcy was discovered insensible on the floor of his cell. Dr. Hooker was immediately called in. He was in the same state at 4 o'clock—the cause is not yet known. He has frequently been heard to say that he never would be carried to the State Prison. Dr. Hooker states that there is no appearance of poison; it is supposed he had eaten ground glass. In the midst of the examination the Sheriff called to convey him to Charlestown. He of course was not removed. *Boston Post.*

Extracts from the Life and Treason of Benedict Arnold Told by Jared Sparks
THE MURDER OF MISS M'CREA.

The murder of Jane M'Crea has been a theme which eloquence and sensibility have alike contributed to dignify, and which has kindled in many a breast the emotions of a responsive sympathy. General Gate's description in his letter to Burgoyne, although more ornate than forcible, and abounding more in bad taste than simplicity or pathos, was suited to the feelings of the moment and produced a lively impression in every part of America; and the glowing language of Burke, in one of his most celebrated speeches in the British Parliament made the story of Jane M'Crea familiar to the European world.

This young lady was the daughter of a clergyman who died in New Jersey before the Revolution. Upon her father's death she sought a home in the house of her brother, a respectable gentleman residing on the western bank of Hudson's River, about four miles below Fort Edward. Here she formed an intimacy with a young man named David Jones, to whom it was understood, she was engaged to be married. When the war broke out, Jones took the side of the Royalist, went to Canada, received a commission and was a captain or lieutenant among the Provincials in Burgoyne's army.

Fort Edward was situated on the eastern margin of the Hudson's River within a few yards of the water, and surrounded by a plain of considerable extent, which was cleared of wood and cultivated. On the road leading to the north and near the foot of the hill about one third of a mile from the fort stood a house occupied by Mrs. M'Neil, a widow lady and an acquaintance of Miss M'Crea, with whom she was staying as a visitor at the time the American Army was in the neighborhood. The side of the hill was covered with a growth of bushes, and on its top, a quarter of a mile from the house, stood a large pine tree, near the root of which gushed out a perennial spring of water. A guard of one hundred men had been left at the fort, and a picket under Lieutenant Van Vechten was stationed in the woods on the hill a, little beyond the pine tree.

Early one morning this picket guard was attacked by a party of Indians rushing through the woods from different points at the same moment and rending the air with hideous yells. Lieutenant Van Vechten and five others were killed and scalped, and four were wounded. Samuel Standish, one of the guards whose post was the pine tree, discharged his musket at the first Indian he saw and ran down the hill towards the fort; but he had no sooner reached the plain, than three Indians who pursued him cut off his retreat, darted out of the bushed, fired and wounded him in the foot. One of them sprang upon him, threw him to the ground, pinioned his arms, and then pushed him violently forward up the hill. He naturally made as much haste as he could, and in a short time they came to the spring where several Indians were assembled.

Here Standish was left to himself at a little distance from the spring and the pine tree, expecting every moment to share the fate of his comrades whose scalps were conspicuously displayed. A few minutes only had elapsed, when he saw a small party of the Indians ascending the hill, and with them Mrs. M'′Neil and Miss M'Cea on foot. He knew them both having often been at Mrs. M'Neil's house. The party had hardly joined the other Indians, when he perceived much agitation among them, high words and violent gestures, till at length they engaged in a furious quarrel, and beat one another with their muskets. In the midst of this fray, one of the chiefs apparently in a paroxysm of rage, shot Miss M'Crea in the breast. She instantly fell and expired. Her hair was long and flowing. The same chief grasped it in his hand, seized his knife and took off the scalp in such a manner as to include nearly the whole of the hair; then springing from the ground, he tossed it in the face of a young warrior, who stood near him watching the operation, brandished it in the air, and uttered a yell of savage exultation. When this was done the quarrel ceased; and, as the fort had already been alarmed, the Indians hurried away as quickly as possible to General Fraser's encampment on the road to Fort Anne, taking with them Mrs. M'Neil and Samuel Standish. The bodies of the slain were found by a party that went in pursuit and were carried across the river. They had been stripped of their clothing and the body of Miss M'Crea was wounded in nine places, either by a scalping knife or a tomahawk. A messenger was dispatched to convey the afflicting intelligence to her brother, who arrived soon afterwards, took charge of his sister's remains, and had them interred on the east side of the river about three miles below the fort.

History has preserved no facts by which we can at this day ascertain the reason why Miss M'Crea should remain as she did in so exposed and unprotected a situation. She had been reminded of her danger by the people at the fort. Traditions relates, however, and with seeming truth, that through some medium of communication she had promised her lover, probably by his advice, to remain in this place, until the approach of the British troops should afford her an opportunity to join him in company with her hostess and friend. It is said that when they saw the Indians coming to the house, they were at first frightened and attempted to escape; but, as the Indians made signs of pacific intention, and one of them held up a letter intimating that it was to be opened, their fears were calmed and the letter was read. It was from Jones, and contained a request that they would put themselves under the charge of the Indians, whom he had sent for the purpose, and who would guard them in safety to the British camp. Unfortunately two separate parties of Indians, or at least two chiefs acting independently of each other, had united in this enterprise, combining with it an attack of the picket guard. It is incredible that Jones should have known this part of the arrangement, or he would have foreseen the danger it threatened. When the prize was at their hands, the two chiefs quarreled about the mode of dividing the reward they were to receive; in the case of captives, one of them in a wild fit of passion killed the victim and secured the scalp. Nor is it the least shocking feature of the transaction, that the savage seemed not aware of the nature of his mission. Uninformed as to the motive of his employer for obtaining the person of the lady, or not comprehending it, he regarded her in the light of a prisoner, and supposed the scalp would be an acceptable trophy.

Let it be imagined what were the feelings of the anxious lover, waiting with joyful anticipation the arrival of his intended bride, when this appalling proof of her death was presented to him. The innocent had suffered by the hand of cruelty and violence, which he had unconsciously armed; his most fondly cherished hopes were blasted, and a sting was planted in his soul, which time and forgetfulness never could eradicate. His spirit was scathed and his heart broken. He lived but a few years, a prey to his sad recollections, and sunk into the grave under the burden of his grief.

The remembrance of this melancholy tale is still cherished with a lively sympathy by the people who dwell near the scene of its principal incidents. The inhabitants of the village of Fort Edward have lately removed the remains of Miss M'Crea for the obscure resting place, and deposited them in the public burial ground. The ceremony was solemn and impressive. A procession of young men and maidens followed the relics and wept in silence when the earth was again closed over them, thus exhibiting an honorable proof of sensibility and of respect for the dead. The little fountain still pours out its clear water near the brow of the hill and the venerable pine is yet standing in its ancient majesty, broken at the top and shorn of its branches by the winds and storms of half a century, but revered as marking the spot where youth and innocence were sacrificed in the tragical death of Jane M'Crea.

NOTICE

All persons are hereby cautioned against purchasing a note of hand signed by the subscribers for $750 payable to SAMUEL SARGENT, Jr., or order on or before the first day of April next, with interest after; said note was dated on or about the 1st day of January 1835. Said note was obtained without any compensation and we are determined not to pay the same unless the said Sargent fulfills an agreement by which the note was obtained.

William T. Sargent
G. L. Sargent

Canterbury, Feb. 24th, 1835.

NOTICE

Is hereby given that I have this day given my son WILLIAM HILL, his time and I shall hereafter claim none of his earnings nor pay any debts which he may contract after this date.   EDWARD HILL

Witness–Francis Dollaff
Bartlett, Feb. 23, 1834

GUARDIAN NOTICE

The subscriber has been appointed by the Hon. Judge of Probate for the county of Merrimack, guardian over the person and estate of EBENEZER BATCHELDER III, of Canterbury, in said county, an intemperate person, and has taken upon him that trust, by giving bond according to law. He will adjust all claims in favor or against his ward accordingly.

       MOSES STEVENS, Jr., Guardian
Feb. 18, 1835

NOTICE

WHEREAS my wife SALLY CLUFF hath left my bed and board without cause and taken with her my infant child; this is to forbid all persons harboring or trusting her or either of them, as I shall pay no debts of her contracting after this date as I have provided suitable provision and accommodation for her at my house in Salem, N. H.

         EZEKIEL CLUFF
Salem, N. H., Feb. 17, 1835

To the Judge of Probate for the County of Merrimack in the State of New Hampshire.

Respectfully shews MARY HAINES, of Canterbury, in the county of Merrimack, that she is guardian of Martha P. Haines, Elizabeth W. Haines, and Abigail P. Haines, minor children of Stephen Haines, late of Canterbury, deceased, by the appointment of the Judge of Probate for the said county of Merrimack that her said wards are seized of a certain tract of land situated in Northfield, in said county and bounded as follows, viz. north, by land of Mary Haines and Smith Sanborn, east by a range road leading from Canterbury to Northfield, south by land formerly owned by Samuel Ames, and west by land formerly owned by Isaac Foss and land of Josiah Haines; containing about one hundred acres, and known by the name of the Nudd farm; and that it is necessary for the support of her said wards, and will be conducive to their interest to have the premises sold; wherefore she prays that she may be licensed and authorized to sell the same at public auction, according to the statute in such case made and provided.

        MARY HAINES, Guardian
Feb. 24, 1835

$25 REWARD

ON the 4th day of February instant, a person by name SAMUEL MINARD, hired of the subscriber a horse to go to Deerfield, South Road, and nothing since has been heard of him or the horse.

Minard is about 30 years old, dark complexion, about 5 feet 8 inches high, a little lame. He wore away a black broadcloth coat and light pantaloons, brown surtout with bright buttons and seal skin cap. The horse is five years old, red color, dark mane and tail. The above reward will be given to who ever will secure and return said horse and thief, or one half of said sum for either.

MARK JENKINS

Deerfield, Feb.16, 1835

GUARDIAN SALE

BY virtue of license from the Judge of Probate for the county of Rockingham, will be sold in public auction on Monday the 23rd day of March next at the late dwelling house of Henry Morrison, deceased, at 10 o'clock, A. M., the homestead farm of said deceased, containing 100 acres of good land suitably divided into mowing, tillage, pasturing and wood land, being well watered and well fenced. The buildings consisting of a house, two barns and sheds, a shop, wood house, corn house and hog house, are in good repair and pleasantly situated.

Said farm lies in Deerfield, on the main road leading through the north part of the town from Portsmouth to Concord, and on the stage road from Lowell to Pittsfield.

ALSO, at 2 o'clock, P. M., of said day, will be sold all the stock that belongs to said farm, together with all the farming tools, &c.

Terms Liberal. For further particulars inquire of John O. Folsom or Samuel Whittier, Deerfield.

ISAAC WHITTIER, Jr.
Guardian of Isaac Henry Morrison

Deerfield, Feb. 17, 1835

MARRIAGES

In this town on the 24th ult., Mr. Joseph Carpenter to Miss Betsey Eastman, both of this town.

In New Chester, Feb. 21., by Rev. Mr. Knight, Mr. Franklin Moseley, merchant of New Chester to Miss Lydia R. Hoyt of Boston, Mass.

In Plymouth, by Joseph Kimball, Esq., Mr. Kimball Corliss to Miss Jane Currier.

In Jaffrey, 18th inst., by Rev. R. Bartlett of Hopkinton, Mr. Hiram Spofford of Reading, Vt., to Miss Paulina Cutter of Jaffrey.

At Lamprey River, Mr. Thomas W. Langley to Miss Charity H. Allard.

In Ossipee, Mr. Benjamin T. Hyde to Miss Lucinda Davis.

In Tamworth by Rev. Mr. Newell, Mr. Nehemiah Stanley, Jr., to Miss Elizabeth D. Folsom, daughter of Levi Folsom, Esq.

DEATHS

In New Boston, Feb. 7, of small pox, Widow Hannah Giddings, aged 90. On the same day her son Mr. Joseph Giddings.

In Sandwich, Feb. 3, Widow Patience Mooney, 86.

In Lowell, Mass., Miss Belinda Young, formerly of this town.

In Strafford, Mr. Samuel Berry, aged 75—also Mr. Jeremiah Foss, aged 83 years and 8 months.

In Charlestown, William Gordon, Esq., Attorney at Law, and a member of the Legislature, 52.

In Portsmouth, Olive Ann, daughter of Mr. Charles D. Carter. Benning Dennett, aged about 10. Elizabeth, daughter of Capt. Robert Lefavor, aged 4 years.

In Roxbury, Capt. Samuel Wadsworth, aged 50. He was thrown from a young horse while riding him to water, and in his fall upon the frozen ground fractured his skull, which put an end to his existence.

In Lowell, Mr. Charles H. S. Ward, Junior Publisher of the Journal and Bulletin, aged 23.

In Hillsborough, Feb. 22., Elizabeth consort of the late John Dutton, Esq., in the 85th year of her age. Printers in Mass., and Vt., are &c.

At Canton, China, July 13, 1834, Mr. William T. Moses, of Portsmouth, aged 24.

In Hopkinton, Feb. 3, 1835, Mr. William Clough aged 58. Death occasioned by the fall of a tree. Printers in New York, are &c.

In Henniker, Feb 2., Mr. Joshua Whitney, aged 80. Printers in Mass., and Vt., are &c.

In Alton, N. H., Feb. 13., Henry March, a Revolutionary pensioner.

In Boston, Oct. 24th, 1834, Amos Place, son of Joshua Place of Alton, N. H., aged 22 years. Printers in New York and Maine, are &c.

In Gilmanton, Feb 21, 1835, of consumption, Mr. Joseph Young III, aged 43.

NEW HAMPSHIRE PATRIOT & STATE GAZETTE
Concord, Monday, March 9, 1835

From the N. H. Patriot

Caution to Mothers. On Monday last, Feb. 16., a very distressing circumstance occurred in the family of Joseph Tuxbury, Jr., of Newton. The father was absent from home; and the mother went out a few rods to one of the neighbors, leaving three small children in the house. The oldest, whose name was Lualla, was nine years old. While she was sitting near the fire, with her back towards it, her clothes accidentally caught fire behind, and burned to a considerable degree before she discovered it. On perceiving that her clothes were burning she became alarmed, and screamed for help. Her brother, five years old, ran for their mother, who upon coming to the house, found the room filled with smoke, the girl lying on the floor, with all her clothes entirely consumed, except her stocking and shoes, a small fragment of her under garment about her shoulders. The whole surface of her body, except her feet and top part of her head was literally burned to an entire crispness. Medical aid was applied, but to no purpose. The child retained her reason to the last, and was able to give the particulars of her clothes taking fire as above described. She survived about ten hours. It is hoped that the numerous instances of this kind, which so frequently occur, will be improved by all mothers, as a precaution never to leave their children exposed to a similar accident. B. F. CARTER

Newton, Feb. 21st, 1835

From the Little Rock (Arks.) Gazette

Fatal Rencounter. By gentlemen from the west we learn, that a sudden rencounter took place at Fort Smith, on the night of the 17 instant, between Mr. William S. Cowan, and Mr. Washington Coffee, in which the former was killed and the latter supposed to be mortally wounded.

Mr. Cowan was shot through the body, and lived only about two hours. His ball entered Mr. Coffee's breast just above the right nipple and is supposed to have lodged near the left shoulder. The latter gentleman has a family residing at Fort Smith. The former was a single man, and his father, we believe, resides in Washington County.

This is one of the evil consequences of the pernicious and too prevalent practice of unnecessarily carrying deadly weapons. Here were two bosom friends—their intimacy of long standing, and even continued almost up to the fatal moment when their hands were raised against each other's lives. Some (perhaps trifling,) dispute arose between them in a large company, which produced angry words—insulting and threatening language followed—pistols were drawn—and, before the by-standers had time to interfere, the parties fired—when one was almost instantly hurried into eternity, and his wretched *friend* so severely wounded as probably to be destined, after dragging out a few days of intense agony and remorse, to follow him to a premature grave.

Extract of a letter, dated Frankfort, Ky., Feb. 10, 1835. On Sunday last, John U. Waring met S. Q. Richardson, at the head of the stairway of the Mansion House, in presence of several persons, and shot him with two balls, which entered the body just above and a little to the right of his navel. Richardson fell, and suffered much until twenty minutes past 8 o'clock last night, when he expired. Waring is in custody.

We regret to learn that Andrew Dunlap, Esq., of Boston, U. S. Attorney, has been seriously indisposed for some weeks, and that his physician thinks a change of climate necessary for his restoration.

Life in New Orleans. We learn from letters received and papers of the 5th inst., from New Orleans, that on the 3rd inst., when the House of Representatives of the state of Louisiana was about being called to order, the Speaker, Mr. Labranche, on entering the hall was attacked by John R. Grymes, Esq., with a cane. Mr. Labranche, to defend himself, drew a small pocket pistol, which he discharged, at Grymes, but without effect. Grymes thereupon drew from his bosom a horse pistol, which he leveled at Mr. Labranche and fired—the pistol proved to be loaded with ball and buckshot. The ball passed between two members, grazing the forehead of Mr. Lavergue, a member, and lodged in the wall of the hall. Two of the buckshot took effect, and were lodge in the arm and hand of Mr. Labranche. The cause of the affray is not stated; the Legislature had passed resolutions to inquire into the affair.

Another Affray. On the 4th inst., Mr. Daussatt made an attack with a cane upon Mr. Samuel Knox in Camp Street. Knox took the cane from his assailant and beat him with it, and while doing so Daussatt drew a pistol from his pocket which he fired at Knox, the ball of which lodged in his neck. Daussatt was immediately arrested.

Hundred of persons assembled Feb. 4th to witness the trial of Grymes by the House of Representatives. The lobby was so crowded that many persons had to go away.

After the necessary preliminary proceeding the Speaker asked Mr. Grymes if he was ready for trial, when the latter offered a protest against the proceedings of the House in his case, denying its right to try him, and contending that the constitution of the state vested that power exclusively in the judiciary.

Mr. Lewis offered a resolution declaring that the House *had* a right to try him—at the same time adducing arguments in support of his resolution. The resolution, after debate was carried.

The Speaker put the question to the prisoner, whether or not he had assailed, beat and shot at Mr. A. Labranche on Monday morning in the hall of the House, at 11 o'clock, being the usual hour for the chair to call the House to order.

Mr. Grymes answered that he did assault Mr. Labranche, but not at the time stated, nor with an intent to insult or act contemptuously toward the House and that he did not shoot at Mr. Labranche, nor show any weapons until Mr. Labranche fired at him.

A committee for the examination was appointed and on motion Mr. Grymes was released on his pledge to appear before the House whenever notified so to do.

There is at this time a great scarcity of seamen in Boston: $18 per month offered.

The Frigate Constitution under the command of Com. Elliott, went to sea at 12 o'clock yesterday, with a fair wind bound for New York. She was towed down the harbor by the steamboat Bangor. At 2 P. M., she discharged her pilot, after having fired a salute in passing down the harbor.

FIRE. The dwelling house of D. C. Churchill, Esq., of Lyme was consumed by fire on the 28th ult. Loss about $800; 400 dollars insured in the N. H. Mutual.

Commodore Hull has been presented with a beautiful vase from a block taken from the timbers of the U. S. frigate Constitution. It was carved by Mr. Ives an ingenious artist of Boston. On one side of the vase is represented the chase of the Constitution by the British squadron on the other, her rencontre with the Guerriere. On the circle of the vase are heads of six principal naval officers. *Nat. Intel.*

Disgraceful—Tarring and Feathering of a Female. A correspondent at Jamesville writes us as follows. "A most disgraceful circumstance recently occurred at Orville, Onondaga Country. About twenty persons assembled at the house of Mrs. Tyler, (whose husband is in the state prison) between 8 and 9 o'clock in the evening, broke open the door, entered her bedroom, gagged and took her off about a mile and a half to a barn, stripped her, and then tarred and feathered her all over. She was found in this state in the barn, on the following morning, and assisted to return to her dwelling.

It is said the cause of such disgraceful proceedings was the fact that Mrs. Tyler's fame was considered doubtful in the neighborhood. Most of the offenders are bound over in $1500 each to appear and answer."

INFANTICIDE

ON the morning of the 25th inst., the body of a full grown male infant was found dropped at the end of a bridge on one of the public roads in this village, bound up in some cotton cloth, under circumstances leaving no doubt how it come to its end. From the investigation made, it is manifest that the child must have been brought from a distance from the village and thus wantonly and inhumanly exposed. A reward of FIFTY DOLLARS will be paid to any person who will give information that will lead to the exposure and conviction of the guilty party, or parties in this infamous transaction.

The verdict of the coroner's jury upon the inquest was that he came to his death feloniously by strangulation, by means of the cloth and bandages bound about him, by some person or persons unknown.

The investigation has been such that no suspicion rests upon any one in the village or town, and no doubt is entertained that the body was brought from some other place.

BRACKETT L. NORRIS } Selectmen
WILLIAM KNOWLTON } of
THOMAS SWETT } Pittsfield

Pittsfield, Feb. 27, 1835.

NOTICE

IS hereby given that I give to my son SAMUEL B. CASWELL his time from this date; he is authorized to trade and act for himself, and I shall demand none of his wages nor pay any of his debts after this date.

ABRAHAM CASWELL

Grafton, Feb. 2, 1835

EXECUTOR'S NOTICE

The subscribers hereby give notice that they have been appointed executors of the last will and testament of PETER HERSEY, late of Sandbornton, in the county of Strafford, deceased, and have taken upon themselves that trust by giving bond as the law directs. They therefore request all persons indebted to said estate to make immediate payment and those having demands against the same exhibit them for settlement.

      SAMUEL HERSEY
      WINTHROP DEARBORN
Sandbornton, March 2, 1835

AUCTION

TO be sold by order of Court on Tuesday the 24th day of March next at the late dwelling house of Isreal Peaslee, Esq., deceased, at ten of the clock, A. M., the homestead farm of said deceased, containing about 300 acres of the first rate land, suitably divided into mowing, pasturing, tillage and wood land, and is well situated for two farms, or one as well best accommodate purchasers. Said farm is in the immediate vicinity of a meeting and schoolhouse, grist, saw and clothing mill, &c. Sale absolute.

ALSO, on the same day at 3 of the clock, P. M., about 150 acres of wood and pasture land, with some pine timber, thereon, and subject to a life estate of widow Abigail Peaslee, and is about one hundred rods west of said homestead farm. Also, on Wednesday, 25th day of March, next, at one of the clock, P. M., all the right of which said Isreal Peaslee died, seized in and unto about six acres of land with buildings thereon, situated near the old mill village and called the Waldo farm.

Conditions liberal and known at the sales.

      MOSES PEASLEE, Adm'r.
Weare, Feb. 9, 1835

MARRIAGES

In Gilmanton by Elder Richardson, Joseph Clifford to Judith Gilman, both of Gilmanton.

In North Hampton, by Rev. Mr. French, Mr. Joseph Fullonton of Raymond, to Miss Abigail D. Robinson.

In Rye by Rev. Mr. Smith, Mr. Obed Rand of Roxbury, Mass., to Miss Anna Y. Jenness.

At Great Falls, Mr. Nathaniel D. Wetmore to Miss Lydia McIntire.

In Milton, by Isreal Nute, Esq., Mr. Isaac Cook of Somersworth, to Miss Elizabeth Peavey of Milton.

In Tuftonborough by Elder William Blaisdell, Mr. Dearborn Copp to Miss Elizabeth G. Burley.

In Ossipee by Elder John Walker, Mr. Ithiel W. Bryant, of Effingham to Miss Hannah Smith of Ossipee.

In Walpole by Rev. Jacob Burnham, Mr. William Barron, of Westminster, Vt., to Miss Eliza Carpenter of the former place.

DEATHS

In Londonderry, Jan. 9., suddenly Mr. James Plath, a Revolutionary soldier, 79. Printers in Ms. and N. Y., are &c.

In Candia, Feb. 7., Elizabeth, daughter of Jesse and Elizabeth Bean, aged 14 years and 6 months. Printers in Vt. are &c.

In Chester, on the 27th ult., Mr. Joseph Carr, *an honest man,* aged 92.

In Portsmouth, Miss Sarah W. Lefavour, aged 18; second daughter of Capt. Robert Lefavour—the fourth child of the bereaved parent has been called to part with, in addition to the loss of his partner in life, in the short space of five months.

In Somersworth, Mrs. Dorcas, wife of Mr. Tristram Horne, aged 67.

In Barrington, 17th ult., Mr. Jonathan Woodman, aged 68.

In Dover, of throat distemper, George, youngest son of Ephraim and Maria Thayer, aged about 18 months. John Leavett aged 5 years, 8 months and 12 days, son of Thomas and Nancy Read.

In Raymond, Feb. 20., of lung fever, Peter H. eldest son of Elder Peter and Betsey Philbrick, aged 18 years. An amiable disposition mingled with constant cheerfulness, together with habits of temperance, industry and economy had gained him the esteem of all who knew him. We could not have selected a youth of more promise and who bid fairer to become a man of worth and respectability. But alas! the bud of our fond hopes had scarcely began to blossom, ere it was blasted by the chilling hand of death.

"Tis God that lifts our comforts high,
Or sinks them in the grave,
He gives, and blessed be his name
He takes but what he gave."

No one could have gone out from us in whose life the happiness of friends was more intimately connected, no one could be more lamented; with the tears of his bereaved relatives is mingled the sympathizing sorrow of a large number of acquaintances.

"Yes, he was dear to all who knew his worth,
Each breast for him the pensive sigh doth give,
Though now united to his kindred earth,
Fresh in their memories will his virtues live."

Printers in Me. and Illinois are, &c.

In Meredith, Feb. 10th, Mr. Moses Merrill aged 81 years and 20 months, a Revolutionary pensioner.

In Kingston, N. H., Feb. 27, 1835, widow Joanna Severance, aged 93 years, 1 month and 12 days. Printer in N. H., are, &c.

In Boscawen, Feb. 17, Miss Eliza Little, aged 47.

NEW HAMPSHIRE PATRIOT & STATE GAZETTE
Concord, Monday, March 16, 1835

Simon Gutmann. A young Polish officer of lancers of this name, a fine looking youth of about 25 years of age, called upon us yesterday, and recounted to us his story, which is one of extreme distress and so blended with romantic and affecting circumstances to make it of painful interest. He was born of respectable parents, and losing his father very young, entered the military school at Warsaw, from which he enlisted with his patriotic comrades in the army, and fought during the bloody conflicts of the late revolution in Poland against the Russian myrmidons. He was a lieutenant of the 11th Lancers, and the eleven deep scars on his body prove that he must have been a youth of most noble and gallant daring. We saw these honorable scars, which he received in four pitched battles from ball, saber and bayonet, and the miracle is how he should have escaped with his life when such vital parts were perforated. From Poland he fled to Switzerland, and was there aid to General Romarino, who commanded the Polish emigrants in their unsuccessful attack on Savoy in 1833. He thence fled to Paris, and arrived in this country from Havre in November last. Since his arrival he has learned the sad news of his brother's death in Siberia, a gallant young officer, a victim to the cruelty of the Russian government. But what gives a still more melancholy aspect to the misfortunes which have pursued young Gutmann; intelligence has now reached him that the young lady to whom he was betrothed at Warsaw, Miss Amanda Karka, has during the recent visit of the autocrat, been condemned to a miserable imprisonment—transmitting to him, before her departure, a lock of her hair as a pledge of her affection which fate has perhaps, forever blighted. He would have braved, as he has done, the dangers of battle and fallen covered with wounds for freedom and his country; but to know that she on whom his last hope was fixed, and for whom he alone wished to live, had been doomed to an ignominious punishment, to die a miserable death in the hands of ruffian monsters, was more than his heroic courage could endure. His personal distress must awaken the sympathy of every generous heart, cast as he is, in the world with out a friend to help him; but we are sure that his appeal will meet with a still warmer response from the generous citizens of America, when it is known that he makes it not so much for himself, but from the chivalrous motive of procuring, perhaps some possible means of effecting the release of the young lady on whom his attachments are placed, and whose cruel destiny has naturally aroused in his bosom every energy into action, that she may survive and be free even if he perishes. *New York Star.*

Melancholy Disaster at Sea. The brig Caroline, belonging to the Greek Company, arrived at Helford, from America, after a long and more tempestuous passage than the captain (Broad) recollect having experienced during a period of 24 years. After having been about a week on his voyage, the man at the wheel cried out "a rock ahead." The captain knowing there could not be any rock, ran forward, and discovered the said appearance to be a boat. It contained six living men but in the last state of wretchedness, and one man dead lying at the bottom of the boat, whose blood they had drank, and a part of whose flesh they had fed on in the morning ! These suffers were the only survivors of a crew of 14, belonging to the brig *Elizabeth*, of Plymouth, from America to Padstow. She had experienced very severe weather: had her main mast carried away, and received so much damage in its hull as to become water logged. Six of the crew, supposing she could not sink, being timber laden, and that she would keep upright, got into the fore top, and there lashed themselves. Unfortunately one side of the vessel was so much stove as admitted an unequal pressure of the water in the hold on the opposite side, and put her on her beams ends, when these were all drowned. The boat, having no food but six or eight potatoes. They had been about nine days in the boat, driving about, suffering what no tongue can describe from hunger and particularly from thirst. The two that died could bear the pangs of thirst no longer, and in bitterness of agony drank salt water (which their comrades tried to prevent;) the consequence was, they became deranged and died! The first victim had been thrown overboard; the second yet remained in the boat, whose mangled body manifested the irresistible cravings of the hunger that his barely surviving shipmates were suffering under. They are now at Helford, under the skill and attention of Dr. Moyle, of Helston. One of them has lost the greater part of one of his feet and all of them some of their toes by cold. *Cornubuan.*

The Hon. Ruel Williams, of Augusta, Maine, has given $10,000 for the purpose of establishing an Insane Hospital in that state. About the same amount has been given by Benjamin Brown, Esq., of Vassalborough, for the same benevolent object.

MAIL ROBBERY!

The great Northern Mail made up at the distributing office in Albany, going north to Middlebury, Burlington and Montreal, was yesterday morning about 4 o'clock stolen from the boot of the mail stage somewhere between this city and the junction post office in Schaghticoke. The robbery was not discovered until the driver stopped at the above post office to deliver the mail. Mr. Abeel, the postmaster there immediately informed the postmaster of this city of the robbery and several individuals were dispatched in pursuit of the lost mail. The mailbag was found yesterday forenoon about 11 o'clock on the Oil Mill Hill, a little more than a mile above Lansingburgh and within 40 rods of the road. The chain was broken and the bag rifled of it contents—the letters and packages mostly torn to pieces. A trunk belonging to a passenger was also stolen from the stage and was found near the mailbag broken open, but none of its contents taken out.

When our paper went to press the postmaster of this city was arranging the mutilated letters in order to forward them to their places of destination, and he had not yet discovered any letters that contained money or remittances of any kind. Sixteen packages were found unbroken, which leads to the idea that the robber was disturbed before he got through pilfering the mailbag.

Troy Budget

Isabella A. Potter, the wife of the notorious *Robert Potter* of North Caroline, lately obtained a divorce from her husband, by the Legislature of the state. She has since petitioned the Country Court of Granville to alter her own name and the names of her children—and has obtained a decree to that effect. In her petition she says: "At the last session of the General Assembly, the said Robert Potter was expelled from the House of Commons, of which he was a member, and is now, as far as she can learn, a wanderer and a vagabond, with whom none but the most debased can associate. Branded as he is by the judgement of his fellow citizens, his name is to be a disgrace, and to his children will be a reproach, from which your worships can, and I hope will save them. They are as yet young in life, and have not learned to blush for a parents shame."

Fire. Early on Thursday morning last the Satinett Factory, belonging to Messrs. Smith & Rockwell, situated about one mile from this village, was discovered to be on fire but too late to be saved. It was wholly consumed, together with the dwelling house of Mr. Rockwell, and the rake factory of Mr. Wilmarth adjoining. We understand that all the machinery, about 3000 pounds of wool, 2000 yards of cloth, 200 yards satinett warp; and all the notes and accounts of Smith and Rockwell, were also destroyed. Total loss estimated at $7000. Insurance on the factory $1000.

Our citizens rallied promptly to the spot but their efforts to stay the progress of the flames ere unavailing.

N. H. Argus

A shocking accident attended with the loss of life occurred on the 28th ult, in the upper part of this county. Two teams belonging to Messrs. Henry Jordan & Co., heavily loaded with pig iron were passing on the public road leading from the Water Gap to Stroudsburg, when the driver of the first team named Gideon Cartwright, well known as a teamster throughout the county as the first of his class, having left his own team, and while engaged in conversation with the other driver, slipped and fell almost directly before the wheel, which passing partly over his head, crushed it, and instantly deprived him of life. He was aged about forty, and has left a wife and eight children to mourn his untimely death.

Eastern (Penn) Whig.

Edward Kavanagh. Our readers will rejoice with us in the annunciation of the appointment of the Hon. Edward Kavanagh, from Lincoln District in this state to the honorable station of Charge d'Affaires to Portugal. There are few, if any of our public men in Maine, who have more warm friends and fewer enemies than Mr. Kavanagh. His mind enriched by a fine education and liberalized by foreign travel, his manner of the most gentlemanly and unobtrusive kind, joined to private virtues of uncommon purity, has made him a great favorite, not only with his immediate constituents but with all the people of Maine. His character and acquisition fit him to an admirable degree for his new station. He is, in every respect, entirely equal to the place; and if the administration at Washington had sought to conciliate and gratify the democracy of Maine by the bestowal of some public honor upon one of their members, the administration could not have been more fortunate in its selection. *Portland Argus.*

Mr. Hill of the Senate and Messrs. Bean, Harper and Burns, members of Congress, arrived in town last Friday evening from Washington.

An arrival at New York brings Liverpool date to Jan. 30. Sir Robert Peel took the oath of office as first Lord of the Treasury on the 27th. The Medical School at Sheffield was destroyed on the 27th Jan. by a mob. The Bank of Gibbons and Williams, in Dublin, stopped payment on the 21st. Its debts are 3000,000 pounds, and occasioned much distress and excitement. *Courier*

NOTICE

WHEREAS, HANNAH my wife had absconded from my residence with other men and has gone to parts unknown; this is therefore to forbid all persons harboring or trusting her on my account as I shall pay no debts of her contracting after this date.

Stephen Thurston

Lebannon, March 5, 1835

NOTICE

THIS may certify that I have given my son MOSES JOHNSON his time to act and trade for himself, and I shall claim none of his earnings nor pay no debts of his contracting after this date.   JOHN JOHNSON

Witness   { Marolin Gross
          { Kneeland Stocker
Springfield, March 4, 1835.

MARRIAGES

In Grantham, March 5th by the Rev. Mr. Himes of Sheldon, Vermont, Mr. Smith N. Stevens of Springfield to Miss Maria Colby of Grantham.

In Mason Village on the 22nd ult, by Rev. Mr. Wellington, Mr. James Bowles of Charlestown, Mass., to Miss Dorcas Russell of the former place.

In Lancaster, by the Rev. Mr. Williams, Capt. Joseph C. Cady to Miss Julia Ann Lovejoy, both of Lancaster.

In Charlestown, Mr. Seth W. Lewis, formerly of Claremont, N. H., to Miss Sarah, only daughter of Col. Phinehas Stone.

DEATHS

In Hawke, Feb. 3., very suddenly, Mrs. Sarah Philbrick, consort of Josiah Philbrick, late of Hawke. Printers in Rochester, N. Y., are &c.

In Dunstable, Lovilia, daughter of Maj. Paul Morrill, aged 4 years and 3 months.

In Nashua Village, on Thursday, the 5th instant, George Cleaves, aged 2 years, son of J. C. Dodge.

In Hollis, on the 28th inst., Mrs. Phebe Cutter, relict of Doctor Benonia G. Cutter, aged 57.

In Cumberland, Me., 27th ult, in a fit of apoplexy, Gen. Aquillia Davis, of Warner, N. H. General Davis was traveling in the stage from the eastward, and taken out of the stage at the Center Post Office in Cumberland in a state of insensibility, about 4 o' clock, P. M., and died the next morning.

In Portsmouth, Lydia A. Bowles, aged 12 years, daughter of the late Capt. Charles Bowles.

In Rome, N. Y., Mr. William Hoyt, formerly of Portsmouth, N. H.

NEW HAMPSHIRE PATRIOT & STATE GAZETTE
Concord, Monday, March 23, 1835

For the N. H. Patriot

ACCIDENT. On Monday the second day of March instant, Mr. Nehemiah Towle of Hawke was engaged in hauling logs in Sandown, and passing over a descending piece of ground, his team suddenly wheeled to the left and caught his leg between the forward end of one of the logs on the sled and a sharp rock and crushed the bones into many fragments. He was conveyed home and after obtaining proper advice, submitted to the operation of amputation, which was performed by Dr. Perry of Exeter, assisted by Drs. Bassett and Brown. He is now apparently doing well and in all probability, will soon be restored to health and usefulness.

Hawke, March 11th, 1835

"*Old Ironsides.*" A new and handsomely carved head of President Jackson was last week placed on the mutilated figure on the frigate Constitution, and probably the gallant ship has already sailed from New York. Com. Elliot will proceed first to Harve, and thence to the Mediterranean or return to the Unites States with Mr. Livingston on board, according to circumstances.

Foundling. The night before last, as a gentleman living at No. 52 Broadway was sitting quietly alone by the fireside smoking his cigar, he heard the hall door open about 9 o'clock; someone entered, and immediately he heard the door shut. He expected an elderly female friend and thinking that it was her he called out for her to come into the parlor, there was no answer save echo to his call; and he went into the hall where, to his surprise, he saw what was apparently a basket of clean linen. "Strange," said he, "that the washerwoman, should set the basket down here—I'll see who it is for." He began to pull aside the upper clothes when to his amazement, he heard the cry and saw the form of a fine male infant, instead of his elderly female friend; and on the bosom of the baby was pinned this paragraph: "I would have come before, but wasn't ready—here I am at last: what do you think of me?" He did not think highly enough of the child to keep it, so it was sent to the Alms House.

Another! As the watchman was going his rounds through Anthony Street, on Monday night, he saw a basket lying at the door of a house which he knew to be unoccupied. He examined the basket and found it to contain a healthy male child. This was also sent to the Alms House. *Boston Traveller.*

Pretended Robbery. It was announced in the beginning of last week that John Herren had been robbed, when passing through the town of Woburn, of the sum of $24,000 which had been placed in his custody for the purpose of conveying it to this city. Facts early came to light of a nature to fix a suspicion upon Herren himself of having secreted the money. He however busied himself in pretended efforts to discover the robber, but at length being charged with the fraud, he confessed it, and on Saturday last was accompanied to Londonderry by one of the directors of the Caledonian Bank, and there produced from its place of concealment in the woods, $13,600 of the money. He pretended that the residue had been paid over to an accomplice who resided in Boston, and promised to conduct the director to the lodgings of this man. They went in the evening accompanied by an officer to a house in Washington Street, in which he said the accomplice boarded, and after inquiring at the door he reported to his attendants that the man was gone. They waited about the door for some time, expecting his return, until at length the rogue contrived to elude their observation, and to make his escape. A reward of $250 is offered for his apprehension and of $500 for the recovery of the thief and the money. We do not learn that there is any reason to suspect, the person indicated by him of any concern in the transaction. *Boston Post.*

Affecting Occurrence. In the midst of the public service on Sunday afternoon last, in the Second Dutch Church, says the Albany Journal, the congregation was thrown into great confusion by the sudden death of the wife of Mr. Anthony Van Santford, an aged member of that church. Mrs. Van Santford had attended church in her usual health, and a moment before the painful occurrence, was observed with her eye intently fixed on the preacher, who, we understand, was preaching on Heb. iii 7; and had just concluded some remarks on the uncertainty of life. The first indication that any thing had taken place was hearing what seemed a loud snore, which directed all eyes to her; her head had fallen forward. She was immediately lifted up, and it was supposed for a moment she had fainted. She breathed a few times, and then it was seen that her spirit had departed.

Most solemn admonition to all. Most affecting seal to the truths the congregation were hearing. The effect of the annunciation from the pulpit at the close of the worship—that she was dead—was indescribable. Mrs. Van Santford was one of the excellent of the earth, and had long adorned the religion she professed.

READ THIS!

I Left Ezekiel Cluff's house on Monday the 16th day of February and went to my sister's to do some washing, because the water in our well was not good—and after finishing, being too much fatigued and unwell to return home, I remained at my sister's all night. When I returned home the next morning I found, to my astonishment, that my bed and all my things were put into a room, locked up and a keeper set over them so that I could not have any control of them. Mr. Cluff was gone I knew not where

SALLY CLUFF

Salem, Feb. 20, 1835

NOTICE

The subscriber having relinquished his business to Hiram K. Merrill, request all persons indebted to him by note or account to make payment without delay.

The Market House will be continued at the old stand by Mr. Merrill, where customers may be supplied as usual with all the articles of provision and produce to be found in the best provided market house.

C. C. HODGDON

March 23, 1835

NOTICE

THIS may certify that I have given to my son EDMUND R. WALLIS his time to act and trade for himself; I shall claim none of his earnings nor pay any debts of his contracting after this date. WILLIAM WALLIS

Witness { Moses Sanborn
{ Samuel Colby
New Hampton, March 19, 1835

NOTICE

ALL persons are forbid harboring or trusting the following persons, paupers on the town of Alexanderia, as the subscriber had made provision for the same: John Folsom and his wife Phebe Folsom, Lucy Folsom, Charles Bumford, Ransom Corlis, Abigail Simonds and Drucells Banfield. CYRUS ROWELL

Alexandria, March 16, 1835

MARRIAGES

In this town on Tuesday last, by Rev. Mr. Bouton, Capt. Charles Chase, of Hopkinton to Miss Mary Evans, of this town.

In Canterbury, Mr. Jeremiah Cochran, of Northfield, to Miss Phebe S. Morrill of Canterbury.

In Wheeling, Va., 26th ult., by the Rev. Henry R. Weed, Major Benjamin Franklin Kelly, formerly of New

Hampton, N. H., to Miss Isabel, daughter of Mr. John Gorshorn.

In Solon, Ohio, Mr. Samuel Gerrish, formerly of Boscawen to Miss Betsey Clough formerly of Canterbury.

In Wilmot, Mr. Emery Baily, Fishersfield, to Miss Susan Clough, of Wilmot.

In Fisherfield, Mr. Isaiah Bailey to Miss Lydia Purinton.

In Bradford, Mr. Smith Morgan of Bridgewater, to Miss Rachel Bagley of Bradford. Mr. Freeman Brockaway of Fisherfield, to Miss Hannah Brown of Bradford. Mr. Huggins to Miss Sarah Smith.

DEATHS

In Amesbury, Mass., Feb. 28th, Mrs. Sarah Colby aged about 77. Printers in New York and Ohio are requested &c.

In Northfield, March 14th, William Whitcher, Esq., aged 76. Printers in Maine and Vt. are &c.

In Pembroke the 4th inst., Widow Mehitable Hutchinson, in the 90th year of her age, by a shock of palsy. Printer in Mass. and N. Y. are &c.

In Hillsborough, Feb. 14., of influenza, Isaac, son of William and Betsey Hartwell, aged 1 years, being their 5th child that has died of the same disease.

"The once loved form, now cold and dead,
Each mournful thought employs;
And nature weeps her comforts fled,
And withered all her joys."

In South Hampton, on the 8th inst., after a lingering illness, Mrs. Nancy Brown, aged 53 years, consort of Mr. Nathan Brown. The deceased sustained an unexceptional character—as all cheerfully admit who shared the pleasure of her acquaintance—as a wife she was faithful—as a mother tenderly affectionate—as a friend and neighbor, kind and obliging. Her funeral obsequies were attended by a large concourse of sympathizing friends who knew and appreciated her many virtues. A funeral discourse was delivered by the Rev. Thomas F. Fing, from 2nd Cor. iv. 17. May this solemn dispensation of Divine Providence, be sanctified to all her surviving relatives and friends, and may they be firmly persuaded with the great apostle to the gentiles, that *"our light afflictions which are but for a moment, shall work out for us a far more exceeding and eternal weight of glory."*

In Salisbury, Feb. 28., after a long and distressing illness of more than two years, Mr. Charles Townsend, son of John Townsend, Esq., aged 23 years; a young man universally respected and beloved by all who knew him.

In Durham, John Henry Young, aged 19.

At Matanzas on the 11th of January last, Mr. Ethan Locke, aged 24, adopted son of Hall J. Locke, Esq., of Kittery, Me.

In Lowell, March 11, after a short illness Mr. Jeremiah Chase aged 34, recently from Weare, N. H.

In Epping, 5th inst., Elizabeth Emeline, daughter of Mrs. Hannah S. Shepard, aged 8 months and 19 days.

"So fades the lovely blooming flower."

Mrs. Shepard has been bereft of a husband and two children, within a few months. May she continue to trust in Him who is the widow's God and friend and be entirely submissive to his will in all things.

In Raymond 20th ult, of lung fever, Peter H., eldest son of Elder Peter and Betsey Philbrick, aged 18.

In Harrisburg, Pa., on the 13th inst., Mr. Abel B. Head, printer, a native of Pembroke, N. H.

In Dunbarton, Mr. Samuel Sargent, after a long illness of about 7 years, aged about 48.

At Hartland, Vt., on the 16th inst. Doctor Rufus Wheeler, Plainfield, N. H., aged 74. He was a Revolutionary soldier—he lived and died universally respected, and has left a numerous family and circle of fiends to mourn his loss. Printers in Vt., Mass., and N. Y., are &c.

NEW HAMPSHIRE PATRIOT & STATE GAZETTE
Concord, Monday, March 30, 1835

The Keene papers announce the death of General SAMUEL DINSMOOR. He died after an illness of a few days of lung fever, at the age of sixty-nine years. His grandfather, a native of Scotland, came to this country more than one hundred years ago with the first Scotch Irish settlers of Londonderry, and pitched in that part of the settlement now known as Windham, in the county of Rockingham. General Dinsmoor was the fifth child of a family of six sons and four daughters, nine of whom lived to the age of adults. His eldest brother, Deacon Robert Dinsmoor, whose rustic muse in the style and mother tongue of Robert Burns, has often charmed others more learned than himself, still lives on the paternal farm at Windham.

Governor Dinsmoor graduated at Dartmouth College in 1789, and settled in the practice of law at Keene about the year 1792. In the honorable pursuit of his profession, although never distinguished as an advocate, he was more successful than most men of the profession. Assiduous in every undertaking, faithful to the interest of his clients, just to their adversaries, generous to every son and daughter of want, true to his friends as well in adversity as in prosperity, few men in this state has been more uniformly confided in and esteemed.

The writer of this article has been acquainted with Samuel Dinsmoor nearly thirty years. He first saw him in the State Legislature in 1808, stemming with John Langdon and other patriots of that day the torrent which was then poured out upon an administration which took its first stand against foreign insult and aggression by the panic orators and writers against the embargo and war. Afterwards he saw him in the Congress of the United States among the few members from New England who had the moral courage to vote for the declaration of war with Great Britain. From that time to the present, as well while in the shades of private life as when sustaining the various trust reposed in him by his fellow citizens, Gen. Dinsmoor has constantly pursued but one course, he has acted the part of a disinterested, concourse; consistent friend to the rights and the voice of the people. During the war, in that part of the state which had discovered a deeper and more intense hostility to the government and it acts than any other, General Dinsmoor for three successive years was collector of internal taxes—an office more odious to the opposition than almost any other; yet such was his prudence, discretion, and spirit of accommodation, that in no part of the state was the revenue collected with greater promptitude: and it is believed that in the whole course of this unpleasant duty in doing business with thousands of persons he never made a personal enemy, or himself added one to our political opponents. After this in 1821, he was one year elected Counselor for Cheshire and was the next year defeated by the perfidy of some who had borne his political name, but whom the people of this state have since repudiated as faithless to their political professions. In 1823, he was the regular democratic candidate for Governor, and was defeated by an unfortunate local division on the part of the republicans and the uniting of political opponents with the minority. Afterwards he was appointed Judge of Probate for the County of Cheshire, in which office he remained until called by the people to the office of Governor in 1831, to which place he was elected for three annual terms in succession by increased majorities, when he voluntarily retired. In every office he has filled he has been more successful than most men in satisfying his constituents. His last office he resigned for a few days before its expiration in May 1834, being unable to attend at the seat of government when the presence of the Chief Magistrate was required in the annual reorganization of the state administration, in consequence of the sickness and near dissolution of a beloved wife, whose demise has been followed by his own in the space of about twenty months. Mrs. Dinsmoor was the daughter of the late Gen. Reed, and a native of Londonderry. Gov. Dinsmoor lost his only daughter about seven years ago; she was the wife of Robert Means, Esq., of Amherst, a most amiable and accomplished lady; she died of a lingering complaint which clouded the prospects of her friends for many months. Three sons in active useful life remain to lament the absence of parents such as few others can claim—so kind and indulgent, so able to gratify every worldly wish, and yet so careful and wary of instruction as when young to lead them in the way they should go, that when old they should not depart from it.

In the future history of public men, SAMUEL DINSMOOR will be numbered in that class of our state who have "acted well their part"—with such men as the elder Bartlett, Weare, Sullivan, Langdon and Benjamin Pierce. The editor of the Exeter News letter, who as not of the same political school may be considered in not a more favorable light than that of an impartial judge, thus speak of the deceased. "Those who were the most intimately acquainted with him, were the most cordially attached to him; and all who knew him respected the honesty of his heart and the integrity of his purpose."

"The public good was his aim; and the discharge of his public duties, in such a manner was most effectualy to promote and secure it was his constant study. In his day he "did the state some service," and "his death is a public loss."

Veteran Stageman. It is just thirty years this week since the worthy Joseph Wyman commenced running his stage between the city and Medford. During the whole of this long period, he has never been prevented by illness from performing his regular advertised trips; he has never experienced an accident or lost a horse, and he has numerous friends who wish he may live thirty years more and be as much prospered. *Bost. Trav.*

Wreck of the ship Emerald. Ship Emerald, Todd, of Newburyport, 28 days from New Orleans for this port, went on shore at Rye Beach on Thursday afternoon. The Emerald had on board 1500 bales of cotton for E. F. Sise for Cocheco, Great Falls, and New Market Manufacturing Companies; she is 17 months old, belongs to Francis Todd, Esq., of Newburyport, valued at 25,000 and insured for 35,000. The ship will probably be lost as her keel is out and she in on a ledge of rocks; we understand her cargo is partly insured and said to have cost $100,000; a part or the whole of which will be saved in a damaged state. The weather through the passage has been severe. *Portsmouth Journal.*

MARRIAGES

In Springfield, Mr. Robert Coburn to Miss Ann Gay.

In Wilmot, Mr. Obadiah Brown to Miss Susan Brown.

In Hopkinton, Mr. Jonathan P. Croell to Mrs. Mary Knowlton; Mr. Charles Tuttle to Miss Hannah Ripley, all of Hopkinton.

In Gilford, Mr. Hiram Gilman to Miss Alice S. Sewell, both of Gilford.

In New Ispwich, by Rev. A. D. Jones of Wilton, Rev. Reuben Bates to Miss Sarah Elizabath Prichard, both of New Ispwich.

DEATHS

In Grantham, Feb. 22, 1835, Col. Henry Howard, aged seventy years nine months and ten days. He has ever sustained himself well as a man, as a citizen, and as a Christian. He was beloved and respected by a large circle of relations and citizens, who were deeply affected by his death. He has been for more than thirty years a respectable member of the Methodist Episcopal Church in this town, and an ornament to the cause to which we was attached. He lived and died in the service of God, at whose altar he bowed and received the sacrament of the Lord's Supper with several other aged veterans of the cross of Christ, but a few minutes before his death. He attended meeting on the day of his death in usual health and was able to take a part in singing of the songs of Zion with as much animation as usual. He left the Meeting House in good health, and said to a man who spake with him when going out of the door of the house,

"I am well." He had not proceeded far from the house before his wife, who was in the sleigh with him, saw him sally partly forward and spake to him, but received no answer. He was taken immediately and carried into a house and laid on a bed, but did not breathe after entering the house. The cause of this sudden death is unknown. Thus in a moment another of our fellows and a Christian has left the shores of mortality for the world of spirits, and no doubt for the world of glory. *Newport Spectator.*

In Lempster, on Thursday the 12th inst., Mr. Asa Way, after a confinement to his house of about 3 weeks of inflammatory fever. The loss sustained by the citizens of this town by this solemn event is beyond calculation.

In Sandbornton on the 20th, very suddenly, Sarah Elizabeth, eldest daughter of Dr. John Carr, aged 19 years—beloved in life and lamented in death by all who knew her.

January 11th, Bradstreet Moody, Esq., aged 64.

In Weare, March 12., Mr. David Favour, aged about 82. Printers in Me., and N. Y., are &c.

In Nelson, March 9th, Mr. Samuel Whiting, a Revolutionary pensioner, aged 84. Printers in N. Y., and the western states are &c.

In New London, Mr. Jeremiah Pingry, 74.

In Springfield, Mr. Trustram Hoyt, aged 54—Mrs. Martha Cross, aged 32.

In Brighton, Mass., March 21, Mary, wife of Mr. Charles Hastings, aged 40.

In Candia, on the 23rd inst., Benjamin Pillsbury, Esq., aged 54. Mr. Pillsbury was a very active businessman, a worthy citizen, a kind parent, a tender husband and an honest man. He was elected on the 10th inst., a Representative to the Legislature for the ensuing political year. His loss will be severely felt by his friends and to fellow townsmen, whose confidence he possessed to a great degree.

In Bartlett, 13th ult., of consumption, Joseph Thompson II, aged 34—after a lingering sickness (incident to the disease) which he bore with Christian fortitude, anxiously waiting the time of his dissolution, that he might depart and be with his God. The subject of this notice is the seventh of this family, which have died by this common but fatal disease. *Com.*

In Acworth, 18th inst., of a lingering illness, Miss Emily M. Barnard, aged 19, daughter of Moses and Polly Barnard. In the death of this young lady the parents mourn the loss of an amiable and beloved daughter. The brothers and sisters a kind and affectionate sister. Her betrothed, the one who was nearest his heart and affections—and in whose society he looked for his future happiness and enjoyment in this life. Her youthful associates and acquaintances deeply regret the death of her in whose company they have oft associated with the highest pleasure and whom they much respected for her amiable qualities and traits of character—but alas, she has gone to that bourn from whence no traveler returns.

In Sandbornton, on Thursday last, very suddenly, Mr. Jonathan Morrison.

In Canaan, March 14th of consumption, Mrs. Elmira Wells, wife of Peter Wells, aged 27. She has left a husband and two small children to mourn her loss. But we trust that their loss is her eternal gain.

"No sickness, or sorrow, or pain
Shall ever disquiet her now,
For death to her spirit was gain,
Since Christ was her life when below.

"Her soul has now taken its flight
To mansions of glory above,
To mingle with angels of light,
And dwell in the kingdom of love."

Printers in New York are &c.

In Andover, Mass., on the 16th inst., Mrs. Mary Bridges, widow of James Bridges, aged 78; leaving her children and friends the consoling reflection that their loss is her gain.

NEW HAMPSHIRE PATRIOT & STATE GAZETTE
Concord, Monday, April 6, 1835

POLICE—March 20. *Poisoning.* A complaint was made by an elderly gentleman of fortune residing in McDougal Street, that his niece, a child under 14 years, had robbed him of $80 which she acknowledged, and said that she had been instigated to do it by the wife of a car-man who lives in Hammersly Street, to whom she gave the money. Mr. Tomkins, police officer, immediately proceeded to the car-man's residence and found his wife and five children suffering from the effects of poison. The unfortunate woman confessed her crime, and informed him of the almost fatal consequences, which had arisen from it. On receiving the money, she determined to make merry with some of the ill-gotten property, and immediately went to a grocer's and purchased flour, as part of the ingredients of a feast. She then made part of the flour into cakes and got them baked in the oven of a woman who lodged with her family in the lower part of the house, to whom she gave some of the cakes as remuneration for her trouble. In the course of the evening the two families consisting of 12 persons, partook of the cakes and were soon after all taken violently ill. A physician was sent for, who on seeing them pronounced that they had taken poison, and on further inquiry into the matter he asked to see the remaining part of the flour, which he examined and found to be highly impregnated with arsenic. The grocer who sold the flour had purchased the arsenic to kill rats and left it on a plate in his store, and some person who saw it there, thinking it was flour threw it into a cask of flour, which was open in the store. From the cask the grocer had supplied the woman who made the cakes if it.

The second case of poisoning brought before the police was on the complaint of Mr. S. Freeman of Reed Street, who stated that on the day before he purchased a large wedding cake from a confectioner in Broadway, of which his family partook in the evening, and were soon after attacked with a most violent vomiting. A doctor was sent for and found that the family had been poisoned, and to such a degree as to endanger their lives. This raised a suspicion relative to the quality of the cake, which they had eaten of, which was frosted with sugar and eggs, and colored with some other material. The physician who was called in analyzed the material of which the color or icing was composed and found that out of every twenty grains of it, there were four grains of a most deadly poison. Although Mr. Freeman's wife and children suffered much from it, it is expected they will all recover.

N. Y. Journal of Com.

A Chase after Dentist. Some times since, two or three persons named Crawcour came to this city from England, set up as dentist, and so successfully advertised themselves into practice, that they received sums of money to an amount almost incredible. Their great merit consisted in supplying teeth of a mineral composition invented by themselves, and which according to their own showing so fully answered the purposes of enunciation and mastification; and were so admirable a substitute for natural teeth, that it mattered very little how soon the latter were lost or decayed, as the Messrs. Crawcours could supply equally good, if not better, at a minute's notice. Some persons, however, who got new teeth from them discovered soon after, that instead of being put in a better way of biting, they were themselves bit and made complaint at the police office, on which a warrant was granted to take one or all the Crawcours into custody. This occurred several days ago; but the police officers could hear nothing of the accused until yesterday morning, when a boat man came up to the police station and stated that he had just put one of the Crawcours on board the Napoleon, which was about to sail for England. Two police officers immediately went down to the river and finding that the ship had already gone off they got a boat and followed her outside the hook, but here they found all further pursuit would be useless, as the Napoleon was then some miles out at sea, with all her sails set, and a strong breeze wafting her on at such a rate that nothing but a steamboat could overtake her, and as they could not procure one they were obliged to let the dentists escape, *in spite of their teeth. N. Y. Jour. Com.*

A Comet. Lieut. Morrison, of the British Navy, has published an account of a comet, which is expected to appear between the months of May and August of the present. He says, "It will afford a degree of light equal to a full moon! that its tail will extend over forty degrees! and when the head of the comet reaches the meridian, its tail will sweep the horizon!" According to the description given of it by Mr. Morrison, the comet is the greatest "Monster," (always excepting the U. S. Bank) which the present generation will have the *pleasure* of beholding.

Hell burnt up. A postscript of the 6th, to the editors says—"You can announce, if you choose, in the Journal, that all Hell is burnt up. Last night about 10 o'clock a fire broke out here (Augusta) in a place called "Hell's Half Acre," and swept it out clean. It was amusing to hear them running in the streets and hallooing, "all Hell's afire." *Geo. Jour.*

The schooner Marian, lying at Liverpool wharf, accidentally took fire yesterday morning, about 8 o'clock from a kettle of boiling tar that had been left in the cabin. Mr. Hill, the wharfinger discovered it, and furnishing buckets from his store it was soon extinguished with trifling damage. *Ibid.*

The Louisville papers are still engaged at their cut and thrust contest. They daily give each other a dose of three or four lines in extent, according to the homeopathic principles of infinitesimal quantities, being more potent in their operation. The following is the latest:—*Noah*

"Passenger from New Orleans inform us that a report of our death has been prevalent in that city. The whole story is a mistake. It's the editor of the Advertiser that's dead—and he is only dead drunk."

From the Portland Courier of Monday
ESCAPE FROM PRISON

Yesterday morning three persons, who had been sentenced to the State Prison, made their escape from the county jail in this city. Their names are Charles Sargent, James F. Hall and William Snow. When Mr. Baily, the jailer, entered their room in the morning in company with one attendant, they seized some clubs which they had prepared from splitting up a bench or bunk, knocked down the jailer and the person with him and went out, turned the key in the door and fled.

Mr. Bailey, we understand was severely injured. The cry of murder raised by his attendant was heard by some of the neighbors, who soon came to their relief. In a short time hundreds of people were in pursuit of the criminals and continued the search during the day. One of them, Snow, was taken before noon near Saccarappa Village. The others have not yet been found, but undoubtedly will be, as the search is diligently and vigorously pursued. A hundred and fifty dollars reward has been offered for their apprehension or fifty dollars for each.

The notorious Walton who escaped from the State Prison in Charlestown last September, was yesterday taken by Mr. Richard Nickols, agent of the warden for transportation of prisoners, and Mr. Samuel Ayers, turnkey in Cambridge Street. Mr. Nickols proceeded up behind him and caught him in his arms. There were found upon him a loaded pistol, razor, powder flask and balls. He was immediately taken to the State Prison.

Mechanic's News Room

Herren Apprehended. Herren, who robbed *himself* of $24,000 belonging to the bank of Calcdonia, Danville, Vt., has been arrested. We learn that after escaping from the officer here on Sunday evening, he contrived to get possession of an old suit of clothes, in which he disguised himself as a vagrant, carrying an old bag, in which he had placed for deception, a piece of salt pork and some crust of stale brown bread. Thus habited, he commenced his journey home. When he arrived at Coventry, N. H., twenty miles from Barnet, Vt., where he resides, he engaged a man to carry him in a wagon the rest of the distance. He was carried within five miles of his residence, and there set down. When the owner of the wagon returned to Haverhill, he stopped at Angier's Tavern, and on being asked where he had been, said that he had been "giving a cast to a poor vagrant devil of an Irishman." A shrewd, guessing Vermont Yankee, who was present advanced a supposition that it might have been Herren.

There was no foundation for the belief, but doubt was excited, and that was soon followed by investigation. An express was dispatched for Barnet, and sure enough there was good Master Herren, in his own house snug in bed, sleeping, away the fatigues of his pilgrimage. On making search, the package of $10,000 was found at the foot of a steep hill near his house, together with his bag of cold pork and brown bread. While on his journey to Barnet, he endeavored by letters written from Boston to produce an impression that he was concealed in the city; and it was to this circumstance that the notice in the Transcript addressed to Jacob Casco had reference.

The bank has now recovered all the money but $150, and there remains $450 on private account to be accounted for. *Boston Trans.*

Murderer Escaped. James Cowan, confined in the jail at Pittsburg, Pa., for the murder of Mr. Young, escaped on Monday night of last week. The sheriff of the county offers a reward of 500 dollars for his apprehension.
Pennsylvanian

The Sea Serpent. Capt. Shibbles, of the brig Manhegan of Thomaston, from Boston for New Orleans, which arrived here on Saturday last, states that he saw when about nine or ten miles from Race Point Light, what he as well as the whole crew, supposed to be a sea serpent—he could distinctly see it with the naked eye

but to be certain he took his glass and saw his eyes, neck, and head, which was about as large as a barrel— the neck had something that looked like a mane upon the top of it; several times he run his head seven or eight feet above the water, and for thirty or forty minutes he swam backward and forward with great swiftness. There were two other vessels near, the crews of which were in the rigging looking at the same object. Capt. Shibbles states that he should think it was 200 to 250 feet long, and that his head, neck and tail, and his motion in the water, was exactly like those of a snake; every time he put his head out of water, he made a noise similar to that of steam escaping from the boiler of a steamboat.
Gloucester Democrat.

Recovery of Stolen Property. Soon after the sailing of Mr. Livingston, minister, to France in the summer of 1833, his dwelling house at Red Hook was broken open and property to the amount of $2000 was stolen. No tidings was heard of it till a short time since, when the goods of a young man by the name of Moore, who had found it necessary to abscond for malpractice, were taken on execution; among which were found, packed in boxes, most of the stolen property. Moore subsequently came to this city, and dashed away at Lovejoy's Hotel under the assumed name of Captain Patterson. Finding that his tricks were discovered and that the officers were in pursuit of him, he bent his way south, and reached Reading, under the name of Chauncy Ludlow, where he was arrested, and brought to this city and thence sent off to Dutchess County Prison. *N. Y. Com. Ada.*

Melancholy Accident. The Bangor Daily Whig relates a melancholy accident, which occurred in Solon in that state on Wednesday last. David Spencer, who was at work near his father's house getting out firewood, was killed, together with his parent's, in the following singular manner. The son had just felled a large beach tree, which lodged in the upper branches against another tree, while the butt of it slipped over the stump, caught his foot and pinned him to the ground. His screams for assistance brought out his parents, and the father seized a stick of wood, with which both of them labored to remove the tree, which being somewhat decayed, suddenly broke in the middle and falling, crushed all three of these unfortunate beings to death.

Never Despair. A London paper gives this account of a whole crew saved by the energy and example of the commander. In the Mangles, from China, came passenger Capt. Theaker, of the late ship Earl of Eldon, which was destroyed at sea by her cargo of cotton igniting when on her passage from Bombay. The captain's conduct affords a striking proof of what may be effected, under the most distressing privations and difficulties by self-possession. In the midst of the Indian Ocean, he safely conducted the crew and passengers, amounting in number to 45 persons, in two boats, one long boat, about 22 feet by 7 loaded to the water's edged by 35 persons, bread, water, provisions, charts, compass, &c.—the other a jolly boat, containing 10 persons, across a space of the Indian Ocean of near 1000 miles, and in 13 days carried them into port (Port Louis,) without loss of a single life, or any real extremity of suffering beyond that inseparable from their situation.

A woman named Pool, recently died at Fitchburg, at the advanced age of nearly 100 years. She had a remarkable appetite. It had been for years her invariable habit to eat a hearty meal during the night, in addition to an uncommon quantity of food consumed during the day. With this habit she could not dispense. Though fortified with a supper of no ordinary dimensions, she was invariably aroused from her slumbers by the pangs of hunger, which could be appeased only by an inordinate quantity of food of the most solid description. Her remaining sisters are afflicted with the same appetite. *Mass. paper.*

A Friend in Need, but Not a Friend Indeed. Yesterday an old gentleman named Warren, arrived in the steamboat from Philadelphia, and a fellow passenger ascertaining that Mr. Warren was a stranger in this city, generously offered to guide him to a house of refreshment. He took the old gentleman to an oyster cellar in Park Row where they ate heartily, and it is supposed the *friend* contrived to put something into the old man's soup, for immediately after his meal he was taken sick, and went out into the yard, the friend supporting him all the while, holding his head; but while one hand was thus engaged, he contrived with a knife in the other to cut the old gentleman's pocket book (containing $8000) from his pocket, and before he recovered, his friend was among the missing.
New York Transcript.

Ira St. Clair, Esq., has been appointed postmaster at Deerfield, vice Enoch Butler, Esq., resigned.

CAUTION
WHEREAS, Louisa B. Parker *my beloved wife,* has this third day of March Anno Domini 1835, left my house without any good cause, and as I have in all cases made ample provision for her support and maintenance, I therefore forbid all persons harboring or trusting her on my account from this date, as I shall pay no debts of her contracting after this date. BRADLEY PARKER
Bow, March 3, 1835

NOTICE
ALL persons are forbidden harboring or trusting Samuel McDonald and wife, paupers of the town of Nottingham, as the subscriber has made suitable provision for their support after the first day of April next.
EBENEZER BUTLER
Nottingham, March 27, 1835.

NOTICE

THIS is to forbid all persons harboring or trusting JOSEPH LOUGEE and wife and his two youngest children on account of the town of Pittsfield, or on my account, as I have contracted with said town and made ample provisions for their maintenance for the present year.   JOHN STANIELS

Pittsfield, March 30th, 1835

NOTICE

ALL persons are hereby forbid harboring or trusting MOSES MITCHELL, a town pauper on account of the town of Campton, as suitable provisions has been made for his support.

David Bartlett   }   Overseers of the poor
John Keniston   }   in Campton.

Campton, March 21, 1835.

I hereby certify that I have given to my son ASPAH MORGAN, his time from this date, and relinquish to him all his future earnings, and allow him to trade for himself, and I shall pay no debts of his contracting after this date.   JAMES MORGAN

Bow, January 1, 1835

NOTICE

THIS is to forbid all persons harboring, or trusting PETER VARNUM, a pauper of the town of Raymond, on my account or on account of the town, as I have contracted with said town for his support, for one year from March 11th, 1835, and shall pay no debts of his contracting, having made suitable provisions for the same.   FRANKLIN DUDLEY

Raymond, March 24, 1835.

CAUTION!

Ran away from the subscriber on the 31st day of March inst., John Small III, an indentured boy about 15 years old. All persons are hereby forbid harboring or trusting him on my account, as I shall pay no debts of his contracting; and all persons are cautioned against employing him, as I shall claim his wages in all cases.

BENJAMIN SMALL

New Boston, March 31, 1835

NOTICE

THE *POLLYWOG* has stated in his slandering sheet, that I gave a toast at the supper on Wednesday evening. It is false! I did not give a toast on that evening. D. S. Palmer has bawled and yelled about this town for some years; now I think he had better mind his own business and leave off clubbing apple trees on Sunday, or go and sell himself to some *soap boiler* to make soap of. I think he would be as good for that as anything. I have had nothing to do with D. S. Palmer, nor do I wish to have; but if he wants anything of me, I will let him have some new rum to preserve himself in, for people do not like to meet him in the streets, he smells so bad,—even his own party.

JOSIAH KNOWLES

March 20, 1835.

MARRIAGES

In Weare, by Jonathan Hobson, Esq., Mr. Cyrus Williard to Miss Sally George, both of Weare.

In Canaan, by Rev. Mr. Evans, Mr. Horatio Gates of Gate's Gore to Miss Sybel Hues of Lyme.

In Gilsum, by Rev. Mr. Arnold, Col. Jehiel Day to Miss Cynthia Hemenway.

In Canterbury, by Rev. W. Patrick, Mr. Nahum Blanchard to Miss Mary W. Tallant, both of Canterbury.

In Newport by Rev. J. Woods, Mr. Joseph G. Hoyt to Miss Catherine C. Parmelee, all of Newport.

DEATHS

In Lancaster, Mass., Miss Elizabeth Grafton eldest daughter of Edmund Toppan, Esq., of Hampton, N. H.

In Claremont, Mrs. Sarah B. Morrill, aged 22.

In Dover, Miss Jenett Pray, 22.

In Farmington, Mrs. Betsey, wife of Luke Furber, Esq., aged 32.

In Durham, John Henry Young, 19.

In New London, Mr. Jeremiah Pingrey, 74.

In Springfield, Mr. Tristram Hoyt, aged 51—Mrs. Martha Cross, aged 32.

In Rochester, of consumption, Mary Ann, youngest daughter of Anthony and Mary D. Pickering, aged 11 years and 7 months.

In South Hampton, N. H., March 18, Mary Ann, daughter of Benjamin and Mary , and grand-daughter of Major John Currier, aged 20.

    Thou hast gone to they rest; the lone tomb
        now doth veil thee
The place that has known thee, shall know thee no more
      But, although we're bereft of thee,
        why should we wail thee
    For God hath but called thee—thy sorrows are o'er.

In Wolfborough, March 21, of a long and lingering illness, Mr. Jonathan Chase, a Revolutionary soldier, aged 86 years. One more of the worthy soldiers, who endured the severest struggles in the glorious context for liberty, has paid the debt due to nature and gone with the sanctified to reap the reward of his labors. Dover papers are, &c.

In Brighton, Mass., March 28, of scarlet fever, John William Eustice, eldest son of John and Susan A. W. Buckman, aged 4 years. Printers in New York City are &c.

In Boston, Mass., Feb. 14, Daniel Jones, formerly of Canterbury, N. H., aged 55.

In Croydon the 1st inst., Mrs. Olive, wife of Major Abijah Powers, aged 49. By this stroke of Divine Providence a husband is bereft of an affectionate partner;

children of a tender and beloved mother; friends and neighbors of an estimable companion; and the whole circle of her acquaintance of an esteemed friend. Her sickness has been long and lingering; and the latter part such as to premise no hopes of recovery. At all times she manifested a perfect willingness to depart, and with those who have gone before into the presence of a God of love.

In Plainfield, Mr. Peter Bugbee, aged 71. He has for a number of years been a member of the Baptist Church in this town. May this afflictive providence be sanctified in the church and the surrounding relatives.

In Cornish, Feb. 26th., Deacon Harvey Demming aged 67. The subject of this notice had for many years been a member of the Baptist Church in Cornish, and had adorned his profession by an upright life.

In Claremont, Feb. 28., Mrs. Olivia, wife of Mr. Samuel Gunnison, and daughter of Mr. Reuben Smith, formerly of Goshen, aged 28. Amiable and unassuming she enjoyed the strong attachment of her friends and the respect of all who knew her; she was called suddenly from her husband and little daughter, and has left them and a large circle of friends to mourn her loss.

In Bradford, 6th inst., Mr. Andrew Aiken, aged 83, a Revolutionary pensioner. He was in the battle of Bunker's Hill, was shot through the body at Bennington, and was in other hard fought battles in the acquisition of our independence.

OBITUARY
MISS SALLY DURGAN

Miss Sally, daughter of John Durgan, Esq., departed this life, Campton, N. H., March 13, 1835, aged 30.

She had been the subject of distressing spasmodic fits from early childhood, which often attacked her without apparent notice. Early in the morning on the 3rd of February, having occasion to going to the cellar in preparing for breakfast, was seized with a fit, and her clothes caught fire from the candle, which she held in her hand. Her father hearing a feeble screech as of one in distress ran down and found his child enveloped in flames. The fire having been extinguished, no effort was spared to heal her wounds and mitigate her suffering, but all was unavailing to arrest her from the hand of death. She lingered upon the shore of mortality in great suffering for nearly six weeks, and passed to that awful bourn,

>That hidden world, that undiscovered shore
>Where the faith gleams of lingering life decay,
>And where the pilgrim shall return no more.

As a child she was dutiful, respectful and faithful, as a sister, affectionate, kind and obliging, and in her connections with society prudent and discreet.

In these and in other respects, she was an ornament to her family and a useful member of society.

But her chief excellence was developed in her unaffected and ardent piety. In 1833 she made a public confession of Christ in the ordinance of baptism, and to the day of her death exhibited the sincerity of her profession by a well-ordered life and godly conversation. To know and to do the will of God appeared to engage her chief attention. Ever ready to duty, she seemed to say to all, "what we have to do must be done quickly." During her confinement, she manifested no anxiety to survive, but a desire to depart and be with Christ. For a short period she appeared to forget her own suffering in her anxiety for some of her friends; but she was enabled to yield them up into the hand of God, and bid them adieu, praying that she might meet them all in heaven. Her parting address as she took them severally by the hand was most affecting and will doubtless be long remembered. Her resignation to the Divine Will and patience to endure suffering, produced conviction in every mind that religion, pure and undefiled before God the Father, is the only thing adapted to the dying bed. It was the spontaneous effusion of every bosom that witnessed the peace and calmness of her mind, "Let me die the death of the righteous, and let my last end be like hers."

On Lord's day, March 15th, the funeral solemnities were attended in Campton Village, and sermon delivered by Rev. J. R. Goodnough, for Phil. 1, 21. "For me to live in Christ and to die is gain."

"Patient, unmoved, amid the varying scene,
Her heart, and hope, and converse were above;
In all the storms of grief, resigned, serene,
Held in the arms of everlasting love."

NEW HAMPSHIRE PATRIOT & STATE GAZETTE
Concord, Monday, April 13, 1835

Steamboat Lost. The steamer Sangamon, which left Apalachicola on the first of March for Porter's Ferry, on the Flint River, succeeded in reaching that place without any difficulty. After her cargo was discharged she proceed 40 miles further up the village of Pinderton, and on her return, when near Newton, under a full head of steam run on a rock while turning a point, which injured her so much that she sunk immediately. She had about sixty bales of cotton in her hold, which will be lost.

Dreadful Storm—Melancholy Loss of Life and Property

Liverpool, March 2.—On Sunday night week, Feb. 22., a violent storm from the N N W swept over this town. Up to midnight the gale was not remarkably violent; as the morning advanced, however, the wind blew with all the force of a hurricane, scattering in the lower parts of the town slates and chimney-pots in every direction, and in the higher parts, un-roofing houses, uprooting and dismembering trees, and leveling walls. The ravages of the storm have, we regret to state been awful and melancholy on the adjacent coast. The loss of lives and the destruction of property at sea have consequently been lamentably great. The ship Norah, from Demerat, went ashore on West Hoyle, and of 15 persons on board including the captain, all were lost except one seaman. The other vessel wrecked on Monday morning was the Robert Peel, of Bristol, Murphy, master, which sailed from Liverpool for South American on the previous Thursday. She was driven on the West Hoyle Bank, and was rapidly going to pieces. The captain and crew (sixteen in number) took to the quarter-deck, which held together until morning; but the captain and three of the crew perished of the cold in course of the night, and their bodies were washed overboard. On Tuesday afternoon and Wednesday morning the Cheshire shore and sands, from the mouth of the Dee, to the Rock–Point in the Mersey, exhibited strong marks of the fury of the storm. In the neighborhood of Holylake not less than seven vessels were on shore, more or less damaged. Various articles of furniture and pieces of wreck were floating in the channel, and the shore was strewed with fragments of the Norah, from Demerara, and of the Robert Peel, for Brazil. The wreck of the Superb, steamer, lay on the Brazil bank, opposite New Brighton, about a mile from the shore; whilst the Rescue, a Torquay schooner, flour laden, from Ireland, was stranded a short distance from the Red Noses. She struck on the North Bank on Monday evening, but rising again to the tremendous sea, which was then raging, she was swept on the main about 8 o'clock at night, where she now lies discharging her cargo, which was considerably damaged by sea water.

Death of the Emperor of Austria

The Moniteur of March 17th, contains a telegraphic dispatch from the French Charge d'Affairs at Vienna stating that the Emperor of Austria died suddenly at one o' clock in the morning of the 3rd inst. He was in his 67th year, and had been Emperor, first of Germany and then of Austria, since 1804. He is succeeded by his son Ferdinand, now 42 years of age. This event, it is probable, will cause a great change in the future of policy of the empire as the present emperor is said to entertain a strong dislike against Prince Metternich.

The trial of *Joseph Reynolds* indicted for the murder of *William Reynolds,* his son, came on before the Court of Common Please, in this town on Wednesday last—Judge Green and Upham presiding. The testimony introduced was similar to that heretofore stated as elicited in the examination before a justice. A few minutes previous to the affray, Mrs. Reynolds, the mother–in–law of the deceased was seen sitting in the door of the house where the family resided, at work. William who had returned a short time before from the village, in a state of intoxication, passed her, when they both disappeared.

Immediately afterwards the mother's voice was heard in a manner which indicated that there was some difficulty between them; soon after which she was seen coming for the house, the deceased following her.

When they left the house and a few minutes previous, the accused was seen standing at an open window; and while the son was pursuing the mother, he left the window and came out of the door with a fire shovel in his hand. Advancing to his son, he struck him on the head with the edge of the shovel. The blow fractured the skull and he died the next day. The testimony depended upon one witness only, a neighbor; no other person having been near at the time of the transaction. Messrs. Bartlett of Portsmouth, and Christie of this town, were counsel for the prisoner; the Attorney General for the prosecution. The jury was charged by Judge Green. After an absence of about twenty minutes they returned a verdict of *Guilty of Manslaughter,* but not guilty of murder. On Friday morning the prisoner was sentenced to ten days solitary confinement and five years hard labor in the State Prison. He is seventy-six years of age.

William Drew, of this town, a lad about eighteen year of age, for robbing a companion while in a boat on the river near Piscataqua Bridge, was sentenced to ten days solitary confinement, and to hard labor for life in the State Prison. At the previous term of the court, an accomplice of Drew's, of about the same age, was sentenced to the State Prison for five years.

Dover Gazette

Hector S. L. Keahan, editor of the Fredrick, (Md.) Citizen put an end to his existence on Thursday morning, by shooting himself through the head with a pistol, in the parlor of his boarding house. The deceased was a gentleman of education. The rash act he committed must have been the result of momentary alienation of mind.

SHIPWRECK. The brig New Packet, Capt. Wilcomb, arrived at New York, picked up on the 10th ult., on the south side of St. Domingo, the jolly boat of the brig Frances, of Portsmouth, and took from it Captain Cutter and two seamen, which brig was cast away on Sloan Island night of the 8th, and totally lost, crew saved with nothing but what they stood in. The mate and five seamen started in the long boat for St. Domingo City, which place they probably reached by the 11th.

Merc. Jour.

John Brown, Esq., of New London, has been appointed Deputy Sheriff for the counties of Merrimack and Sullivan.

NOTICE

THIS is to forbid any person harboring or trusting EDWARD AVERY or any of his family on account of the town of Barnstead, as we have made suitable provision for their support, and shall pay no bill of their contracting.

          Samuel J. Edgerly } Selectman
          Jeremiah Clark, Jr. } of
          Jacob Saunders } Barnstead

Concord, March 21, 1835

NOTICE

THIS may certify that from and after this date, I declare my son GREENLEAF LEAVITT, free to trade and act for himself; and I shall demand none of his wages nor pay any of his debts after this date.

                                  Josiah Leavitt

Witness { C. Smith
          { A. Merrill
Springfield, April 9, 1835

COMMISSIONER'S NOTICE

THE Hon. Horace, Judge of Probate for and within the county of Merrimack, has extended the time for the allowance and adjustment of claims presented against the estate of GIDEON MORSE, late of Bow, deceased. The subscriber will therefore attend to that duty at his office in Concord, in said county, on the last Saturday of June and July, next between the hours of one o'clock and seven o'clock, P. M., on each of said days.

John Whipple, Com'r

Concord, March 23, 1835.

NOTICE

THIS is to certify that I have given my son JEREMIAH HARDY, his time to act and trade for himself, for the age of sixteen years; and that I shall claim none of his earnings for the above date.   Silas Hardy

Attest { Phinehas Clough
       { Reuben Hardy
       { Silas Hardy
Hopkinton, March 4, 1835

NOTICE

THIS may certify that I have given to my sons Charles A. Morse and John S. Morse, their time to act and trade for themselves; I shall claim none of their earnings nor pay any debts of their contracting after this date.

Charles A. Morse

Witness {Thomas Clough
        {Hannibal Haines
Canterbury, March 31, 1835

NOTICE

IS hereby give that I have relinquished to my son HENRY QUIMBY, his time to act and trade for himself. I shall claim none of his earnings nor pay any of his debts after this date.

his
Jeremiah X Quimby
mark

Witness {William W. Sargent
New Chester, March 7, 1835.

NOTICE

THIS may certify that we have sold all of our accounts from the date 1834, up to present date 1835, to John Homes. Therefore we have no claim on them.

Joseph Brown
Joseph Greely

Boston, Mass., April 1, 1835

NOTICE

THIS certifies that I have given to my son, THOMAS SPAFFORD AMES his time till he shall arrive at the age of twenty-one years, and I shall claim none of his earnings, nor pay any debts of his contracting.

STEPHEN AMES

Witness { Nathan W. Ames
{ Ruth Baker
Chichester, Feb. 25th, 1835.

MARRIAGES

In this town, by the Rev. Mr. Bouton, Mr. Daniel Harvey of Nottingham, to Miss Sarah Ewes of Concord.

In Weare, Mr. Cyrus Willard to Miss Sally George.

In Candia, by Elder B. S. Manson, Major Benjamin F. Carter to Miss Sarah Bagley, daughter of the late Dr. Moses Bagley, of Candia. By William Turner, Esq., Mr. Samuel Woodman to Miss Samuel Fisk to Miss Eliza Ann Moore, all of Candia.

In New London, Mr. Seavey to Miss Rosaline Woodward.

In Bath, by the Rev. David Sutherland, Mr. Daniel Patterson to Miss Harriet S. Dean, all of Bath.

In Actworth, by Rev. Joseph Merrill, Capt. Nathaniel Grout Davis to Miss Sally Anne Gilmore, daughter of Gawin Gilmore, Esq.

In Bridgewater, by Nathaniel P. Melvin, Esq., Mr. Enoch O. Garland to Miss Mary B. Marston.

In Plymouth, Mr. Moses Pillsbury, of Bridgewater to Mis Roxana Corliss, of Plymouth.

DEATHS

In Candia, Mr. Benjamin Eaton, aged 76. Mr. Nathaniel Burpee, 78. Mr. Moses Russell, 89, all soldiers of the Revolution.

In Deering, April 4, widow Lucy Hobson, aged 79 years 6 months.

In Goffstown, March 20, of consumption, Mr. John Orr, Jr., aged 30. Printers in N. Y., and Ohio, are &c.

In Newtown, March 28, Polly Dorinda, daughter of Mr. Timothy Whittier, aged one week.

"The dear delights we here enjoy
And fondly call our own,
Are but short favors of the Lord,
To be unpaid anon."

In New London, March 27, Capt. Solomon Adams, a Revolutionary pensioner, 76.

In Swanzey, on the 31st ult., Mr. John Whitcomb, a Revolutionary pensioner, aged 103 years, 4 months and 7 days. He lived a long life, blest with unusual health—always industrious, always temperate, both in eating and drinking, cheerful and sociable, with intellects, less impaired, at his great age, than many others at 70. But a few weeks before his death he rode to Keene, a distance of eight miles, to receive his pension money.

In Epping, widow of Elizabeth Elliot, aged 93.

In Salem, Miss Mary Hopkins Emerson, eldest daughter of Rev. Brown Emerson, in the 27th year of her age.

In Washington, Charles Pinkney, Esq., aged 39, Junior Editor of the Sun, and son of the Hon. William Pinkney, of Maryland.

In Coventry, N. H., Mr. David Whicher, aged 38.

In Lancaster, Mrs. Lydia Hart, aged 93, the oldest person in the town. Also, Mr. David Greenleaf, aged 83.

In Weare, Mr. Jonathan Philbrick, 48. Printers in L. C. are &c.

In Actworth, April 3, of a short illness, Mr. William Heywood, Jr., aged 28, son of Mr. William Heywood of Bangor, Me.—a young man much respected for his uprightness of character, moral and gentlemanly deportment, and although he was called for this world at a distance from his parental home, yet his friends will have the consolation that his last painful moments were smoothed by every kindness the generous, and disinterested hospitality of the family with whom he resides could afford, and that he has left behind him a memory which his associates will long cherish with grateful recollection. Printers in Me., and Mass., are &c.

In Acworth, April 7, of a short but painful illness, Mr. John L. Brown, aged 36 years, formerly of Lancaster. An industrious upright and respected citizen. He bore his last distressing sickness with that patience and resignation which characterized the humble Christian—and died in the full assurance of an immortal glory beyond the grave.

NEW HAMPSHIRE PATRIOT & STATE GAZETTE
Concord, Monday, April 20, 1835

Fatal Trick of Conjurer. A dreadful accident occurred at Armstadt, on the 10th of November. On that day, Linsky, the celebrated legerdemain performer, gave in the presence of the family of Prince Schwartzburg Sonderhauser, a grand exhibition, in which he distinguished himself by an extraordinary display of his art. Six soldiers from the garrison were introduced to fire with ball cartridges at Madame Linsky, the young wife of the conjuror. They were however instructed, in biting the cartridge, to bite off the ball and keep it in the mouth as they had been shown how to do on a rehearsal. Madame Linsky was for a time unwilling to perform the part allotted to her in this trick; but by the persuasion of her husband, she was induced to consent. The soldiers were drawn up before the company, took aim at Madame Linsky, and fired. For a moment after the firing, she remained standing upright, but the next moment she sunk down, saying, "Dear husband, I am shot." One of the musket balls which had not been bitten off, passed quite through her abdomen. The unfortunate woman never spoke another word, and died on the second day after she received the wound. Many of the spectators fainted, and the horror of the scene has given a shock to the reason of Linsky. It was indeed a spectacle which might have unmanned the most firm. It is to be hoped that this will serve as a warning to all conjurers, as well as to the spectators of their tricks, who usually show too inconsiderate confidence in the art of the performer not only with respect to cases of risk of life, but to other practices of a dangerous nature. *Austrian Observer.*

Horrible Outrage! The Albany Evening Journal contains a particular account of the recent brutal outrage upon a Mrs. Tyler, of Orville, Onondage County, compared with which the Morgan abduction dwindles into insignificance.

The wife of ____ Tyler, who was sent about a year since to the State Prison, was left residing at Orville. It was rumored, during the fall that an improper intimacy existed between this woman and a Mr. Young, and although no evidence of it existed, and none of the decencies of life were known to be violated a village "excitement" was raised against her. The embers were finally fanned into a blaze, and having possessed themselves of a bucket of tar and a bag of feathers, eight men proceeded in a sleigh, at 12 o'clock at night, to the house of the offender, where the confidently expected to surprise her in bed with her paramour. Breaking into the house they found the woman in bed with her children. After searching in vain for Young, they seized the woman, dragged her, with nothing but her night clothes, into the street, put a gag in her mouth, threw a blanket over her shoulders, put her into the sleigh, and drove off leaving *three little children alone, without a fire or a light, shrieking with terror!!*

The monsters drove off about three quarters of a mile, took her into a field, tore off her night clothes, and with the instruments of torture prepared for the purpose, these eight unfeeling wretches perpetrated upon a defenseless and unfortunate female, an outrage of the most horrible character.

After literally enveloping the miserable woman in tar, they rolled her in the blanket, took her to an unoccupied and unfrequented barn, where they left her, entirely helpless, and still gagged, to perish with cold, unless found, as she was, by accident.

The cries of the children, in the morning, attracted the attention of the neighbors, and upon learning what had occurred, a search was made for the woman. Nothing, however, was discovered, till nearly dark, when a quantity of tar and feathers were found on the snow in a field where the outrage was committed. From this spot the villains were tracked to the barn, where George Grinnell found the poor creature, alive, but speechless and senseless! She was taken home and a physician sent for, who discovered that her *jaw had been dislocated!*

Several benevolent ladies kindly assisted in relieving the suffering woman from her dreadful condition, and after several weeks, her health was restored. A strong feeling of indignity ran rapidly through the community. The monsters were soon identified, and prosecutions commenced. The causes were to have been tried during the present month, but were settled, a short time since by the payment of FOURTEEN HUNDRED DOLLARS, from the defendants to the victim of their barbarities.

LITCHFIELD, April 9.

LIGHTNING. The house of Mr. Samuel F. Peck, in Sharon, Ellsworth Society, occupied in part by Rev. F. Gridley, was struck with lightning on Sabbath the 5th inst., between 2 and 3 o'clock, P. M. The shock was sudden and awful. The main body of the fluid struck the north end of the house, a little below the ridge, tearing a hole into the chamber six feet in height by four in width. It then passed down and made a breach of about equal dimensions in the lower part of the house, into the room where the family of Mr. Gridley was sitting, consisting of six persons. A clock which was fastened to the side of the room was shivered to pieces, and a table, by which one was sitting was turned over and hurled into the middle of the room. At the same instant a small portion of the electric fluid struck the chimney, passed down to the fire, and bursting, scattered the ashes over the room. An opening was made in the roof at some distance from the place where the main body of the fluid was expended, the door fast of the outside door shivered, and some adjoining boards torn off. Mr. Gridley had just returned from church, had passed through the door, entered his room and cast a glance upon his family, when the awful explosion took place. The room in which the family was sitting is 14 ½ by 12, and although literally surrounded by the devouring element, yet through the good providence of God, no one was materially injured. There was no lightning rod attached to the house. *Enquirer.*

Murderers Punished. We published sometime ago an account of the piracy and murder on board the ship Matilda, in which Capt. Livingston was barbarously destroyed, and $200,000 on board the ship carried off by the mutineers, in September, 1834. We learn from information received by a mercantile house in this city, that the pirates had been arrested at Patjiton, and have been tried and executed at Java. We are not informed how many of them, nor where the money is, but certainly much praise is due to the promptness and decision of the Dutch government in arresting and punishing these atrocious pirates. *N. Y. Star.*

Slander—Actionable. Not content with representing "Squire Pierce as a *'pretended* Republican," his quondam friends speak of him as *associating* with the editor of this paper! If the 'Squire' chooses to institute a suit, we are ready to testify. He is innocent of the crime alleged, and we cannot look on and be silent when we see one of the human family so outrageously abused. *N. H. Sentinel.*

Siam and Cochin China

Edmund Roberts, Esq., of Portsmouth, N. H., is to sail shortly in a sloop of war to Siam, charged with presents to the king of that country, with whom we some time since concluded a treaty. He thence proceeds to Cochin, China to form a commercial arrangement similar to that subsisting with Siam.

Loss by Fire. A few days since the wheelwright shop of Mr. Daniel Kennedy, in Bristol, Grafton County, with all its contents was consumed by fire; whereby Mr. Kennedy, the owner and occupant has lost "his all." Mr. Kennedy is a young man just settled in life, industrious and prudent, and had by the strictest economy laid up enough from his labors to purchase the shop, machinery and tools. We think he is entitled to the sympathy of his friends. *Bristol.*

A Young Victim. Yesterday morning about 4 o'clock, the moans of a person were heard by a resident of the neighborhood of Sixth and Pine Streets, and on examination a young woman, in the last agonies of death was found prostrate on the ground in Sixth Street. She was immediately carried from the public highway, while the person who first discovered her, hastened for assistance, but she died before it could be obtained. We learn from the coroner, that she was apparently not more than sixteen years of age—quite handsome—four feet ten inches high—had on a striped calico dress, but was without a bonnet or shawl.

We have since learned that the history of the poor creature is truly melancholy. She was not seventeen years old when she perished—perished miserably in the street. But two weeks before she died, she was the object of the fond care of parents and friends—beautiful, beloved, innocent and happy. Fortunately she did not long survive her fall. In the short space that intervened between her departure from home and her death, she passed through every grade of wretchedness, and died as we learn, from mere anguish of mind. *Phil. Gaz.*

From the Brooklyn (Con.) Advertiser, April 2.

Distressing and Fatal Accident. Never have we been called to record so shocking an event as that which occurred last week at Woodstock, the details of which well be found heart rending and painful in extreme. It appears that Mr. and Mrs. Marcy set out on a journey on Tuesday of last week, expecting to be absent from home but a few days, and leaving the house &c., in the charge of their daughter, Nancy Ann Marcy aged about 26. On the following Thursday, two days after the lifeless body of the young lady was accidentally discovered near the "wood pile" a short distance from the house. From appearances in the house and near the spot were she was found, it is supposed that on Tuesday afternoon, the same day on which her parents left home, she went out about tea time to get fuel, and that a large *log* rolled down and caught her by the arm, in which awful situation she remained until her death, being unable to extricate herself, or to raise a cry sufficiently loud to arrest the attention of any of the neighbors. The exact period of her distress and agony can not be known, but from the fact that her constitution was such as would not easily yield to physical suffering, she must have died from actual pain and exposure, and it is quite propable that the spark of life had not been long extinguished when this discovery was made! The poor creature, it is said had struggled so hard to extricate herself with the hand which was at liberty, that her fingers were very much mangled and torn.

Report speaks very highly of the respectability and intelligence of this unfortunate young lady, and the family to which she belonged. Her sudden and untimely death, and especially the circumstances attending it, will not soon be forgotten in the neighborhood where she resided.

The Wife of Benedict Arnold. Col. Burr, in 1780 was on a visit to Mrs. Provost, the lady who not long after became his wife, when Mrs. Arnold stopped at her house, on the way to join her husband. At the first news of his treason, Mrs. Arnold excited the sympathy of every one. Her lamentations and screams might be heard at a distance, and many feared that her reason would be shaken from its throne. Several of the officers at West Point, at that time, wrote most affecting descriptions of her wretchedness; and went so far as to think that the wounds given to the heart of an elegant and accomplished woman deserved as much punishment as the treason Arnold had committed. Washington was deeply affected by her situation and rendered her every assistance in his power, and with great gallantry sent her a letter of safe conduct to the lines. Mrs. Provost was the wife of a British officers, and to her Mrs. Arnold could unbosom herself; and being assured that no one was near but those of strict honor she threw off the mask, and thanked God that the farce of hypocrisy was over, for she hated to be an actress any longer. She said that she had commenced the correspondence with the British commander, and had brought her husband to the deed at last; stating also that she had long abhorred the American cause and was happy that she was free from the rebels. This spoils the pathos of many a brilliant description of her patriotism and sensibility, but nevertheless, the generous feeling in which they were written will still remain as proofs that there was nothing revengeful or low in the dispositions of those who achieved our independence. [Knapp's Life of Aaron Burr]

An Honest Fellow. Eight or nine prisoners effected their escape from the jail of Chester County, Pa., on the night of the 3rd inst., of whom one voluntarily returned on the following Monday. He thought the escape of his colleagues afforded him a good opportunity to visit his friends in another part of the country, and having employed his liberty to that object, he of his own accord returned to durance. The nature of the offense charged against him is not stated; but if it is not *very* heinous, his honesty should be rewarded by a discharge. *N. Y. Sun.*

NOTICE

I HEREBY certify that I have given my son, JOSEPH B. DOW, his time to act and trade for himself, and I shall not hereafter claim any of his earnings nor pay any debts of his contracting after this date. SAMUEL DOW

Witness, William Dow

Concord, April 11th, 1835.

Look out for a Knave

ON the 13th inst., I was robbed, in the following polite way of two promissory notes, amounting to one hundred dollars, by Jeremiah F. Brown, of Bradford, N H. Said Brown knowing that I had the above mentioned notes, and that I was under the necessity of raising the money on the same, came to my house, the distance of two miles on the 12th inst., and offered without my request, that if I would fetch the notes to him the next day, he would get the money on them for me. I accordingly called on said Brown: he then wished me to go out with him by ourselves—accordingly did. He then said to me that I must let him take the notes to raise the money on; so he took the notes promising to return in a few minutes with my money. At length he returned, I asked him if he had got the money; he said he had not, and added that he had the advantage—he had my notes and I had no proof of it, and utterly refused to give them up, denying to all others any knowledge to case whatever. Said notes were endorsed to me.

EDWARD CRESSY.

Merrimack, ss. April 15, 1835

Personally appeared the above named Edward Cressy and made solemn oath that the above affidavit by him subscribed, it true. Before me—

JASON H. AMES, J. Peace.

Editors in general will confer a favor on the community, especially those in the state of Ohio, by giving the above affidavit, together with these remarks, an insertion in their respective columns, that they may be on the look out. He has lived in Chester, and his father-in-law now resides in Orange, Meigs County, Ohio. It is expected he will flee to that part of the state; it is evident that he intends to leave this state for Ohio as soon as possible. Measures are taken to arrest and bring him to justice. EDWARD CRESSY

April 20, 1835.

TAKE NOTICE

ALL persons are cautioned against purchasing a note of hand signed by George Ashley of Bradford, in the county of Merrimack and state of New Hampshire, for the sum of forty-eight dollars and 50 cents, running to Daniel Cressy or his order payable in one year with interest, dated Sept. 24, 1831, as said note has been transferred and endorsed over to the subscriber. Said note has been lost or fraudulently obtained from me.

EDWARD CRESSY

Bradford, April 15, 1835

NOTICE

ALL persons are hereby forbidden harboring or trusting Widow Sarah Jacobs, Alfred C. Jacobs, Andrew Jacobs, Levina Pickering, on account of the town of Barnstead, as suitable provisions are made for their support and we are determined to pay no bills for their support hereafter in place.

    Samuel J. Edgerly   }   Selectmen
    Jeremiah Clark, Jr.   }   of
    Jacob Saunders   }   Bristol
April 10, 1835

MARRIAGES

In Bow, on Thursday evening last, by Rev. Mr. Boswell, Edward Gould, Esq., of Dunbarton to Miss Harriet Maria Heath of Bow.

In Center Harbor, Mr. Eliphalet Hazeltire, of this town, to Miss Caroline S. Senter of Center Harbor.

In Boscawen, 15th inst., by Rev. Mr. Cummings, Mr. Oliver Shaw, of Salisbury, to Miss Jane Stanwood, of Boscawen.

In Bradford, Mass., by Rev. T. G. Farnsworth, of Haverhill, Ebenezer G. Pressey, formerly of Sutton, N. H., to Miss Hannah H Stickney, of Bradford.

In Springfield, April 8th, N. W. Westgate, Esq., of Enfield to Miss Lydia Jane Prentiss.

In Candia Mr. Aaron Knight, to Miss Melinda Patten. Mr. Joshua Griffin to Miss Sally Towle.

In Raymond, Mr. Timothy Quimby to Miss Eliza Brown. Mr. Samuel Healy to Miss Drusilla Robinson.

In Candia, Mr. Sameul Woodman to Mrs. Sally Woodman. They had previously lived together in a marriage state for nearly thirty years. At the last term of the Superior Court in this county, the wife's petition for a divorce, on account of the husband's extreme cruelty, was presented, the charges proved—and a bill of divorce granted. A new courtship commenced—the hatchet was buried—and the fond couple, too impatient to abide "the laws delay" of a fortnight, for the usual publishment, repaired incontinently to a magistrate who united the ardent lover and the blushing bride in those sacred bonds that nothing but death—or the Superior Court—can sever!

> "Divorced like scissors rent in twain,
> Each mourned the rivet out;
> Now whet and riveted again,
> They'll make the old shears cut."

N. B. The court does not sit again till December.—News letter.

In Portsmouth, Mr. Nathaniel Balch, to Miss Elizabeth M. Tucker. Mr. Charles Quincy to Miss Eliza Smith. Mr. Andrew B. Vennard to Miss Ariadne Locke both of Newcastle.

DEATHS

In Croydon, on Tuesday, April 7th., Mrs. Anne Barton, wife of Benjamin Barton, Esq., aged 49. In all the relations of life, the deceased was a pattern of female excellence. As a wife she was affectionate, industrious and frugal, looking well to her household, and eating not the bread of idleness. As a mother, kind and indulgent, imparting to her children as well by example as instruction the maxims of virtue, and giving to them precepts calculated to train them in the way they should go, that in maturer years they might not depart from it. As a friend and neighbor she was benevolent and obliging, ever ready to extend to others the offers of kindness and charity. She has left a husband and a large number of children and relatives to mourn their loss, and her death has created a void in the family and neighborhood circles, which cannot well be supplied. But having faithfully discharged all her duties on earth, the rewards of the just are her portion in heaven.

In Conway, March 25, of consumption, Mrs. Judith Cutler, wife of Zarah Cutler, Esq., and daughter of Mr. Enoch Coffin of Concord, aged 36. In her life Mrs. Cutler exhibited the meekness of a Christian, and in her last sickness the patience, faith, and hope of one who knew in whom she believed. For the comfort of her Christian friends it should be said that they who saw her in the time of her greatest need had pleasing evidence that she drank of living water; and would never thirst again. Printers in Mass., Conn., &c. Com.

In Enfield, April 7th., of lung fever, George C., only son of Thomas Merrill, Esq., aged 11 months.

In Bartlett, March 30, Mrs. Abigail Pitman, 38. At the age of fifteen years, she was left the eldest of nine orphan children, all of whom, with one exception, have died of consumption within a year. She became a disciple of Christ at an early age, and is now, we trust, in possession of the crown of life, which He hath prepared for all those who love Him and obey His commandments. She has left a husband and three small children to mourn the loss of an affectionate wife and tender mother.
Com.

In Andover, the 9th inst., Josiah Langley, Jr., son of Josiah and Sarah Langley, aged 29 years and six months. After a long and distressing sickness of about three years, which he bore with patience and resignation to the will of God, and then resigned his body to the dust, and his spirit to God who gave it, with full assurance of a blessed immortality in Christ his redeemer. He has left an numerous circle of friends and relatives to mourn their loss. He was amiable in his disposition, engaging in his manners, and died beloved and lamented by all who knew him. Com.

In Brentwood, April 3., Mrs. Hepzibah Marsh, wife of John Marsh, aged 67, of lock –jaw.

In Warner, Jan. 25, 1835, Caroline Hoyt, aged 24 years and 2 months. Funeral service on the 28th; a sermon which was calculated to comfort the afflicted, was delivered by Rev. Robert Bartlett, of Hopkinton, from Isaiah 40th and 1st.

In Washington City, George Beale, Esq., late Purser of the U. S. Navy. Andrew Jackson, son of Amos Kendall, Esq., aged 6 years.

NEW HAMPSHIRE PATRIOT & STATE GAZETTE
Concord, Monday, April 27, 1835

Distressing Accident. On Friday last, the chimney of the house in which Mr. Isaac Silver, resided about a mile and half from this village, fell in, and one of Mr. Silver's children, a boy about six years old was instantly killed. Mrs. Silver was sitting upon the hearth with three of her children about her, the eldest about nine years old, when the sudden falling of the chimney carried them all into the cellar, where the water was two feet deep. Mrs. Silver escaped with slight injury from the falling bricks, and succeeded in rescuing two of the children, who were both more or less injured; but the third was covered with the rubbish and literally buried in the water, from whence its lifeless body was taken about half an hour after the accident happened. The falling of the chimney awakened the youngest child, about a year old, which was asleep on the bed, from which it fell crawled to the edge of the floor and was taken down and held in the arms of Mrs. Silver who was standing in the water. She succeeded in raising the oldest to the floor who was sent too alarm the neighbors, but a traveler passing by, assisted her and the children from the cellar. The water had undermined the arch on which the chimney stood, and which it seems, had rested on a single stick of timber, the sudden breaking of which precipitated the chimney, and the family together into the cellar.

TORNADO. A most furious tornado was experienced at Columbia, Tennessee, on the night of the 21st ult. Its entire duration is said to have been but a few minutes, in the course of which houses were torn from their foundations, trees uprooted and piled together, fences prostrated and every thing within the scope of its fury beaten down and destroyed. Eight persons were killed and fifteen or twenty badly wounded. The account says that a Negro girl belonging to a family in which four persons were killed was blown into the fire and there confined by a beam until the storm was over, when directed by her screams assistance was afforded. In this excruciating situation she lay literally roasting for nearly an hour. She is still alive. Some conception of the velocity of the wind may be had from the fact that a green lynn tree near Mr. Lusk's dwelling, is to be seen sticking about twenty feet from the ground, a broad piece of poplar plank, firmly driven in to the depth of four or five inches and at an angle of about 45 degrees across the grain.

A thief was discovered in the President's house at Washington, on Friday night last. The President was awakened by someone at the door of his chamber endeavoring to gain admittance, and who, upon being asked his business replied that he was trying to get out. It seems that he broke in for plunder, and had lost his way. He was locked up for safe keeping in an apartment usually occupied as a stable but at the time vacant, and escaped before morning through a window which was at such a height from the ground, that no one supposed he could possibly reach it.

COMMISSIONER'S NOTICE

THE Judge of Probate for and within the county of Merrimack, having extended the time to the 24th June, 1835 for the allowance and adjustment of claims that may be presented against the estate of Jeremiah Adams, late of New London, deceased, the subscriber will therefore attend to that duty at his dwelling house in Sutton, on Saturday the 16th day of May, and at the office of S. C. Badger in Concord, in said county, on Tuesday the 21st day of June next, between the hours of one of the clock and five of the clock, P. M., on each of said days. REUBEN PORTER, Com'r.
Sutton, April 9, 1835.

DEATHS

In New Durham, April 6, 1835, in the 67th year of her age, Hannah, wife of Lieut. Joseph Willey, departed this life and we hope for a better. She with her companion have raised up seven children, who with their father have met with an irreparable loss, for in her life she was a kind, affectionate and obedient wife, a tender and loving mother. She was pious, virtuous and charitable. Benevolence was a leading trait in her character—to feel others woe and relieve the distressed whenever in her power. She embraced religion about 18 years ago and could say to her companion just before she expired, "the Lord will receive me." About five years ago she complained of a pain in her side, which terminated in a large hard swollen body, which bore some resemblance of the dropsy. Her complaint was unknown to her attending physicians, which she bore with Christian fortitude and resignation to the divine will of Christ, with whom she went to sleep without a groan.

An able and appropriate discourse was delivered on the occasion by Elder Nathaniel Berry from Rev. 14, 13, "And I heard a voice from heaven saying unto me right blessed are the dead that die in the Lord, &c."

In Chester, April 17th inst., Esq. David Patten aged 76, a soldier of the Revolution. He was in the battles of Bunker Hill, Bennington and others during the Revolution. In politics he was a Republican of the Jeffersonian school and although far advanced in life, yet he felt a lively interest in the welfare and prosperity of this great and happy republic. With President Jackson's administration he was highly pleased and cordially approved of all his public measures. In religion he was neither an atheist, or a skeptic but died as he had lived, an honest man.

In Epsom, April 18th, Elder Daniel Philbrick aged 82 years—leaving 10 children, 46 grand-children and three great grand-children. Elder Philbrick had been a professor of the Free Baptist communion 56 years and came to the grave like a shock of grain fully ripe in the same hope of entering that rest when the wicked cease from troubling and the weary are at rest. Elder Philbrook entered the service of his country during the Revolution, was in the battle of Bennington, Stillwater and Saratoga, and during life was a firm supporter of the republican form of government which he fought to establish—an appropriate discourse was delivered at the funeral by Elder Dyer from the words—"all these died in faith."

Drowned in Hopkinton, on Sabbath afternoon, the 12th inst., Mr. Charles Cary. He was engaged with some others in making fast a boom log across the river to prevent logs from floating over the falls.

On the island of Cuba, Matanza, March 18, Mr. Prentice Cheney of Newport, aged 19. Mr. Cheney was a young man of high promise. He commenced the study of medicine about two years since and was a member of the medical class at Hanover when his health first failed him. He visited New Orleans hoping that a southern climate might be favorable to restoration of health, but finding no relief he proceeded to Cuba, where far from kindred and home he closed his earthly career. Letters received from him at Cuba by his friend's show that he had the support of religion, which must be a source of strong consolation to them in this time of affliction. It was expected that a discourse would be delivered on the occasion at the Baptist Meeting House in Newport last Sabbath afternoon.

In Deerfield, Sept. 30th, 1834, Abigail, aged 18—April 15th, Seth, aged 24—children of the widow Lucy Langley, making with her husband, six which have died since 1826 all of consumption.

In Gilmanton of the 16th, Betsey Sargent, wife of the late Joseph Sargent. After a long and distressing sickness which she bore with patience and Christian fortitude, in the exercise of that faith that purifieth the heart and in the hope that is an anchor to the soul; Christ was her life, her joy, her hope, nor could she sink with such a prop. Printers in Me., are &c.

NEW HAMPSHIRE PATRIOT & STATE Gazette
Concord, Monday, May 4, 1835

GENERAL JACKSON

The number for last month of the London New Monthly Magazine contains an article entitled *General Jackson,* and contributed avowedly, by an American "from the north," who had an interview with him in 1831. We subjoin two passages of the article, in order that our readers may know how Andrew, *Volente de Fer,* has been exhibited to the British public.

General Jackson is very tall, bony, and thin, with an erect military bearing and a head set with a considerable *fierte* upon his shoulders. A stranger would at once pronounce upon his profession: and his frame, features, voice and action have a natural and most peculiar warlikeness. He has (not to speak disrespectfully) a *game-cock look* all over him. His face is unlike any other; its prevailing expression is energy, but there is, so to speak, a lofty honorableness in its thin worn lines, combined with a penetrating and sage look of talent, that would single him out even among extraordinary men, as a person of more than usually superior cast. He looks like the last person in the world to be "humbugged," and yet a caricature of him would make an admirable Don Quixote. In the days of chivalry he would have been the mirror of tried soldiers—an old iron-grey knight invincible and lion like, but somewhat stiff in his courtesy. His eye is of a dangerous fixedness, deep set, and overhung by bushy gray eyebrows, his features long, with strong, ridgy lines running through his cheeks; his forehead a good deal seamed; and his white hair, stiff and wiry, brushed obstinately back, and worn quite with an expression of a *chevaux de frize* of bayonets. In his mouth, there is a redeeming suavity as he speaks, but the instant his lips close, a vizier of steel would scarcely look more impenetrable. His manners are dignified and have been called high-bred and aristocratic by travelers; but to my mind, are the model of republican simplicity and straight forwardness. He is quite a man one would be proud to show as the exponent of the manner of his country.

"General Jackson would be a bad diplomatist in Europe, or any where without power. He has but one *cheval de bataille*—he rides down and breaks through everything that other men would think of avoiding or circumventing. He cut all Gordian knots. His is no "head to creep into crevices." Having made up his mind as to his aim and trusting to his own directness of purpose, he shuts his eyes, like the monarch of the herd, and charges—generally with success. His passions are said to be tremendously violent:—and a long life has but little subdued their warmth. His paroxysms are not unfrequent;—and sooth to say, he has often cause; for never man was so crossed and thwarted as he has been in his administration. His stern uprightness and singleness of mind, however, bring him generally well through. His immediate passion is soon over, but his purpose does not evaporate with his anger; and he has shown, since he has been in power, some rather startling specimen of his inflexibility. This extends to the desire of serving his friends, *hine illæ lachrymæ,*—it is the only thing like a breath on his justice. Immediately on his inauguration, he turned out inexorably every officer of the government, from highest next himself, to the clerks in the post offices, and rewarded his partisans with the places. Offering no pretence of excuse or apology however. He is quite above that. His reasons were openly avowed; he thought that where there was an advantage in his gift, his friends had the first claim. And a sacrificing business he would have made of it if America had not been a country where a man may turn his hand to anything at half a day's notice."

Conflagration of the Mails and Baggage on the Railroad. A few minutes after the railroad cars left Bordentown for this city, yesterday it was discovered that the car containing the baggage was on fire. The guard perceived a volume of flame and smoke issuing from the lower part of the baggage beneath him. The locomotive was stopped as soon as practicable on the alarm being given, but not before the fire had made such progress that the whole car was enveloped in flames, which rose in a column of fifteen or twenty feet. The passengers rushed confusedly from their several cars, each eager to save his own share of the property; but owing to their want of method in their efforts and the rapid spreading of the conflagration, they succeeded in rescuing only a few trunks and packages from destruction. The burning car after some delay was overthrown from the track, and its blazing contents thus disintegrated and scattered, but not before much the larger portion was rendered wholly worthless by the fire. There were about one hundred passengers, sixty or eighty of who have lost their entire baggage, and some of them articles of great value. The following particulars are gathered from the morning papers, mainly the Gazette.

A lady of Boston lost a large quantity of very valuable clothing, estimated to be worth fifteen hundred dollars. Her diamonds and other jewelry were saved.

Miss Austin, of the theatre, lost all her baggage, including many valuable articles of dress, but saved a box of jewels, which was taken from the center of her trunk.

Mr. Knowles, of Amherst, Massachusetts, had a package in his trunk, containing $15,000, which was fortunately rescued from the flames, the top of the trunk having been burnt up. We understand the money was put into his charge by one of the Philadelphia banks for a New York bank.

A German gentleman and his wife, who lost all their clothing, were fortunate enough to recover a tin box, which was in one of their trunks, containing documents necessary for the recovery of a large estate in Europe, whither he is proceeding for that purpose

This morning mail from Philadelphia was in the crate and shared the fate of the rest. A scorched bundle, which remained was brought to the post office, and out of it, the subscription on forty-four letters were deciphered. This mail usually contains but few letters and those not of the most valuable kind. How the fire originated is not certainly ascertained. It had probably been burning for a few minutes fanned by a fresh breeze, which blowing diagonally across the tracks, served when added to their motion to carry the smoke off to the rear, so as to prevent its being seen.

The passengers made a rough estimate of the loss and it was computed to the amount to upwards of five thousand dollars.

We understand the agent of the company acted with great coolness and intrepidity and did every thing in his power to arrest the progress of the flames.

When the passengers got on board the steamboat, a meeting was called to take the matter into consideration. Joseph P. Grant, Esq., of Baltimore, was appointed chairman and J. J. Smith, Jr., of Philadelphia, secretary. A committee of three was appointed to call upon the company and represent the nature of the accident, and request remuneration to the sufferers.

Since the above was in type we learn from another passenger, that the opinion was very prevalent among them that the fire was the result of design, and that it did not originate from sparks from the chimney. He says that the baggage was covered with a thick tarpaulin, and the fire evidently proceeded from the center of the baggage.

The fragments of forty-four letters were received at the New York post office last evening and have been repacked to be returned to Philadelphia this day. One of them contained a check for five hundred dollars.

N. Y. Eve. Post.

Lexington Battle. In accordance with previous arrangements by our fellow citizens of the town of Lexington, an interesting celebration was held in that place on Monday, to commemorate the events of the 19th of April 1775. The concourse of people from that and the neighboring towns and from Boston was very great. At 11 o'clock, a procession escorted by two military companies in uniform, under the direction of Gen. Chandler as Chief Marshall, aided by several Assistant Marshals, was formed in front of the "Monument House," and proceeded to the burying ground. Here the remains of Munroe, Parker, Hadley, the two Harringtons, Muzzey, Brown and Porter, the men who fell a sacrifice to the cause of liberty and their country on the morning of the memorable nineteenth, (which had previously been taken from the grave and placed in a sarcophagus,) were received into the procession drawn on a hearse by a white horse, and the whole proceeded to the meeting house. The sarcophagus was placed in the aisle fronting the pulpit, the two military companies standing in the aisle. Religious and solemn services were then performed and an address delivered by the Hon. Edward Everett.

At the close of these services, the procession was again formed and the remains were taken to the monument, where a new tomb had been prepared for their reception. Having completed this interesting ceremony the procession returned to the Monument House in the rear of which, and under a spacious pavilion a collation was prepared. The interior of the pavilion was decorated with flags and scrolls bearing the names of the patriots distinguished in the war of the Revolution. Elias Phinney, Esq., presided at the table.

In was not the least affecting circumstance of the day, that there were present, in the procession, and on the stage with the orator *ten* of the men who were engaged in the battle. These ten are all, except *one,* who survived to tell the story of the awful tragedy in which they are actors to the present generation. *Bost. Courier.*

Matthais the Impostor. This extraordinary and villainous impostor, self-styled prophet, &c., who made considerable noise and trouble in New York, the past year, was tried last week in Westchester County, of that state, on the charge of murder. He stood indicted for the murder of Elijah Pierson, one of his followers, who died last August by poison or ill treatment. When arraigned in the courtroom, he became exceedingly boisterous, and singular in manner, indicating insanity. This being supposed to be feigned, a jury was impaneled to try the question of the prisoner's insanity. The jury in a few moments returned the verdict that Matthias was of *sane* mind. The trial for murder then proceeded and resulted in his acquittal. The jury, under the direction of the court, gave the verdict of not guilty. The trial elicited much that was curious and audacious in the previous conduct of this extraordinary individual.

The prisoner was then arraigned on another indictment for cow-hiding Isabella Laisdell, his daughter, and a married woman of 18 years of age. Upon this indictment the jury returned a verdict of guilty. He was then sentenced to thirty days imprisonment for contempt of court, and three months for the assault. Previous to his trial he had been confined in jail seven months.

Judge Ruggles, after pronouncing sentence, addressed Matthias as follows: —"We now tell you that the time for practicing these foolish impositions is past. The court is satisfied that you are an impostor, and that you do not believe in your own doctrines. We advise you therefore when you come out of jail to shave off your beard, lay aside your peculiar dress, and go to work like an honest man. *Salem Observer.*

Horrid Murder. A murder was committed in a rum shop kept by a man named John Rogers, No. 15 Peck Slip, New York, on Thursday last, on the person of a seaman named Joseph Sheridan, of New Bedford, in this state. It appears that Sheridan, the landlord, his barkeeper and hired girl, were all drunk during the evening. A quarrel took place between Sheridan and Rogers, and the latter struck the former a violent blow with a poker across his right eye towards the temple, which caused a concussion of the brain, and also broke the bone of the right upper arm, immediately above the elbow joint. Sheridan was subsequently carried up stairs and put to bed, where he remained until 12 o'clock on Friday night without any thing given him but a cup of coffee. On Friday night, an old shipmate by the name of Cooper called and inquired for Sheridan, and was shown to him by the servant girl. He immediately called the watch who on their arrival ascertained that Sheridan was dead. On Saturday afternoon a party of sailors, indignant at the supposed murder of their comrade, assembled and toward evening proceeded to the house of Rogers, broke it open, demolished the furniture and destroyed the bed, &c., and then tore the whole front part of the house to pieces, breaking doors and all in their power to destroy, and left it a tottering ruin. A posse of police officers, headed by the high constable, proceeded to the place and arrested Joseph Brown, William Evans, James Nugent, Harvey Marstin and three others who were committed to prison for riot. They also discovered a quantity of bones, which are supposed to be human, under the floor of the house, and a part of a shirt completely saturated with blood, which were carried to the police office. Rogers, his barkeeper and female servant were, after an examination at the police court, remanded to prison. *Boston Post.*

Dreadful Fire—Burning of 51 Horses. A terrific fire, threatening the destruction of the fairest portion of our city broke out last night a little after 12 o'clock on Market Street. It commenced in the interior of the extensive livery stable owned by Messrs. Laveilee and Morton, and at the time in the occupancy of Mr. John Calvert. The first intimation of the fire was given by the flames bursting from the building, and as it was built of wooden materials, and contained a large quantity of hay, and other provider, all efforts to save it were fruitless. Attention was instantly directed to the rescue of the horses, but horrible to say fifty-one of those noble animals are supposed to have been burnt with the building. Others were let loose, wild with agony and fright—their manes on fire, and presenting a terrific spectacle; to relieve them from suffering several were shot down.

From the stable the flames communicated to the old Catholic church, which having been abandoned was temporarily occupied as a warehouse. The walls of this building alone are left standing. The goods—from eighty to one hundred crates of china, queens and glassware—are all destroyed. Mrs. Perry's row of buildings, running from Second to Main Street, were in imminent danger, as was indeed all the property in the neighborhood—a brisk wind prevailing at the time directly from the west. The new Catholic Church having a fireproof roof, was uninjured, except in the burning of two or three windows.

The loss cannot new be accurately estimated. Morton and Laveille, John Calvert and R. D. Watson—the latter, the owner of the goods—are the principal sufferers. The loss of the horses will be very heavy, but divided among their several owners in the city. Altogether the damage cannot be less than fifteen thousand dollars. It is not, as yet, known how the fire was communicated.

Fires. A fire occurred last midnight, which destroyed the Hook and Eye Manufactory in Arnold Street near Boston and Roxbury line, together with a barn. Whilst the engines were at or on their way to this fire, they were recalled by an alarm from the city. As Engine No. 15 was on its way to the South End, the company discovered fire in the extensive wooden ware store of Messrs. Parkes and Palfrey in Hanover Street. They immediately gave the alarm, proceeded with their engine to the nearest reservoir and went to work; but the fire had got so well under way that before it was subdued, Messrs. Parkes & Co., establishment was entirely destroyed, together with a range of ten foot wooden buildings in the rear of the store. The crockery ware store of E. B. McLaughlin, on the south, and the dwelling house and shop of Mr. Rice, saddler, on the north, were much damaged. Messrs. Parks & Palfrey, and Mr. McLaughlin, were insure, but Mr. Rice, whose loss is considerable has no insurance.

An incident occurred at this fire which ought to be related. It puts humanity to the blush. When the fire was first discovered, a member of Engine Company 18, who was coming up Hanover Street at the same time 15 was on the way, was one of the first at the fire, and remembering that the passage way between the store where the fire broke out and the one above it led to a court, where there was a number of wooden tenements, occupied by indigent families, he ran up in company with one or two other persons, to notify them of their danger. The wooden-ware store was then nearly all in flames, and the wind blowing directly across the court, but they found every soul sound asleep.

Bursting into one house, they saw a large family of helpless children. The member of No.18 took two in his arms, and two members of No. 15 took two others, rushing with them into the street, carried them for protection from danger and the cold midnight air to an opposite house, occupied by Mr. W.R. Frost, and begged him to take then in. He refused their request, and shut the door in their faces!! They applied to the next house—the residence of the Misses Foster. These benevolent ladies opened their doors and received not four children only—but eight children and two women. One of the children whom Mr. Frost refused to receive was an infant only one month old and its mother was sick in her bed, and could not move without assistance.

Destructive Fire. Six building were destroyed by fire in Albany on Friday night, viz:—a livery stable (where the fire originated) occupied by Hazard & Carter, corner of Beaver and William Streets—a three story frame building on William Street, occupied by 7 or 8 families, most of whom lost their all and are left entirely destitute; the Rising Sun Tavern, corner of South Pearl and Beaver, occupied by Hazard & Carter; the two adjoining buildings, occupied by William Richards as a sugar factory, and John Sampson as a porter house. The building were owned by Isaac Dennison, and insured for $3,900. Several other buildings, including the theater, were partially injured. During the fire a railroad car coming into the city came in contract with a fine horse running the other way. The shaft of the car entered his breast, and killed him almost instantly. The horse is supposed to have been turned loose from the stable burnt. *N. Y. Gaz.*

From the Blairsville, (Penn.) Record.
Distressing Accident. On Wednesday last, Capt. John F. Greer, of Pittsburg, was drowned in the dam at this place. He was coming down the slack water on the canal boat "Fireman," which he owned and commanded, and just after throwing off his tow line, to pass under the Conemaugh Bridge, a flaw of wind struck the boat and drove her into the stream, which was high and running rapidly. An effort was instantly made by a person on the shore to take out a line with a flat, but failed in reaching the boat. On seeing this Capt. Greer stripped off his upper clothing, took the end of a line in his hand, plunged into the river and swam to what appeared to be a stump sticking up through the water. When he reached it, which he did with great exertion swimming against both the wind and the current he found it to be the roof of a floating tree which sunk as soon as he touched it! He then turned round, despairing apparently of reaching the shore and cried out to those on the boat "pull me in—pull me in." Most unfortunately the piece of rope he still held had slipped the loop by which it was connected with the bowline and consequently left him beyond the reach of assistance. At this juncture two of the hands on board the boat, jumped into the water and made for Blairsville shore, which with much difficulty they reached, within a very few feet of the dam, and were rescued by those on that shore. In the meantime the boat with four persons still on board, and Capt. Greer swimming after it, approached the verge on the dam, and the next instant both pitched over—a fall of twelve and a half feet. The boat was not injured except in the breaking of her rudder, and the persons in her were perfectly safe, and were shortly afterwards relieved by a skiff from the shore. Mr. Greer was seen to go over the dam in a swimming posture and rise three several times

on the swell below, but the reaction of the water carried him back as often, in spite of his efforts, and he sunk to rise no more.

An interesting exhibition of cool deliberation that took place on board the boat and witnessed by the persons on shore is worthy of notice.

A lad apparently about 15 years of age named Francis Martin, of Allegheny Town was observed when it was evident that the boat would go over the dam, to walk over the deck, and deliberately gather up Capt. Greer's coat, hat, and waist coat, and a saw and carry them below, and as deliberately close the hatches and cabin doors after him. No sooner had he finished his work then the boat took the pitch.

From Cape of Good Hope. Capt. Felt, of the Derby, brings information that one of the Caffree Chiefs had commenced a sanguinary war on the colonist, murdered many of the farmers, burnt their houses, carried off their cattle, &c. The survivors fled to Graham Town for safety. The governor at Cape Town dispatched Col. Smith, with detachments of troops to Graham Town, and in January, he was mustering all the force he could collect, English and Hottentots to meet the enemy. The inhabitants at Cape Town were raising funds for the relief of the distressed colonists. *Salem Reg.*

A White Slave. A most extraordinary and outrageous abuse of usurped authority over a fellow creature was developed at the upper police office on Saturday. Mr. James McEnally of Fourth Street, applied to Mr. Palmer the magistrate to send a little girl about fourteen years of age to the House of Refuge, as he said she was so very badly disposed that it was impossible to get any good of her. Mr. Palmer consented to take the girl and send her to the House of Refuge or the Alms House and Mr. McEnally brought her to the police office. When he was leaving the office he stretched out his hand to shake hands with her, but instead of putting out her hand to meet his, she shrunk back from him as it his attempting to touch her had terrified her. Mr McEnall then left the office. Mr. Palmer had observed the occurrence and perceiving that the girl was from some cause or other, in a state of extreme terror, he addressed her in a solacing manner, and endeavored to encourage her by saying that she should be taken good care of, and made comfortable. Whilst he was speaking to her he took her by the hand. On doing so he perceived that it was black and bruised from some hurt. Mr. Palmer asked her what had happened to her hand, and she replied in the most piteous manner, "Oh, sir, my *master* had beat me, and my back is very sore." Mr. Palmer then examined her person and found that from the small of her back down to the calf of her leg she was covered with black marks, bruises and cuts, some of which were festering.

On making this discovery Mr. Palmer made inquirers into the matter, and from what has as has been developed it appears that a Mr. R., formerly of the city, obtained possession of the girl. By what means is unknown–when she was only a few years old, and reared her and treated her completely as a slave. A few months back Mr. R. left this city and went to reside in New Jersey, and when going there hired out the girl to McEnall, in the same way that any slave owner would hire out a slave, at twenty shillings a month, the money to be paid to R., and the girl to get nothing but food and raiment. The unfortunate little girl possesses an extremely agreeable and rather pretty countenance, and evinces too much simplicity in the history she gives of herself, to leave any ground for doubt of its being true. She is altogether ignorant of her name or parentage, and only remembers that she once lived in the country. When she came into the possession of Mr. R., he named her *Philadelphia*, which, when speaking to her, he generally abbreviated to the word *Philly*, and this is the only name she recollects to have been ever called by. By her own accountshe has always been treated as a complete slave, and since she has been with her last master, with the exception of food, of which she says she got sufficient, she has been treated worse than most slaves have been treated in this country during the last half century. She was obliged to sleep on the garret floor without anything but one blanket for a bed and covering, and as to her apparel she says it was never better than what she now wears, and her outer garment is seemingly composed of a piece of an old sack. There was a gentleman of strong nerves, and by no means given to the "melting mood," present, when she was examined at the police office and so much was he affected by her story, and the horrible appearance which her person presented, that he wept like a child. As soon as Mr. Palmer examined her and heard her story, he immediately had McEnall brought to the police and bound over to answer whatever charge might be brought against him for ill-treating her. *N. Y. Jour. Com*

U. S. Ship Peacock. This fine vessel has just been fitted out for a long voyage to the eastern seas. She will carry out E. Roberts, Esq., the diplomatic agent in whose labors were are indebted for the treaties with the Sultan of Muscat and King of Siam. He bears with him the ratification of those treaties and goes in to complete and establish relations of amity and commerce for which his enlightened services have already laid the foundation. He will be accompanied by scientific agents, and from their joint observations during the long voyage of the ship, we may expect to derive much information regarding those comparatively unknown countries that will be valuable to commerce and to science.
Boston Gazette

The Great Foot Race of ten miles within the hour took place on the Union Course, Long Island, on Friday. Nine persons started for the purse. After performing two miles, says the New York Gazette, one of them gave up and by the time of the eight mile was completed, only four were left on the ground, but three of whom performed the whole distance, and one alone within the time. The successful individual is named Henry W.

Stannard, a native of Killingworth, Connecticut, about 24 years of age, and six feet one inch in height. He performed the distance in 59 minutes and 50 seconds, having ten seconds to spare, and, of course, won the whole sum offered by Mr. Stevens, (one thousand dollars) and the additional sum of three hundred dollars offered by the club. The other two men were about 15 or 20 seconds over the house, but Mr. Stevens came forward with a praise–worthy liberality, and gave each of them two hundred dollars.

Mysterious. A Mr. David Woods, who has for considerable time driven a team between Greenfield and Boston, disappeared in a mysterious manner on the evening of Monday last. He was with his team and load of goods on his way from Boston in company of a Mr. Dow, and put up for the night at Washington House in this village and was seen about 10 o'clock on that evening about the premises. The next morning, it was discovered that he did not lodge in the house, and he has not since been seen. Some anxiety for a time was manifested for his safety, but it is now generally believed that he has absconded. *Nashua Gazette.*

Loss of Life, Chief Justice Marshall. We learn that the steamboat *Chief Justice Marshall* on her passage from New York to this city was wrecked yesterday morning, off New Haven. Her engine became unmanageable during the violent storm of the preceding night and she was driven about for several hours until she struck upon the rocks in attempting to enter New Haven harbor. We understand that the passengers and crew were landed in safety, with the exception of the pilot (Hascall) who was drowned. A stage passenger this morning reports when he left New Haven last evening it was there reported that the Marshall had nearly gone to pieces.

Hartford Times of Wednesday

The Earl of Mar. This nobleman, who commanded the army of the Pretender in the Scottish rebellion of 1719, is said to have left a son and a daughter at Newcastle upon Tyne, when he and the unfortunate prince made their escape into France. Soon after the son, quite a boy, came to America and landed at Portsmouth, N. H., where he lived a short time, and finally married at Kittery, Me. After the British government granted a pardon the Earl, with permission for him to return to his estate at Newcastle, he sent for his son, who went to England and had an interview with his father. It was agreed that the son should return to American, and accompany his wife to England, but circumstances of an extraordinary nature detained him for two or three years in this country; at last he was suddenly taken sick and died. He left six children who settled in different parts of Maine and New Hampshire, from whom originated nearly all this part of America, who bear the name of Mar. The heirs have lately taken measures to recover the immense property left by the Earl of Mar in England, and have sent an agent to Newcastle Upon Tyne for this purpose. The property is said to amount to the enormous sum of sixty or eighty million dollars.

Whaleman Burnt At Sea. In the brig Alexander, arrived last night from Trinidad, Cuba, came passengers Capt. E. C. Joy and mate, late of the whale ship Lydia, of Nantucket, which was destroyed by fire in the Pacific Ocean on the 31st of January last, in lat. 4 18 S., lon 84 20. All the crew were saved in their boats, and picked up by the bark Washington, and taken to Payta, whence Capt. Joy and his mate crossed the Isthmus of Darien, took passage to Jamaica, and thence to Trinidad. *Trans.*

Fatal Accident. On the 24th April, Henry S., a promising son of Martin Wilder of Worcester, aged 6 ½ years was killed, while at play in a factory at South Worcester. He thoughtlessly moved a belt from the place where it was usually kept when no in use, so that it caught on a shaft, which was revolving seventy times in a minute. His foot becoming entangled in the belt, he was carried round the shaft about 30 times before the wheel could be stopped, his head striking against the timbers above each time. He died in about four hours.

Worcester Spy.

MARRIAGES

In Groton, Mass., Mr. Reuben Simpson of this town to Miss Jane Day of Groton.

In Hanover by Rev. Mr. Morey, Elbridge G. Chase of this town to Miss Caroline Maria Easton, of Hanover.

In Peterborough, Mr. William S. Roberts, of Sudsbury, to Miss Sophronia Danforth, of Peterborough.

In Gilmanton, Mr. Reuben Page, to Miss Mary A. Gilman.

In Mason Village, by the Rev. B. Knight, Rev. Joel Wheller of Dunbarton to Miss Julia Ann Elliot of Mason, Mr. Luther Wetherbee of Rindge, to Miss Ester Jeffts of Mason.

In Canterbury, by Hon. J. M. Harper, Mr. Joseph W. Scales to Miss Sarah N. Shaw.

In Center Harbor, Mr. Life A. Hazeltine, of Concord to Miss Caroline S. Senter, of the former place.

In Portsmouth, Mr. William Johnson to Mrs. Charlotte Cummings.

In Greenland, Capt. Ammi R. Cutter, of North Yarmouth, Me., to Mrs. Martha Ann M. Leighton of Portsmouth.

DEATHS

In this town, Miss Hannah George, aged 26, daughter of David George, Esq.

In Lee, April 27th, after a distressing sickness of 27 days, John Jay son of John and Parna Wilson, aged 23 months. Printers in Va., N. Y., Me., are &c.

In New Boston, April 22., Mr. Joseph Webster, aged 73, a soldier of the Revolution, formerly of Springfield.

In Wentworth, 21st ult., Enoch Page, Esq., 52.

In Canterbury, of consumption, Mrs. Anna F. Hedge, 42.

In North Hampton, Mrs. Persis C., wife of Abraham Towle, formerly of Boston, aged 27.

In Kentucky at the residence of Col. M. R. Johnson, Black Coat, a distinguished Chief of the Cherokee tribe of the Indians. He was on a visit to the Choctaw Academy.

In Lexington, Mass., Rev. William Mussey aged 63, for thirty years pastor of the Congregational Church and society in Sullivan, N. H.

In Hawke, March 31st., Mr. Peter Stevens, after a few days confinement to his house, aged 70. He had been a member in the Methodist Church, about 39 years.

In Henniker, 22nd ult., of consumption, Mrs. Betsey B. Kimball, 37, wife of Mr. Samuel Kimball. Mrs. Kimball was a person of inestimable worth and one whose memory will long live in the hearts of all her friends, and acquaintances to whom by the amiability and sweetness of her temper, joined with correctness of department, has most affectionately endeared her. In this dispensation of Providence a husband is bereft of a beloved wife, a mother of a beloved daughter and brothers and sisters of a kind and affectionate sister. As a neighbor she was ever ready to extend the hand of sympathy and friendship and notwithstanding, she has been an invalid for many years. Her sufferings have been great yet her "strength was equal to her day" and her reliance was on her God, to whose will she was perfectly resigned; and her hope was in Christ—having the fear of death removed from her—she died in the triumphs of faith, leaving an evidence behind that her last moments were her happiest. *Com.*

In Charlestown, Mr. Hudlah R., wife of Rev. J. Crosby, and daughter of Rev. Sylvester Sage, of Westminister, aged 42.

In Portsmouth Rev. Joseph W. Clary, late pastor of the church in that place, formerly of Dover.

At Lawrence, N. Y. Mrs. Mary Whitney, formerly of Gilsum, N. H., aged 77. Printer in Me., and Mass., are &c.

In Bow, Miss Noami Noyes, aged 24, daughter of Mr. Clement Noyes.

In Dunbarton, 18th ult., of fever and canker rash, Celana, daughter of Joshua F. and Olive Hoyt, being the sixth daughter of these parent have been called to part with—aged 3 years and 9 months.

In Hanover, Mr. William Knight, aged 86, he was a soldier of the Revolution, during life a firm supporter of the republican form of government. He came to his grave in full faith of entering that heavenly kingdom where trials and troubles are no more. Printers in N. Y., and Mass., are &c.

In Dunbarton, Wednesday, April 22nd, Miss Susan, daughter of M. P. P. Ray, the 18th years of her age. By this dispensation of Providence, parents are bereft of an amiable and lovely daughter; one in whom was concentrated every quality calculated to render her an object of the warmest love and strongest attachment. A brother and sister are called to mourn the loss of the affectionate, kind and obliging companion of their youthful days.

The circle in which she moved is deprived of its brightest ornament, its most beautiful gem. Her whole deportment was ever much as to secure the highest esteem of all which whom she had intercourse. Possessed of a character tarnished by no stain and a disposition more congenial with a heavenly than an earthly soil, she seemed a perfect pattern of female excellence.

Long will her virtues be revered and her memory cherished with fond delight. Times ruthless hand will strive in vain to erase her name written on the tablet of the heart of every one who knows her. And though death has sundered a golden chain, which bound her to the hearts of her numerous friends, yet she will live in their affections till time with them shall cease to be. From the dark portal of the tomb her virtues shine forth with redoubled luster and the smile which but a few days ago would sometimes light up her blooming countenance and which would have graced an Angel's cheek still seems to beam upon her mourning friends.

Her voice seems to whisper in every gale that blows that youth and beauty are no shield against the shafts of the fell destroyer. So insidious were the ravages of her disease that no apprehensions were entertained with regard to her recovery till the afternoon before her death. A few hours before her spirit took its flight to the eternal world, not knowing how soon reason might lose its throne never more to regain its empire over the mind, she with a calm and heavenly composure bid her weeping parents and friends a last adieu. When her tender frame was racked with pains poignant and severe, when death was fast encircling her in his icy embrace, when friend were standing in almost breathless suspense around her dying pillow, and when all earthy objects that are held dear were fast receding from her closing eyes she with Christian triumph and " joy unspeakable and full of glory" exclaimed *"Father I am happy,"* and with strong and unwavering faith in her Savior and a full assurance of a blessed immortality added, *"I shall be happy when I die."* Yes although the cold and silent grave contains her much loved form, yet her immortal spirit has soared to the mansion of eternal rest to meet the beatific smiles of her approving judge and to chant forever in the sweetest and most melodious strains the song of redeeming love.

>Ye mourning friends do not complain,
>Your Susan's gone to endless rest;
>No sorrows now or tort'ring pain,
>Shall e'er corrode her peaceful breast.
>In Jesus' arms she, happy, lies
>And sweetly sings a Savior's love;
>With joy sublime beyond the skies
>She waits to meet you all above.
>   *Com.*

NEW HAMPSHIRE PATRIOT & STATE GAZETTE
Concord, Monday, May 11, 1835

SAMUEL SLATER. The Rhode Island papers announce the death on Monday last, of Samuel Slater, Esq.,—long known as one of the most enterprising and respected citizens of that state, and as the father of the cotton manufacturing business in this country. The first cotton mill built in the United States was erected by him in Pawtucket, and was yet in operation at the time of our last visit. There is a curious anecdote connected with the original machinery of this factory, which, as it is strictly true, we will relate for the edification of Doctors Abercrombie and Macnish, and other inquirers into the philosophy of dreams. Mr. Slater was an ingenious machinist and all the machinery was constructed under his immediate direction. Of course, in the earliest infancy of the business, and before the machinery to be constructed was itself thoroughly understood, or the means for making it as ample as could have been desired, imperfections to a greater or less extent were to be anticipated. At length, however, the work was complete, and high were the hopes of the artist and his employers. All was ready, but the machinery would not move—or least it would not move as intended or to any purpose. The disappointment was great, and the now deceased machinist was in great perplexity. Day after day did he labor to discover that he might remedy the defect—but in vain. But, what he could not discover waking was revealed to him in his sleep.

It was perfectly natural that the subject which engrossed all his thoughts by day should be dancing through his uncurbed imagination by night, and it so happened that on one occasion having fallen into a slumber with all the shafts and wheels of his mill whirling in his mind with the complexity of Ezekiel's vision, he dreamed of the absence of an essential band upon one of the wheels. The dream was fresh in his mind on the following morning, and repairing bright and early to his works, he in an instant detected the deficiency! The revelation was true and in a few hours afterwards the machinery was in full and successful operation.

Such is one feature in the history of American manufactures. The machinist has since led an active and useful life—sustaining in all the relations of society, and unblemished reputation. *N. Y. Commercial*

Novel Expedient for Catching a Thief. A short time since a miller residing near Beverly whose premises had been entered for some time past nightly, and a considerably quantity of corn abstracted, hit upon an ingenious expedient of the detection of the offender. The means of the ingress was by putting the finger through a hole in the door, which uplifted the latch. On the night in question the miller set a common rat trap and hung it inside the door so that the thief would be obliged to touch the spring in opening the door. Having taken this precaution he left it for the night, and on going the following morning his expectations were realized by finding a fellow suspended from the door by his finger. The miller after severely admonishing him for the crime, and taking into consideration the sufferings the poor wretch had undergone, gave him the choice of abiding by the law, or a good horsewhipping. It is needless to add he preferred the latter alternative, which the miller administered pretty freely and then released him.

Hull Rockingham

A Horse in a Printing Office. Saturday last while all hands were attentively engaged at the types, a large and likely horse came dashing through the back alley, mounted the platform at the door, for a moment took a look, then made a sudden spring into the office and struck our large iron press, on which lay the outer form of the Sentinel. The violence with which the press was struck, moved it several inches, and brought the animal at full length upon the floor, amidst our cases, stands, &c. After nearly recovering his feet he again fell, but finally rose, made a jump and stood—his eyes flashing, and showing symptoms of great fright. He was seized and lead to the front door, upon reaching which, he ran off at full speed and we have not since heard of him.

How he escaped with so little damage appears miraculous. *Augusta Sentinel*

Nine barns were blown down in Unity, N. H., during the late severe gale.

Cincinnati Going the Whole Hog. It is said the merchants of Cincinnati will clear $800,000 this season upon the single article of pork. They go the whole hog, feet and ears, middlings, tail and snout in the way of making money.

The private fortune of Louis Phillippe, King of France is said to amount to twenty-five millions dollars.

The Rev. E. K, Avery is preaching in the interior of New York.

JUDGE BUCHANAN of Maryland lately attended in court at the trial of his son for shooting a railroad laborer who made an attempt upon his life–the prisoner was acquitted. The conduct of his father is said to have been just and impartial, and indicative of a degree of moral firmness seldom equaled.

NOTICE

IS hereby given that I give my son Levi Tucker, Jr., his time from this date; he is authorized to trade and act for himself, and I shall demand none of his wages nor pay any of his debts after this date. LEVI TUCKER

Witness–Micajah M. Smith
Orange, March 28, 1835

NOTICE

THIS is to forbid all persons harboring or trusting Rachel Stevens and Esther Raynoe, town paupers of New

Chester on my account, as I have contracted with said town for the their support for one year, and have made suitable provisions at my house in said town.

SAMUEL MARTIN

New Chester, March 13, 1835.

NOTICE

THE subscriber cautions all persons against purchasing five certain notes dated April 8, 1833 for $433.33, with interest each, payable in two, three, four, five and six years from date, running to Stephen P. Breed, or order, and signed jointly by us—as said notes have been obtained under fraudulent pretences, and for no valuable consideration, we will not pay the same.

DUDLEY THING
JOSEPH CARTER

Concord, April 24, 1835.

NOTICE

THIS certifies, that I have given my son Stephen Morse, the remainder of his time during his minority; I declare him free to act and trade for himself after this date and that I relinquish all claims to his earnings.

PETER MORSE

Witness { William Gibson
{ Alice Blodgett

Poplin, Feb. 10, 1835.

MARRIAGES

In Bartlett, April 29, by Rev. Daniel Elkins, Mr. John B. Deering to Miss Hannah Thompson, both of Bartlett.

In Keene, Levi Chamberlain, Esq., Attorney at Law, to Miss Harriet A. Goodhue.

In North Hampton, Col. Josiah Dow, Jr. to Mrs. Eunice Moulton, both of Hampton.

In Haverhill, Mr. Joseph Hartwell, of Piermont, to Miss Ruth Keyes.

In Goshen, on the 7th inst., by Rev. Ira Person, Mr. Benjamin S. Broton, to Miss Miriam Libbey.

In Newport, by Rev. J. Woods, Mr. George W. Howe, to Miss Sarah M. Carr, both of Newport.

DEATHS

In this town, of scarlet fever, on Saturday, May 2, at the house of Richard Bradley, Esq., Harriet Osgood Ayer, youngest child of the late Doctor Samuel Ayer, of Eastport, Me., aged 12 years. She was a child of remarkable intellect, mild in her disposition, affectionate, sensible and so promising to have attracted ordinary attention. Also, on Thursday, May 7, at the same house, Mrs. Sarah Newman Ayer, widow and mother to the above deceased, aged 44. Mrs. Ayer was the only child of the late Capt. George Connell, formerly of Newburyport, and afterwards a resident of this vicinity. Caressed by fond parents and friends in early life, she lived to drink deep of life's bitter cup in privation of parents and husband, and nearly every blood connection, saving two remaining children. Her two last years were spent with the friends and connections of her deceased husband, upon whose arms she threw herself, and a zealous but humble follower of the meek and lowly Savior on whose name her last faltering accents whispered praise.

Mr. Robert Davidson, aged about 60. May 3, Elbridge Chase, son of Mr. Jacob Perkins, aged 4 years. May 6, Georgiana, aged 2 years, child of Mr. James Kendrick. May 1, Valara Ann Capen, aged about 18.

Drowned at Canaan, on Tuesday last, George S., son of Nathaniel P. Rogers, of Plymouth, aged 11.

In Warren, Nathaniel Batchelder, Jr., only son of Nathaniel Batchelder, aged 19.

In Rumney, of the scofula and pulmonary consumption, Rev. Joseph Dearborn, a member of the Methodist, N. H. Annual Conference, aged 29.

In Great Falls, Mrs. Elizabeth S., wife of Mr. Ezra Harthan, aged 33 years; Mrs. Eliza, wife of Mr. Solomon Ham, aged about 30. In Andover, N. H., George Gilbert Thompson, of Boston, about 6 months.

In Middleton, of consumption, Mrs. Mary Whitehouse, wife of Mr. John C. Whitehouse, and daughter of Nehemiah and Elizabeth Kimball, aged 18 years.

In Newport, Edwin C. Brown, aged 31. Printer in New York, are &c.

In Nottingham, April 20, Mrs. Thankful Newhall, wife of Mr. George P. Newhall, aged 43. She had been confined to her bed but a few days, and was then called to leave a world of pain and suffering for one of the unclouded felicity. She has left a kind husband and 7 children to mourn the loss of one who in all her relations of life was kind and affectionate and by her example testified to the world, that she sought a desirable inheritance. An able and appropriate discourse was delivered upon the occasion by Elder Daniel P. Cilley, from Matthew 24 44. Printers in Me., and Mass., are &c.

In Hopkinton, April 18, after a few days sickness of inflammation of the bowels, Mrs. Palfrey, wife of Deacon John S. Palfrey, aged 41. Mrs. Palfrey was a member of the Baptist Church in Hopkinton. In her life she was beloved for her social virtue and Christian meekness, and in her death lamented by all her acquaintances. She lived an ornament to her profession, and died the death of the righteous. She has left a fond husband and a large family of children and many relatives to lament her sudden departure. Printers in N. Y., and Mass., are &c.

In Dunbarton, Isreal Clifford, in his 90th year. Printers in Me., Mass., and Vt., are &c.

In Gilmanton, Ezra, son of Ezra D. and Nancy Nute, aged 13 months.

At the Alms House in Derry, Mary Riddle, at the advanced aged of 116 years.

In Providence, R. I., Mr. Nehemiah Bartlett, in the 36th year of his age, formerly of Nottingham, N. H.

In Alton, Mr. Enos Whitehouse, in the 53rd year of his age. He was a wealthy farmer and a firm Republican. Printers in Me., and &c.

In Bow, April 11, Miss Naome A. Noyes, aged 23. Printers in Me, and Mass., are requested to notice the above.

NEW HAMPSHIRE PATRIOT & STATE GAZETTE
Concord, Monday, May 18, 1835

Thomas Jefferson's Opinion of Farmers. "Those who labor in the earth," he early declared, "are the chosen people of God, if ever he had a chosen people, whose breasts he has made his peculiar deposit for substantial and genuine virtue. It is the focus in which he keeps alive that sacred fire which otherwise might escape from the face of the earth. Corruption of morals in the mass of cultivators, is a phenomenon of which no age or nation has found an example. It is the mark set on those who not looking up to heaven, but their own soil and industry, as does the husbandman for their subsistence, depend for it on the casualties and caprice of customers. Dependence begets subservience and venality, suffocates the germ of virtue; and prepares fit tools for the designs of ambition. This, the natural progress and consequence of the arts has sometimes perhaps, been retarded by accidental circumstances but generally speaking, the proportion which the aggregate of the other citizens bears, in any state to that of its husbandmen, is the proportion of its unsound to its healthy parts and is a good enough barometer hereby to measure its degree of corruption."

Thomas Laws, Esq., has been appointed postmaster at Washington, N. H., vice C. C. Boutwell, Esq., resigned.

Jason Allen, Esq., of Lebanon, has been appointed County Treasurer for Grafton, in place of Enoch Page, deceased, by the Court of Common Pleas.

The property of the late Samuel Slater, who died recently in Rhode Island is said by the Pawtucket Chronicle, to be estimated at nearly two millions of money.

Great Fire at Wilmington. A destructive fire occurred at Wilmington, N. C., on the 2nd inst., which destroyed property to the amount of $70 or $80,000 dollars.

Death of President Cushing. Jonathan F. Cushing, Esq., President of Hampden College, died in Raleigh on the 25th April, of a pulmonary affection with which he has been afflicted for many years. He was a native of New England and has been President of Hampden College about eighteen years.

NOTICE

I hereby give CHARLES C. DEARBORN my son, a minor, his time to trade and transact business for himself and claim none of his earnings after this date and pay no debts of his contracting. ABRAHAM DEARBORN

  Noah G. Smith   } Witness
  Thomas R. Crosby }
    Northfield, May 14, 1835

NOTICE

IS hereby given that I have this day given my son DAVID ORDWAY his time, and I shall hereafter claim none of his earnings, nor pay any debts which he may contract after this date. JOSEPH ORDWAY

  Witness–Thomas R. Taggant
    Hooksett, May 18, 1835

MARRIAGES

In Gilmanton by the Rev. Mr. Clark, Mr. Peter Perkins to Miss Mary A. Greene, all of Gilmanton.

In New Boston by Rev. J. Atwood, Mr. Joshua E. Woodbury, Jr., to Miss Rachel Walker. Also, Mr. Joseph B. Cochran to Miss Elizabeth Dodge, all of New Boston.

In Saco, Me., Dr. Ezra Bartlett of Haverhill, to Miss Sarah, daughter of Josiah Calif, Esq.

In Strafford, Mr. Daniel B. Waldron to Miss Druzilla W. Parshley.

In New London by the Rev. O. Tracy, Mr. Nathaniel Seavey, of Andover to Miss Rosaline Woodward.

In Salisbury, Ms., Mr. Peabody Ilsley of West Newbury to Miss Mary Perkins of Seabrook.

In Wilton, Rev. H. W. Strong of Dublin to Miss Cyrena L. Winn.

In Castleton, Vt., Mr. W. S. Fairfield, editor of the Vermont Statesman, to Miss Mary Ann Goodwin.

DEATHS

In Northfield, very suddenly, Mrs. Lydia, relict of the late Thomas Clough, Esq., 73.

In Raymond, of small pox, Widow Deborah Richardson, 72.

In Hopkinton, suddenly of the apoplexy, Widow Meriam Farrington, 83.

In Newport, Widow Anna Hurd, 74.

In Acworth, Mrs. Gregg, consort of Mr. John Gregg, aged 41, of consumption. Mr. George Anson Merrill, aged 22, son of the Rev. Joseph Merrill, a graduate of Dartsmouth College and recently a member of the medical class of that institution.

Drowned in Canaan, George S., son of Nathaniel P. Rogers, Esq., of Plymouth, aged 11.

In Dover, Miss Lydia Daniels of Barrington, aged 25; Miss Sophronia Tasker, aged 21; Widow Mary Taylor, 75.

In New York City, Mr. Otis Ferrin, aged 28, son of Capt. Enos Ferrin, of Hebron in this state.

In Exeter, Miss Frances C. Conner, aged 36, youngest child of the late Benjamin Conner, Esq.

In New Chester, Mrs. Betsey, relict of the late Mr. Charles Bean, aged 100 (?) years, and 5 days. She had been a worthy member of the C. B. church about 70 years. A sermon was preached at her funeral by Rev. B. H. MacMurphy from Rev. 14 13. Printers in Mass., and Vt. are &c. *Com.*

In Deerfield, March 17, Mr. Samuel G. Goodhue, a worthy member of the Baptist Church in that place, aged 28. It may be truly said of Mr. Goodhue, "the memory of the just is blessed." His memory will long live in the hearts of beloved parents, brothers, and sisters; of a large circle of affectionate friends; of the people of God and of numerous youth, whose minds he successfully directed in the delightful fields of science, and impressed with the importance of early being devoted to religion. It was his object in all his connections and relations in life to lead those with whom he associated to a more entire consecration of themselves to the service of God, and a preparation for death and eternity. He enjoyed excellent health and had commenced a regular course of study preparatory to the practice of medicine; but about three years since, while attending the medical lectures at Brunswick, Me., he was taken with bleeding at the lungs. With the advice of his physicians, he soon left no more to return to the fond object of his pursuits, the acquisition of knowledge, and a preparation for future usefulness. He however so far regained his health that he taught at a number of schools, (his favorite employment in which he was uncommonly successful) and engaged in some other business, but not without frequent returns of bleeding. While visiting a sister, a few miles distant a few weeks before his decease, he was very violently seized, and after being conveyed to his parents, the fatal disease, which had already prostrated his strength continued its ravages and soon brought him to the cold embrace of death. But death to him had lost its terrors. From a child he possessed an amiable disposition and was upright in all his conduct. But it was in religion he shone the brightest. From the first openings of his benevolent mind he believed in the necessity of experimental religion, and was often convicted of his sinfulness in the sight of Holy God. The prayers, exhortations, and holy example of pious parents, and Christian friends were often blessed for his good, in keeping alive a sense of divine things in his youthful heart. It was not, however, till about eight years before his death that he gave up his heart to God through Christ, and experienced the witness of the Holy Ghost that he was born of God. His faith in the atoning merits of the Savior, and his hope in His pardoning mercy were not merely speculative principles, which glow in the head but leave untouched the heart, but they possessed that life-giving power that led him to loathe and abhor himself and pant after the image of his divine Redeemer in the service of God. He was not that self-confident professor that goes about boasting of his engagedness in religion and of the strength of his faith and love, but that meek, humble, devoted Christian, that feared, labored and pressed forward in the path of duty least he should be wanting. Nor did he rest upon his virtuous efforts for salvation; the righteousness of Christ was all his hope. Nor did he live for himself. Next to the glory of God he sought the present and eternal welfare of all with whom he associated. His brothers and sisters shared largely in his pious efforts, and he had the happiness of seeing many of them pious before he was called from them. His neighborhood too, will long remember with what delight they listened to his many prayers and expostulations in the meetings he helped sustain; and the many youths and children he instructed will never forget his wise counsels and ardent prayers, while he pointed them to that Savior who says, "those that seek me early shall find me."

During the last confinement of Mr. Goodhue he complained much of the languor and darkness of his mind, which he attributed in a great measure to his extreme weakness; but never lost his confidence in God, nor in the fullness and willingness of Christ to save the chief of sinners that came to him. He conversed freely with the numerous friends who called to see him, and would often remark, "are you prepared for such a hour as this?" Addressing a pious sister, who watched his last moments, he said, "I can give you up, and say, farewell dear sister. O live near thy Savior and it will be but a short time before we shall meet to part no more. And looking from time into eternity, I have had a sweet glimpse of the saints above, all with immortal lungs singing praises to God." He often repeated the verse,

"Lord at thy temple we appear,"

and finally, he breathed out his soul into the bosom of the Savior no more to experience pain and sorrow.

Printers in Me., Mass, and Vt., are &c. Com.

NEW HAMPSHIRE PATRIOT & STATE GAZETTE
Concord, Monday, May 25, 1835

Mrs. Tyron, about 20 years of age who resided in Vandam Street, New York, and who had been married about six months, swallowed a shilling's worth of laudanum on Monday evening, and died about 10 o'clock on Tuesday morning. She had been *deserted by her husband* and this is supposed to have prompted her to the fatal act. A man who will desert the woman he has sworn to love, cherish and respect—under any circumstances,—is a brute, and hanging is too good for him.

From the N. Y. Com. Advertiser of Tuesday

FIRE—Death of Five Persons. At two o'clock this morning a fire broke out in a two story brick front house, No. 4 Front Street, occupied by Mr. Dalton, on the lower floor, as a grocery, and several families above. The flames spread so very rapidly that the inmates of the house, near twenty in number, would all have perished, had they not in part retreated from their slumbers through the second story windows. One of the families was that of a laborer by the name of Mooney, who, in making his escape, fell upon the pavement, and broke his leg; and is so much injured otherwise, that his situation is deemed critical. He was followed to the window by his eldest son, aged ten year, who recollecting that his mother, and the other children, one seven, and one a year old were left behind, went to their relief, but the flames prevented his noble purpose, and all four perished. Their remains have been taken from the ruins and a coroner's jury was summoned this forenoon to take an inquest. Another person, a young man whose name we have not learnt, aged 22 years, a shoe maker, who landed from St. Johns on Tuesday, also perished, making five in all. Another person was severely injured in leaping from a window.

A bill to abolish imprisonment for debt has recently been introduced into the British House of Parliament.

The Tomb of Byron. It is but a few years ago that I stood by the grave of one of the greatest poets and one of the most extraordinary men of this or any other age. It was in a miserable little village!, and he had gone and dwelt in the lands of old renown—in the lands of present and perpetual beauty he had walked with the mightiest, the wisest and the most illustrious of the earth, and not only the multitude, but they also had looked upon him with wonder and admiration. He had desired pleasure and reaped it down to the coarse and jagged stubble of pain and barrenness; he had panted for renown, and had won it in its fullness; he had rejoiced to sail on wide seas; had sat amid the eternal and most magnificent mountains, and gathered up thoughts of everlasting grandeur; all that was lovely in nature and in man he had seen and partaken without scruple, and without measure. He had even turned in scorn from his native land and sworn that his bones should never lie in its bosom; but death stood before him, and his heart melted and acknowledged its allegiance to the mighty power of nature—to the irresistible force of early ties—and here, from all his glory, to this little obscure, unattractive nook of earth, he was brought! Not a spot of all those distant and beautiful ones might defraud this of its rightful due; nature was more powerful than time, or space, or passion, or fame—dust must mingle with its kindred dust. *Howill.*

Distressing Shipwreck. The schooner Tarborough, Capt. Canfield, was capsized and sunk in six or eight minutes, Nov. 5th, on her passage from St. Thomas for New York, and all on board, consisting of five or six passengers, and five hands were lost, except the Captain, who saved himself in the boat. He was eight days and nine nights without food or water.

A Righteous Verdict. The Springfield, Mass. Gazette, contains notices of several interesting cases decided at the recent term of the Supreme Court in that county, among which is the following.

Contracts for labor. William Fowler vs. Henry Bliss.

This was an action brought to recover wages for five or six month's labor, done by the defendant at so much per month. The defense set up was, that there was a special contract between the parties for a year's service and therefore that the plaintiff could have no claim for wages for a less time, unless he fulfilled the whole contract. Such being the evidence and such the instruction of the court, the jury gave a verdict for the defendant.

The principal involved in this case is of great importance, especially in reference to contracts of labor, and accords perfectly with the dictates of equity and common sense, as well as with the decisions of our courts. It is too apt to be the case that persons employed by others, feel and act as if they were at liberty to leave their employment whenever they please—no matter what the contract may be or what the damage to their employers; but it ought to be known and remembered that whenever there is a contract to labor for a man for any specific time, say a year, the laborer can recover nothing for any portion of his work, it he does not continue in his service the whole time, unless indeed the contract has been waived.

Fatal Casualty. On Monday last as Mr. Samuel Ward of Goshen Gore was rolling logs over a defective mill yard to the saw mill he slipped from one of the string pieces, fell about 12 feet, struck his neck across the sharp edge of a slab which broke it and produced instant death. Mr. Ward was 53 years of age—a respectable citizen—a member of the Christian church—and has left a large family and circle of connections to mourn his sudden exit. "In the midst of life, we are in death." *Danville, Vt. Star.*

CURIOUS REMINISCENCE

The French paper, published in New York, (the Courier des Etas Unis) has copied from a Paris print a very curious historical document which goes to prove that nearly two hundred years ago a man was confined in a mad house for having had the genius to discover the power of steam. The document is in the form of a letter dated Paris 1641, from a French gentleman to his friend in the country, in which the writer describes his doing the honor of Paris to an English Marquis of Worcester, represented as a man of strong and original mind.

"Among other places, they visited together the inmates asylum at Bicetre where their attention was attracted by a man crying out to them, "I'm not mad; I have made a discovery which will enrich the country that shall apply it." On being asked what it was he said, shrugging his shoulders, "Ah, it is something very simple—you would never discover what it is; it is the employment of the steam of boiling water." The keeper said his name was Solomon Decaus. He came from Normandy four years before, in order to present to the king a memoir of the wonderful results that might be obtained through the invention. To listen to him, one would think that machinery and carriages could be set in motion by steam. Cardinal Richeliue dismissed him without a hearing. Decaus however, continued to repeat his applications until the Cardinal, tired of being constantly beset by him, and importuned "by his nonsense," ordered to him to be confined in the lunatic hospital at Dicetre. He had written a book on the subject, and the Marquis of Worcester after examining it, said, "This man is not mad—and in my country, instead of being confined he would be loaded with wealth." On conversing with him the Marquis said that he was now deranged and that he had been rendered so by captivity and suffering.

Such is the substance of this letter, which is another instance added to many which prove that when a man is much beyond his age he is much more likely to receive persecution than honor. The great discoverers and improvers among men have generally been neglected, despised, imprisoned, or put to death by their contemporaries.

The number of physicians in the state of New York is 2650.

MARRIAGES

In this town on the 21st inst., by Rev. Mr. Cummings, Mr. John Munroe to Miss Mary Epps, both of Concord.

In Bradford by S. Jones, Esq., Mr. William H. H N. Robey, to Miss Julia M. Downing, both of Sutton.

In New Chester by Benjamin Emmons, Esq., Mr. Edward Buzzell of Wilmot, to Miss Sarah Emmons of New Chester.

In Dover, Mr. John Kenney, of Lagrange, Me., to Miss Elizabeth Willey. Mr. Stoten Austin to Miss Sarah Varney.

In Lyman, Mr. Samuel Gilpatrick of Dover, to Miss Susan Clark of Lyman.

In Bradford by the Rev. Mr. Thatcher, B. F. Long, M. D., of Alton, Illinois to Miss Lucy Martin.

In Boston, Mr. John Quinn to Miss Elizabeth Morse, of Sandwich, N. H.

In North Hampton, Mr. George W. Flagg of Warwick, R. I., to Miss Abigail Marston, daughter of Jonathan Marston of the former of the place.

In New Ipswich, Dr. William Gallup to Miss Rebecca A. Shed, daughter of Samuel L. Wilder, Esq.

DEATH

In this town, of throat distemper and canker rash, Edward, son of Col. Stephen Brown, aged two years.

In New York City, Joel P. Tibbets, Esq., formerly of this state.

In Farmington of consumption, Mr. Charles Colbath, 47.

In Madbury, Mrs. Patience Hodgdon, 84.

In Hanover, Mr. William Knight, aged 86; he was a soldier of the Revolution.

At Detroit, M. T., Mr. Samuel Chandler, Jr. aged 23. He was a native of Bedford, N. H., and graduated at Union College last July.

In Goffstown, Mr. John Entman, aged 34.

In Hollis, Mrs. Sarah Jewell, wife of Mr. James Jewell, 80.

In Windsor, Mr. Benjamin Davis, 37.

In Dunbarton, on the 12th inst., Widow Agnes Stewart in the 91st year of her age.

In Raymond, April 28, Mrs. Sarah H., wife of Mr. John M. Stevens, aged 31, leaving a husband and four children, two in infancy to mourn and regret her loss. During her last illness Mrs. Stevens was deeply impressed with the importance of religion, sought and as she trusted and all who witnessed her last moments believe, found the delights of redeeming love. When her end approached she conversed with her friends on the advantages of piety, entreated them to make their peace with God and in prayer commended her husband, children and friends to the protection of a beneficent Providence. Printers in Me., Mass., and Vt., are &c.

In Deering of a long and lingering illness, Deacon James Whitaker, aged 79. He was a soldier of the Revolution, fought in the Battle of Bunker Hill and was at the taking of Burgoyne, and afterwards settled in life and enjoyed the liberties which were so dearly bought. He was a good citizen, a regular member of society and of the Church of Christ, and died in full faith of a glorious immortality. Printers in Me., and N. Y., are &c.

In Hopkinton, Saturday evening May 16, Mr. Enos Jones, in the 45th year of his age.

NEW HAMPSHIRE PATRIOT & STATE GAZETTE
Concord, Monday, June 1, 1835

A Severe Character. The New York Morning Herald gives an account of a man by the name of John Allen Williamson, who began business in Vermont at the age of 17, being now only 32. He married a young woman by the name of Mary Taylor whose face was somewhat marked with small pox. Mary was otherwise a tight girl and had a farm, two cows and a young horse left to her by her grand-mother. The first month after marriage Williamson sold the cows for half their value, and rode off with the horse to see the world. This was the last Mary saw of him. Mary cried for a week, wiped her eyes, got married and is now a matron with four boys. His next exploit was in the lower part of Massachusetts. He was teaching school and boarding round among his patrons. In this capacity he prevailed upon Mrs. Walker, the Elder's wife, to run away with him and leave her four children. Williamson carried her with him to the interior of Pennsylvania, where he gave evening lectures on Grammar and Elocution. One morning early he got up and left poor Mrs. Walker asleep, and ran into Maryland with Biddy Leiper who was a nice Dutch girl. This was for love entirely, as Biddy, had nothing to call her own, but a bible which her mother had left her. Williamson sold the bible for a glass of brandy, stole a horse in Maryland, decamped to Western Virginia, and set up for a politician. This trade he found the poorest trade of all. He soon re-crossed the mountains, got into North Carolina, and went digging for gold. He was much pleased with this business, and pictured to himself a long vista of wealth and grandeur. He got up early, and dug deep, made trenches, worked hard, until his eyes fell upon the wife of a neighboring small tobacco planter. He got acquainted with Mrs. Napier, the planter's wife and asked her one evening to walk out with him, she did so; both walked away, leaving the tobacco planter the gainer by a tongue's less noise in his domicile. Williamson next came up like a duck in Savannah, where he was a captain of a small coasting vessel that traded to St. Augustine. From St. Augustine he ran away with John Feld's fourth wife, to Tallahasse—from Tallahasse into the Creek Nation, with a widow. Here he set up a grocery, married the Chief's daughter, got a piece of land, left it, daughter and all and taking a long dive, came up like another duck, somewhere in Oneida County, New York.

Distressing Casualty. Killed on the Monday, 11th of May, at L. R. Falls, Lebanon, Maine, John Bodwell, oldest child of Increase S. Kimball, Esq., aged 3 years and 2 months. The manner of the accident and the circumstances attending it are substantially as follows:-

On Monday the 22nd inst., Mr. Kimball went in his carriage to a lot of land belonging to him at a short distance from his residence taking along with him his little boy; and having completed his business there, was about to return home—having first put his child into the carriage he was about to get in himself when the horse suddenly started, wrested from him the reins which he had hardly yet secured, threw him under the carriage, passed over him, and ran furiously, with the child alone in the carriage, for a little distance, when sheering somewhat to the side of the road, he crossed a causeway or sharp pitch which tossed the vehicle (by this time going at full speed,) and dashed from it the child, dropping him head foremast on a sharp rock, the blow from which severely fractured the skull of the hinder part of the head and leaving him before the carriage, directly in front of the carriage wheels which also passed over his face, cutting and bruising him in a shocking manner—all of which wounds caused almost instant death.

Dover Enquirer

A Storm in a Teapot. A great meeting was held in Boston to nominate Daniel Webster for President. None but those friendly to him were invited, and strange to say, he was nominated *unanimously!* Wonder that we are not told that the spirit and *unanimity* manifested at this meeting insures the defeat of Van Buren.

Post Office Robbery. [From the Baltimore American.] No small degree of astonishment and regret pervaded this community yesterday as the report circulated rapidly through the city that the editor of the Baltimore Gazette, William Gwynn Jones, had been arrested yesterday morning on the charge of having robbed the post office letters containing enclosures of money. Subsequent inquiries, we are pained to state, proved the report in question to be but too true. For at least a month past, as we learn from an authentic source, the Baltimore post office has been in the unpleasant predicament of hearing the complaints of merchants and others, who alleged that their letters, sometimes containing money, had failed to come to hand. In several instances it was ascertained that letters thus missed had been regularly mailed at distant offices, and as they had not reached the individuals here to whom they were addressed, the position of the clerks in the office was rendered extremely unpleasant. The missing letters were uniformly, we believe those due by the southern and western mails, the delivery of which was in the morning. Mr. Jones was accustomed to visit the post office at a very early hour in the morning, and obtained his papers before the office was opened for general delivery. In doing so he was daily within reach of the tables on which the letter mails are spread. Complaints of loss of letters within a few days past were again repeated, and the suspicions of the clerks were at length directed towards Mr. Jones. On Thursday morning he went as usual into the post office and when he retired, certain letters which had been placed in a particular spot near him had also disappeared. The discovery is may be well imagined was truly astounding to the clerks, but as neither of them could testify to the fact of having seen him take the letters, it was deemed prudent to await further developments. Yesterday morning Mr. Jones again entered the post office for his papers, and was seen by a clerk who was on the watch, to take a double letter, the address of which had been previously noted. He was also seen to take from the table five entire packages of southern and western letters, which had not yet been opened. Immediately afterwards he left the office and as he was proceeding to his own office was arrested by a deputy marshal, who had been in waiting for the purpose. The double letter and also the entire packages, containing from fifty to hundreds of letters, were found in his possession. He subsequently made admissions, which show the purloining of upwards of a thousand dollars from letters at various times. The unhappy man—who, up to this period, has enjoyed a full share of the public confidence and respect—has been committed to prison, to take his trial at the regular term of the U. S. Circuit Court. He ascribes the act to a ruinous course of speculation.

Mill Dam—Loss of Lives, &c. We went up yesterday to the Mill Dam which really presented a scene of desolation. Early yesterday morning the water which has been rising rapidly for several days, tore away the cross dam above the mills, and made a breach through which it rushed with such fury as for a time to overflow the floor of the mills; the cross dam struck the main dam and carried off nearly the whole length of this, together with the fender dam on the out side of the mills. A man by the name of Kent belonging to Sebec, was upon the cross dam at the time it started, and if his presence of mind had not deserted him, would have remained upon it safely, but in attempting to leap on shore he fell into the rapids and being unable to swim was drowned—he was about thirty years old, and a man of family. Mr. Cyrus Stinson of Farmington, was lost from off the fender dam, and we left his fellow workmen grappling for the body.

Stinson was about twenty years old, and his father had suffered the loss of one of his limbs at the Mill Dam a short time before.

Twenty or thirty men were upon the main dam when it broke loose, and all escaped (as is supposed) in safety—some leaped on shore and others were taken off in boats—one man escaped by clinging to a log in the river.

The actual damage to the Mill Dam is not great but will cause a suspension of the works for some time until the dams can be repaired. The two men above named are all whose loss is certainly known, although particular inquiry may prove that others are missing. The number of men employed at the Mill Dam is about 220—probably one half of them will be discharged until the necessary repairs are made. *Bangor Whig.*

[By Request]
GEN. LEAVENWORTH

At a meeting of the officers of the 3rd Regiment of Infantry, at Fort Jesup, La., on the 23rd day of April 1835, Colonel James B. Many, was called to the Chair, and Lieutenant and Adjutant George Wright, was appointed Secretary.

The Chairman then stated the object of the meeting was to express the thanks of the officers of the 3rd Infantry to the civil authorities and inhabitants of Natchitoches, for the respect which they paid to the remains of the late Brigadier General Henry Leavenworth, Colonel of the 3rd Infantry.

On motion it was resolved that a committee of three, to consist of Major Nelson, Capt. Walker, and Lieut. Wright, be appointed to draft suitable resolutions.

The committee presented the following resolutions, which were unanimously adopted.

Resolved. That the officers of the 3rd Regiment of U. S. Infantry stationed at this post, duly appreciate the respect and honor, shown by the civil authorities and inhabitants of Natchitoches, for the character and memory of the late Brigadier General Henry Leavenworth, Colonel of the 3rd Infantry.

Resolved. That the officers of the 3rd Regiment of U. S. Infantry, stationed at this post present their thanks to the civil authorities and inhabitants of Natchitoches for their attentions on this melancholy occasion.

Resolved. That a copy of the foregoing resolutions be transmitted to the Mayor of the city of Natchitoches, and also published in the "Frontier Reporter," after being signed by all the officers of the 3rd Infantry, at this post.

    JAMES B. MANY, Col., 3rd Infantry, and Chairman
J. S. Nelson, Major U. S. Army
A. Lewis, Captain 3rd Infantry
T. J. Harrison, Captain, do.
H. H. Loring, Captain, do.
B. Walker, Captain, do.
O. Wheeler, 1st Lieut., do.
J. Bonnell, 1st Lieut., do.
N. C. MacCrae, 2nd Lieut., do.
A.G. Blanchard, 2nd Lieut., do.
H. Swartwout, 2nd Lieut., do.
George P. Field, Brevet, 2nd Lieut., do.
J. L. Coburn, Brevet 2nd Lieut., do.
P. N. Barbour, Brevet 2nd Lieut., do.
G. Wright, Adjutant and Secretary.

    A Noble Reward. Some years since Mr. Joseph Wood, of Trenton, N. J., heroically saved the life of a son of a Mr. Jones of England who had fallen into the Delaware from a steamboat. The grateful parents of the child long pressed munificent rewards upon Mr. Wood but he invariably declined their presents, satisfied with the consciousness of having done a noble deed. Mr. Jones recently died, since which event Mr. Wood has received due notice from the agent of Mr. Jones in this country that he has thus become by the will of the deceased, heir to £27,000 sterling. *Sun.*

    Destructive Fire. On Sunday evening last at half past 11, the mills in Marlborough, owned by G. & N. Converse, consisting of a saw and fulling mill, (the saw mill, wheels and gearing entirely new,) machinery for the manufacture of powder kegs, (new and ready for operation) and a new shingle mill were discovered to be on fire and were entirely consumed, with a large amount of hoops, only insured at the Springfield office, previous to the repairs and putting in the machinery. There had been no fires for 10 days in the premises. How it caught is involved in a mystery.

Fatal Mistake. We learn from the Frederick Maryland Examiner, two members of the family of Mr. Samuel Atkins who resides a few miles north west of that city, were accidentally poisoned on Saturday night last by the introduction of arsenic by mistake, instead of pearlash, in making bread. The mother of Mr. Atkins, who was the person that made up the bread, and one of the children, died on the following morning from the effects of that poison.

Æronautic. Mr. Clayton attempted on the 14th inst., to make his promised ascension at Cincinnati. When every thing was nearly ready a sudden gust of wind struck the balloon, which being released by those who were holding it down, was carried a great distance in the air. There being, however, too much ballast on board, it soon fell to the earth with great violence. Mr. Clayton, who was in the car, threw out ballast as fast as possible, and was dragged by the balloon through the streets and over the tops of the houses, until he came in contact with a chimney with such force as to separate the car from the house. The balloon soon disappeared in the air, but as it was seen to turn upside down, it is hoped the gas may have escaped and that the balloon may yet be recovered. Mr. Clayton was not severely injured. His loss was about $1300.

A young man by the name of Horace Kimball, an indented apprentice to Mr. James K. Remick, printer, of Kennebunk who absconded from Mr. Remick in October last, was yesterday arrested in this city and lodged in Leverett Street Jail for safe keeping. This is one consequence of apprentices deserting their masters, and of parents neglecting to restore them when so deserting.

From the Pensacola Gazette of 25th April

HORRIBLE. The annals of crime and infatuation can scarcely furnish a parallel to an outrage committed in this city on Saturday night last. A Mr. Whittaker, who has for some years been engaged here in business, after returning to his residence from a public assembly with his wife, cut her throat from ear to ear, and then made an unsuccessful attempt to destroy himself by cutting his own throat. When the alarm was given they were found lying on their piazza, the wife, of course, entirely dead, and Whittaker himself in a dangerous situation. It is said he will recover. He was actuated by jealousy.

GUARDIAN NOTICE

THE subscriber has been appointed by the Hon. Judge of Probate, for the county of Merrimack, guardian over the person and estate of EBENEZER BATCHELDER, of the town of Canterbury, in said county, and has taken upon himself that trust by giving bond according to law. He will adjust all claims in favor or against his said ward accordingly. G. L. SARGENT, Guardian.

Canterbury, May 14, 1835.

MARRIAGES

In this town by Rev. Mr. Bouton, Mr. Charles W. Underhill to Miss Susan F. Kimball.

In Hanover by the Rev. Henry Wood, Mr. Charles E. Thompson of Mobile, Ala., to Miss Mary Olcott, daughter of Hon. Mills Olcott.

In Groton by the Rev. J. G. Adams, Mr. John Kidder, Jr., to Miss Betsey Metcalf.

In Somersworth by Rev. Mr. Caverno, Mr. James Goodwin of Berwick, to Miss Sophia S. Hanson, of Somersworth.

In Bellingham, Mass., by Rev. Adin Ballou, Mr. Albert McKeen, of Nashua to Miss Vienna Paine, of Bellingham.

DEATHS

In Francistown, of consumption, Mr. John Petterson, aged 21.

In Conway, Mr. Oliver Sparhawk Steward of Harvard University, and son of the late Samuel Sparhawk, Esq., 29.

In Lowell, Caleb W. Kimball, of Sandbornton, N. H., 22.

In Plaistow, Moses, son of Mr. Henry Sleeper, aged 2.

In Derry, of consumption, Miss Ruth Maria Kimball, 20.

In Mason, Mr. Silas Bullard, 80.

In Meredith, after a long and distressing confinement of 10 months, which was borne with Christian patience and steadfast reliance on the mercy of God, Mr. James Quincy, a Revolutionary pensioner, aged 80. He served in the army of the Revolution 5 years, and was engaged in some of its most important battles. He was in the battle of Bunker Hill and in the battle of Hubbardton, and was there made prisoner and was held enemy two months, and treated with their usual barbarity when he escaped from them and joined the army under General Gates a few days before the surrender of Burgoyne's army. He was likewise at the memorable and hard fought battle of Monmouth. He suffered much while in the army with fatigue and hunger, cold and nakedness as did many others, which exposure caused a cough to settle upon his lungs which continued until his death, a term of more than 50 years. He was a good citizen and neighbor, a kind husband and tender parent and strongly attached to those democratic principles for which he so long fought and suffered for himself and posterity after him to enjoy.

NEW HAMPSHIRE PATRIOT & STATE GAZETTE
Concord, Monday, June 8, 1835

DARING EXPLOIT

Mr. Clarke, in his Natural History, relates the following instance of cool intrepidity, which exhibits very forcibly the daring character and adroit manoeuvres of our naval heroes in the war of the Revolution.

"In June 1797 an expedition of Unites States vessels was fitted out and sailed from Boston. It consisted of the Providence, thirty-two guns, Commodore Whipple: The Queen of France, twenty-eight guns Capt. J. P. Rathburne, and the sloop of war Ranger, Capt. Simpson. About the middle of July, near the banks of Newfoundland as the squadron lay in a fog, signal guns were heard at intervals, the sound of ship's bells striking the hours. From this they supposed themselves to be near a fleet. About eleven o'clock the fog began to clear off when the crew of the Queen of France to their great surprise, found themselves nearly along side of a large merchant ship and soon after they perceived themselves to be in a fleet of one hundred and fifty sails under the convoy of seventy-four and several frigates and sloops of war. The Queen of France immediately bore down to the large ship and hailed her. She answered that the fleet was from Jamaica bound to London. The English ship then hailed the American, and was answered his Majesty's ship Herthusa, from Halifax, on a cruise. The American then inquired if the had seen any rebel privateers. The English replied that several had been driven out of the fleet. The American Capt. Rathburne, then requested the Captain of the English vessel to come on board, which he did; when to his great astonishment he found himself a prisoner. Capt. Rathburne then sent one of his own boats and the English captain's boat, both well manned, to the ship of which they took quiet possession without exciting the least alarm in the fleet, notwithstanding many of the vessels were nearly within hail of the one captured. Rathburne then went along side another large ship and captured her in the same manner. Soon after the capture of the second ship, Commodore Whipple came along side and ordered Capt. Rathburne to edge away out of the fleet as soon as possible as he was persuaded they would be discovered and overpowered. Capt. Rathburne pointed out the two large ships he had captured, and requested permission to remain. The Commodore at first disapproved of this project; but was at length prevailed upon by Captain Rathburne to stay in the fleet all day and capture as many vessels as they could in the same cautious manner. As soon as it was dark they left the fleet after having captured eleven vessels without giving alarm. The squadron arrived safe at Boston with eight of their prizes—three of them having been retaken by the English.

Another Dreadful Accident. Just as our paper was going to press, we are informed that a coal car ran over a person by the name of John Patterson of the Schuylkill Valley railroad, which nearly severed his legs from his body. He survived but a few minutes after the accident.
Miner's Journal

Joseph Blunden—Attempt to Escape. On Sunday night last this unfortunate man made a bold attempt to escape from prison. The fire in his room had as usual been carefully put out but, previous to the last visit of the keeper he had contrived to secrete a few coals in an earthen vessel, by which he rekindled his fire, and having previously sawed off his irons, burned a hole through the floor, passed through into the cellar below and from thence into the yard. He had cut up his bed, made it into a rope and fastening an axe to it, cast it over the wall—with the help of some wood he succeeded in getting nearly to the top of the wall, when the axe slipped from the rope, and he fell back into the yard so severely injured as to prevent any further attempt, where he was discovered in the morning. *Doylestown Democrat*

Blunden was under sentence of death and was to have been executed on Friday. *Post.*

Mail Robber Convicted. At the recent session of the Circuit Court of the United States holden in Windsor, Vermont, *Sylvester W. Sheldon,* formerly postmaster at Londonderry in that state, was tried for violation of the post office laws by a robbery of the mail. It was proved that he had in many instances abstracted money from letters passing through his office, and a portion of the money so obtained was found upon his person. He was sentenced to 12 years hard labor in the state prison.

Fatal Accident in the Coal Mines. Two deaths have recently occurred in quick succession in coal mines in this vicinity, owing as we understand, to a spirit of rashness and indifference which unfortunately but too generally prevails among miners in this neighborhood. A respectable young miner by the name of Taylor, having a parent with 9 children, his brothers and sister dependant upon him for subsistence, fell a victim on Friday week while engaged in the work of undermining in the collieries of Dr. Palmer—and another by the name of Bobb, on Tuesday last while similarly employed in the works of Messrs. Lawton and Weaver. In both instances the individuals were crushed by the superincumbent mass of coal. We trust that these mournful occurrences will operate as a salutary warning to all engaged in the business. *Miner's Journal*

A Hook to Catch Gudgeons. A meeting has been held in Maryland by Josiah Hook, Thomas Hook, Nelson Hook, Gustavus Hook, Samuel Hook, Jacob Hook, Jr., Rudolph Hook, John Hook, Isaac Hook, Richard Hook, and Solomon Hook, and others at which Solomon, who seems to be a very bright Hook presided; and at which meeting it was resolved that they would support no person for the presidency except a friend of the present administration; and that they would support Judge White for that office. This seems to be a Hooking business, but we are sure that none but the smallest fish would bite at such a bare Hook. *Boston Post.*

The Detroit Free Press of the 13th ult., gives the following account of a mighty water snake which has recently paid a visit to the waters of the west:—

"Yesterday between the hours of 5 and 6 p.m. a regular built *Snake* destitute of all appearance of a mane and of those phrenological bumps or bunches which are said to be appurtenant to the old sea serpent—of slim formation, and apparently not less than 75 feet in length, and in the middle about 5 feet in circumference, or 20 inches in diameter—floating down the Detroit River, and passing the city, generally with his head elevated from 5 to 8 feet, as in an attitude of surveying, alternately, the scenery presented on either shore—sometimes carried along by the current, coiled as if prepared to spring upon his prey, and other times stretching forward at full length as if to exhibit himself for the gratification and astonishment of his beholders—his back of a brown color, his side a deep green and his belly a dingy white, without fins—with small green but glistening eyes, encircled with red—at last plunging forward as in sport and disappearing in the depth of the majestic river, was not seen again.

A Man Gone Over Niagara Falls. Two men who were attempting a few days since to pass from Grand Island to the Canada shore were forced into the rapids near the great cataract, and they both jumped out of the boat. One of them was rescued by the people on the shore but the other, a Mr. Bratly, was hurried over the falls and was seen no more. *N. Y. Cur. & Eng.*

ACCIDENT Three of the Irish laborers engaged upon the land of the late Gardiner Greene were partially buried up on Wednesday morning by the falling of an embankment. They however succeeded in disengaging themselves from their uncomfortable situation without having received any serious injury.

Mercantile Journal

MARRIAGES

In Shelburne the 17th ult, by Elder A. Wheeler, Benjamin R. Pinkham, Esq., of Pinkhams Grant to Miss Sarah Ann B. Evans, of Shelburne.

In Jackson April 13, Mr. Daniel Meserve to Miss Joanna Meserve, both of Jackson.

In Salisbury, Mr. John S. Pressy to Miss Rhoda Stevens. Captain John Couch III, to Miss Almeda Greeley.

In Plymouth by Robert Barber, Esq., Mr. Daniel Rowe of Bridgewater to Miss Lucy Morrison of Plymouth. Also, by same, Mr. William B. Nichols of New Hampton to Miss Sally Jewett of Bridgewater.

By Rev. Mr. Storrs, Mr. Samuel Dow, Jr. of Westfield, Mass., to Miss Belinda R. Robinson, of this town.

DEATHS

In Sharon, N. H., May 16th 1835, of the inflammation in the bowels, after a short but distressing illness of four days, Betsey Russell, second daughter of Benjamin Russell, Esq., of Sharon, aged twenty-one years and seven months. Printers in Maine, New York, Pennsylvania and Ohio are &c.

In Springfield, Vt., Moses Chase, Esq., formerly of Hopkinton, N. H., 72.

In New London, Mrs. Betsey Bunker, 68.

In Goffstown, May 3, after an illness of only 24 hours, Mr. John Butman, aged about 35.

In Grafton, on the 10th Feb., last, Mr. Henry Springer, a Revolutionary pensioner, 76. Printer in Me. and &c.

In Lowell, on the 30th ult., very suddenly, Mr. Charles Haselton, son of Lieut. Daniel Haselton of Hebron, N. H., aged 30. His remains were removed to Hebron for interment.

In Jackson, May 20th Miles, son of John Chesley, Esq., aged 7 years, 6 months and 26 days.

In Antrim, Col. David McClure, 77, a respected citizen and Revolutionary pensioner.

In Atkinson, May 23, Samuel N. Little, &c. Printers in N. H., are.

In Alexandria, N. H., on the 28th of May 1835, Mary Ann Fogg, aged 12 years. She came from Stanstead, L. C. in the fall of 1834. She was the daughter of Josiah and Mary Fogg, formerly of Meredith, both deceased. Although an orphan child, few of her age have been more fortunate in securing the favor of all those with whom she became acquainted, her sickness was short but very distressing; this sudden death is much lamented by her young acquaintances. Printer in New York and Lower Canada , are &c.

In Alexandria, May 9, 1835, John Atwood, son of David Atwood, aged about 10 years.

NEW HAMPSHIRE PATRIOT & STATE GAZETTE
Concord, Monday, June 15, 1835

Confessions of a Pirate. The public no doubt, remembers the story of the daughter of Aaron Burr, who was the wife of Governor Alston, of South Carolina. On the return of her father from Europe, about the year 1812, she embarked from Charleston on a visit to him at New York, on board a privateer built vessel, and was never heard of afterward. It seems that her friends at first thought the vessel had fallen into the hands of pirates and afterwards concluded that it was wrecked and lost. It appears from the statement of a respectable merchant at Mobile that a man died in that city recently who confessed to his physician on his dying bed that he had been a pirate and helped to destroy the vessel and all the crew and passengers, on board which Mrs. Alston had embarked from New York. He declared, says this gentleman, that after the men were all killed there was an unwillingness on the part of every pirate to take the life of Mrs. Alston, who had not resisted them or fought them, and therefore they drew lots who should perform the deed, as it had to be done. The lot fell on this pirate who declares that he effected his object of putting a lady to death by laying a plank along the edge of the ship, and made Mrs. Alston walk on that plank till it tilted over into the water with her. The dying pirate requested his physician to make the story public, but his surviving family will not permit or consent that the name of the deceased should be known. *Alabama Journal*

GEN. LEAVENWORTH. We last week published by request the proceedings had by the officers of his regiment on occasion of the death of this gallant and lamented soldier. The following brief biographical notice is from the New York Journal of Commerce:

General Leavenworth was born in the state of Vermont, and in the year 1806 came to the town of Delhi, in Delaware County, N. Y., where he studied law under

General Root, when he entered the army as Captain at the head of a volunteer corps which he raised himself, and from that period till his death he remained in the army. He commanded a battalion in the 9th Regiment at the battles of Chippewa and Bridgewater. After the first of these battles he was made Lieutenant Colonel, and after the second, where he particularly distinguished himself for his gallantry, he was made Colonel. At this battle most of the officers were wounded and for a part of the day nearly the entire command devolved upon him. Whilst he was holding out his arm pointing towards the enemy, a cannon ball struck his arm and knocked him from his horse. After the battle he retired to Delhi where he remained five or six months, and then joined the army. When peace took place he was appointed to the command of Sacketts Harbor and was subsequently stationed at Jefferson barracks, a little below St. Louis on the Mississippi, afterwards at the Falls of St. Anthony on the Mississippi and other outposts until the summer of 1834, when he marched in command of the dragoons, on an expedition to the settlements of Pawnee and Camanche Indians. This was unfortunately his last campaign; he died of the 24th July 1834 of fever, at a place called Cross Timbers on the False Washita. His remains were at first taken to Cantonment Jessup and from thence to New Orleans, from which place they were shipped for this port about six weeks ago. Prior to the shipment the flesh was separated from the bones and nothing but the latter was brought here. They arrived a few days since, and were put on board a steamboat to be conveyed to Delhi, where his wife, who died in 1811 lies interred. She was the sister of Dr. Knapp of this city. In all his different relations of life he sustained the character of a brave, intelligent and highly honorable man.

Mason and Dixon's Line. The question is often asked, "What line is this?" and as often answered, "I don't know." At the suggestion of an intelligent friend we state what this line is. It divides Pennsylvania and

Maryland, commencing at a point at a certain distance north of Cape Henlopen, on the Delaware, and running west to a certain point of longitude. Long and vexatious chancery litigation were had between the proprietors of Maryland and Pennsylvania respecting this line. It was finally run and established under an order of the English Court of Chancery. The surveyors were two gentlemen of the names Mason and Dixon. Hence it is called Mason and Dixon's line. *Cincinnati Gazette*

The Commercial Advertiser published the following letter.
U. S. SHIP VANDALIA, HAVANA }
May 15, 1835 }

An event of melancholy nature occurred to us this afternoon. Commodore John D. Henly, Commander of the West India Squadron, suddenly expired on board the ship; he had been in ill health for some months, but not sufficiently so to alarm his friends. He yesterday afternoon went on shore for the purpose of riding out of the city and returned on board at sundown, apparently as well as usual, but in the night had an attack of diarrhea for which our surgeon, Dr. Osborn, prescribed, little thinking him to be dangerously ill.

I was dining in the cabin today in company with Dr. Osborn and Mr. Miller, the Commodore's Secretary, when suddenly a servant attending upon the Commodore in his state room called to Mr. Miller, who, on entering it requested Dr. Osborn's attendance. We suddenly arose from our seats and on approaching his couch found him in the agonies of death. It was so sudden and so unexpected that we were all astounded—it has cast a gloom over us all.

We shall sail tomorrow morning with the body for Pensacola.

A painful accident occurred last Monday at the military academy at West Point. Two of the cadet were amusing themselves at fencing, when in the heat of the play the foil of one was thrust into the eye of the other, and penetrating to the brain, inflicted a wound of which the unfortunate cadet, a son of Capt. Carter, of Virginia, died in a few hours. The anguish of mind experienced by the survivor is we understand so intense, that the liveliest apprehensions are entertained that grief will wholly overthrow his reason. The two cadets were intimate friends, and were practicing at their foils for mere sport before a number of their companions. The classmates of the deceased entered into a subscription to erect a suitable monument to the memory of their ill-fated associate.

A singular fatality seems to attend the family of Mr. Carter; this is the third of his sons who have died violent deaths. The elder was killed in a duel, the second came to his death by accident, and the fate of the third is recounted in the above statement.

NOTICE

THE subscriber most respectfully begs leave to announce to the public, that he will exhibit to all desirous, the way to enter heaven, obtain forgiveness of former sins and receive eternal life, which alone has power to remove those maladies of the mind resulting from a misspent life.   BENJAMIN GREEN.

Concord, June 8, 1835.

NOTICE

WHEREAS Sarah, my wife has left my bed and board and conducted with impropriety; this is to forbid all persons harboring or trusting her on my account, as I shall pay no debts of her contracting after this date.

JOHN R. PAINE

Center Harbor, June 7, 1835.

NOTICE

THIS certifies that I have given to my son JOSIAH W. WHITE his time to act and trade for himself and I shall claim none of his earning, nor pay any of his debts after this date.   JOSIAH WHITE

Attest—Moses Norris, Jr.

Pittsfield, June 9, 1835.

NOTICE

THIS certifies that I have given to my son JOSEPH REED his time to act and trade for himself; I shall claim none of his earnings nor pay any of his debts after this date.   AARON K. REED

Attest—Benjamin Dow, Jr.
J. G. Perley

June 1, 1835.

NOTICE

THIS certifies that I have given my son LYMAN ROBY his time and authorize him to act and trade for himself and shall claim none of his earnings in future.

ICHABOD ROBY

Sutton, June 10, 1835

MARRIAGES

In Nashua, by Rev. Mr. Pratt, Mr. Joshua D. Pierce to Miss Louisa L. Corbin.

In Dover, Mr. Eli French to Miss Hannah R. Draper.

In Boston by Rev. Mr. Barrett, Mr. James M. Thompson to Miss Caroline Matilda, daughter of Gurdon Steele, Esq.

At St. Petersburg, Russia, in the chapel of the British Factory, on the 2nd April last, by Rev. Edward Law, John Randolph Clay, secretary at the American Legation to Frances Ann Sophia, daughter of Harry Leake Gibbs, of St. Petersburg.

DEATHS

In Northwood, of consumption, Mrs. Mary, wife of Benjamin Batchelder, and daughter of Mr. Samuel Crockett, aged 37.

In Goffstown on the 5th inst., Miss Mary Stark.

In Franklin, Mrs. Nancy, wife of Jeremiah Green, 29.

In Deering, Margaret Armour, in her 99th year. She left 2 children, 20 grand-children and 22 great grand-children. Printers in Me., N. Y., and Ohio are &c.

In Peterborough, Mr. Reuben Melvin, aged 67. Printers in Mass, and Vt., are &c.

At sea, Mr. Robert Dinsmore of Exeter, N. H., aged 23. He fell from the main top and was instantly killed.

In Gilsum of a cancer, Mr. David Dean, 66.

In North Hampton, Elder John Lamprey, in his 87th year.

In Fryeburg, Me., Gen. James W. Ripley, Collector of Passamaquoddy District and late a member of Congress.

In New Market, Capt. Nathaniel Weatherby, aged 72, formerly of Dorchester, Mass. He was a patriot of the Revolution and was at West Point at the time of Arnold's treason. He has sustained many respectable offices; was a good citizen, good husband and good father. Although his wife, children and grand-children may mourn their loss, yet they have the consolation of knowing that they did all in their power to make his last days comfortable and happy. Printers in Mass., are &c.

In Newport, on the 9th inst., of consumption, Aaron Nettleton, Jr., for several years Register of Probate for Sullivan County, aged 36.

In Raymond, Mrs. Hannah, wife of Deacon Jeremiah Fullerton, aged 56. She was a member of the Freewill Baptist Church 36 years and lived an ornament to her profession. In the church her great aim seemed to be the glory of God and the good of souls. In the family circle she was an example of modesty, meekness and sobriety, and in the neighborhood, a pattern of peace and love. She was remarkably industrious, so that it may be said of her in the language of scripture, "She arose while it was yet night and worked willingly with her hands. She looked well to the way of her household, and ate not the bread of idleness. She opened her mouth with wisdom and in her tongue was the law of kindness." Her last sickness was the consumption. Three or four weeks previous to her death, though she was then able to walk about she made arrangements for her funeral, ordered her grave clothes prepared, and in a few days, took to her bed. She was now remarkably happy. She entreated her children to make religion the business of their lives and gave a solemn warning to the unconverted to flee from the wrath to come. At length death came and she calmly yielded her spirit to God who gave it. On the funeral occasion agreeably to her request, Elder John Kimball delivered a discourse from Matt. 24 44. "Therefore be ye also ready &c." Her husband is now left to mourn the loss of one whose constant aim was to make his journey of life pleasant. Seven children are deprived of a mother who strove by her prayers and wise councils, to have them pursue the narrow way to life; and the church lost a bright and shinning light. Printer in Me., Vt., and Michigan, are &c.

NEW HAMPSHIRE PATRIOT & STATE GAZETTE
Concord, Monday, June 22, 1835

The Hartford Riot. A letter from Hartford says—"we have had some exhibition of mob law this week. They began on Tuesday night. Some whites and Negroes had a quarrel, which ended for the time, in a white fellow was shot—not killed, but dangerously wounded. On Wednesday night a mob of whites pulled down two Negro houses. Last night, (Thursday,) two independent companies of the military were ordered out and kept on guard all night. A mob of some hundreds collected in the streets, but no attempt was made to do any mischief. The black man, who shot the white and several of the rioters have been arrested. The provocation is said to have been given by the whites at the African Methodist Church. *Courier*

Another Mexican Outrage. The schooner St. Croix, Elliot Ward, master, sailed from this port sometime in October last bound to Arranso Bay, in Texas, with colonist and freight. On the arrival of the captain, he was visited by the Collector of the place, who, without assigning any reasons seized the vessel and cargo, and lodged him in prison where he was confined twenty-nine days, suffering much for the want of proper food and from the loathsomeness of his situation. When liberated he found the schooner plundered of her sails and stores. The crew having deserted and fearing another incarceration in prison, he was forced to abandon everything together with his vessel and quit the country with all possible expedition! It was in vain to remonstrate and no satisfaction could be obtained.
N. Y. Star

COUNCIL WITH THE INDIANS. We understand that the Secretary of War has appointed Gov. Stokes, Gen. Arbuckle, and Major F. S. Armstrong, commissioners of the part of the United States, to hold a council with as many of the civilized and uncivilized Indians west of the Arkansas as can be convened at the time which shall be appointed to hold it, for the purpose of effecting a general treaty of amity and friendship between all the various nations and tribes roving on our western frontiers, including those in Texas in the neighborhood of the Rocky Mountains, &c., &c. This council can hardly fail to be a very interesting one, as we understand that several thousand of these untutored sons of the forest and of the prairie are expected to attend. It was not known when the steamboat Arkansaw left Fort Gibson, on Thursday last, where the council will be held—possibly at that post but more probably at Fort Arbuckle, or perhaps somewhere in the prairies. Three Camanche Indians had been at Fort Gibson several weeks, and excited considerable curiosity. They were highly delighted with the Arkansaw and Compromise, which were the first steamboats they ever saw. They were to leave in a few days under escort of a company of Dragoons for the purpose of inviting the various tribes or bands belonging to their nation to attend the council. *Arkansas Gaz.*

The bank at Darien, Georgia was robbed on the 7th inst., of specie and bills amounting to $100,000. False keys were used and the robbery, which took place Saturday night was not discovered until Sunday evening. A reward of $5,000 is offered for the detection of the robber and the recovery of the money.

Col. Johnson. The federal editors commenced their *smutty* abuse of Col. Johnson the moment he was nominated by the Democratic Party for Vice-President. This was to be expected. The Colonel's services against their *allies* and *friends*, the *British* and *Indians* were of too important a nature ever to be forgiven him by those who declared that "England was the bulwark of our religion," and who voted against and withheld supplies to carry on the war. Col. Johnson's gallant conduct in that war was such as to procure for him the mortal hatred of the federal party. *They* can only support men for the highest offices, who, like *Daniel Webster,* voted against supplies to feed and clothe the soldiers who were fighting their country's battles. In this they are consistent—and they are welcome to all the advantages to be derived from personal and scurrilous attacks upon the prominent men of the Democratic Party. They accused JEFFERSON of the same offences they now charge upon COL. JOHNSON; and have frequently accused JACKSON of even worse offences. The consequence has been that the people have more zealous sustained them all. So it will ever be, the men who receive the greatest share of federal malignity will always be sure of the more constant and unwavering support of the democracy of the county.

LA FAYETTE

Without tiring, the writer of this notice sat two hours and half last winter to listen to the address in commendation of the character of the illustrious Gilbert Mortier De Layette delivered in the National Hall of Representatives by JOHN QUINCY ADAMS, late President of the United States. That address was rendered more interesting from the circumstances that the author had probably a better personal acquaintance than any other man in America with the principal men of eminence who have figured in Europe during the last forty years, having for much of that time resided near the principle courts of the transatlantic states and kingdoms. Mr. Adams portrayed the character of the great man in its true colors, and then, to our recollection uttering no sentiment that would be offensive to the most astute democratic ear. On Wednesday last the writer sat nearly two hours to hear the eulogy of NATHANIEL G. UPHAM, one of the Justices of the Superior Court of New Hampshire, who had been appointed to deliver an address before the members of the Legislature of this state, *commemorative of life and services of the man who must ever live in this nation's gratitude so long as that liberty and those republican institutions procured by the valor and devised by the wisdom of our father's shall be continued to us.* He can say with truth that scarcely less interest was felt and kept up in the last than in the first performance. Mr. Upham exceeded the high expectations which had been formed of him. His introduction which united the birth of Lafayette with the commencement of the contest first waged, principally in America between two great rival powers of Europe, terminating in the conquest of the French possessions of North America, and attributing to the death of the father of Lafayette in the battle of Minden fought during that war, the first breathings of hostility in the breast of the youthful hero to the nation whose soldiery had made him an orphan while yet an infant was ingenious and appropriate. In the path of dull narrative which had been often trodden Mr. Upham strewed flowers, which would have embellished any production of even the veteran historian. He evinced throughout talents which reflect credit both on himself and on the judgment of the executive which had selected him, while but a youth in the practice of his profession, for a conspicuous station on the bench requiring deep research and the best talents. It is presumed the address of Judge Upham will be printed; and if so, it cannot fail to be perused with pleasure and profit.

Lightning. James Sherburne of Epsom, had (about ten days since) six cattle killed in his yead, by a single shock of lightning. He was within a few feet of them but escaped without injury. *Com.*

THE INSANE

By the report of a select Committee consisting of two from each county made to the House on Friday last, it appears that returns have been received from only 48 towns, concerning their insane. These towns contain a population of about 60,000, and the number of persons insane reported is 115, of whom 53 were males and 62 females. The duration of their insanity varies from 2 to 55 years, excepting in one instance, which is of 6 months continuance. The whole number of years all have been insane collectively, is 1527 or more than 13 on an average. More than half are supported as paupers, about one fifth part by the charity of friends, not legally liable for their support. If the insane in our state is in proportion to the towns heard from according to the proportion, the whole number of years would be 7038. By the same report it was abundantly proved from tables of all the principal hospitals in France, England and the United States, that in cases of not more than 3 months duration 90 percent recovered; those of not more than a year standing, 70 percent and in cases of every length of continuance, degrees of severity and difficulty of cure, over 41 percent. If the recoveries in our state would have been the same in proportion as in the vast number of cases alluded to by the committee treated at hospitals, the saving to us by an asylum in a pecuniary point of view, would have been immense to say nothing of the thousand of years of mental anguish avoided. Let anyone go into the calculation, reckoning the cost of supporting them at $100 per year, and the value of their time at $75 on an average, he will be startled at the enormous amount to which it swells. The committee reports that from investigation and the best information they could obtain, the cost of erecting an asylum suitable for accommodating 120 patients, furnishing the same, erecting the out buildings, fencing out the yards, &c., would not exceed $25,000, and that the whole expense of supporting the institution if divided among 120 would not exceed $48 1/3. Taking into consideration the cases at the numerous hospitals in foreign countries and our own and also that the treatment of our insane without an asylum must from necessity be such in most cases, as is directly calculated to prolong and inflame the disease, there can be no doubt as to the expediency in a pecuniary point of view of establishing an hospital.

MARRIAGES

In Gilmanton, Capt. John G. Page to Miss Mary Jane Gilman, both of Gilmanton.

In Acworth, Mr. Joel B. Smith to Miss Harriet Maria Mills.

In Gilmanton, June 7, by Rev. H. D. Buzzell, Mr. Jonathan Hill, Jr., to Miss Eliza Chesley of New Durham.

In Bristol, by Rev. Mr. Winter, Moody U. Sawyer, M. D., of Meredith to Miss Sarah Brown of Bristol.

In Haverhill, Mr. James Dean to Miss Sarah Lothers.

In Plymouth, Mr. Daniel Rowe, of Bridgewater to Miss Lucy Morrison, of Plymouth. Mr. William B. Nichols of New Hampton, to Miss Sally Jewett of Bridgewater.

DEATHS

In this town, of dropsy on the brain, William Eaton, son of Jacob and Harriet Perkins, aged 3 ½ months. A wise Providence has seen fit to call the afflicted parents to mourn the loss of three lovely and interesting sons, the two last of which were taken within the short period of 6 weeks—one in the early bloom of childhood and two in infancy.

In this town on Sunday June 7, Mrs. Nancy Hazen Brigham, relict of Mr. Levi Brigham of Boston, a daughter of the late Capt. Richard Ayer of this town, aged 42 years. For the last twenty-five days of her life she endured a most intense suffering under an entire obstruction of intestinal passage; her disorder had been gradually increasing for nearly ten months. From the moment she was taken down she assured her friends that there was no hope of recovery knowing better then her physicians the nature of her disorder. And all the time it was a source of gratification to all whom visited her to witness the calm resignation with which she anticipated her earthly dissolution. No business of her was performed with more cheerfulness and alacrity than were her preparation to "throw off this mortal coil," and enter on that "dread borne from whence no traveler has returned." To one of her fellow mortals who in more youthful days had been accustomed to look on the last struggles of expiring nature with a sort of instinctive horror, the witnessing of the subject of this notice from day to day, even while enduring great bodily suffering— the quietude with which she anticipated her great change—the desire she had to depart and be with her

Savior—imparted a strong conviction that evanescent mortals should teach themselves that the going out of the world is an event to be scarcely less dreaded than to be born into it. Mrs. Brigham has left two interesting children, a son and a daughter, at a tender age to mourn the loss of their only surviving parent.

In Gilmanton, of a cancer, April 29, Mrs. Judith, wife of Mr. Paul Sweat. She was an amiable woman and a humble follower of the Redeemer. Printer in N. Y. and &c.

In Pembroke, 8th inst., Mr. John Ladd, aged 81.

In Acworth, May 6 of consumption, Mrs. Lucy Keyes, wife of Mr. John Keyes, aged 35 years. May 28, Mr. Ezra George, Jr., aged 27 years, son of Mr. Ezra George. June 15, Miss Fanny Cummings, aged 19 years, daughter of the Rev. David Cummings.

In Antrim of consumption, May 18, Ruth Merriam Tenny, aged about 20. Printers in Mass., are &c.

In Piermont, on the 12th inst., Miss Sally Learned, aged 37 years after a severe sickness of sixteen months.

In Dover, Mrs. Susan Allen, aged 29 years, wife of Mr. George W. Allen.

In Corinth, Vt., May 8, Mr. Samuel C. Stevens formerly of Dover, aged 37.

Drowned at New Market, Lamprey River on the 15th ult., Mr. John Perkins, aged 68 years and Mr. John Perkins, Jr., aged 25 years—father and son.

In Meredith, Louisa Ann, youngest daughter of Col. J. S. Hoit, aged 3 years and 8 months.

In Thornton, Mr. William McDearmid, Miss Martha Gilman, and Martha Sargent.

NEW HAMPSHIRE PATRIOT & STATE GAZETTE
Concord, Monday, June 29, 1835

From the N. H. Gazette

HORRID MURDER—A correspondent has politely furnished us with the following particular account of the shocking murder, committed at Kittery during the past week—

On Thursday morning the 11th inst., Theodore Wilson, of Kittery, Maine, about 56 years of age, was brought before Justice McIntire charged with the murder of Sally Wilson, his wife, on the afternoon of the 10th inst. Wilson appeared a perfect maniac during the examination. He refused to plead either guilty or not guilty.

From the evidence given in the case it appeared that for years past, he had been habituated to drunkenness; had frequently abused and beaten his wife when intoxicated, but no symptoms of insanity had ever been observed in him, excepting when under the influence of spirituous liquors.

On the morning that the fatal act was committed he appeared insane though it was not known that he had drank any spirits for the last three days.

About 4 o'clock in the afternoon of the 10th, a female in the house of Benjamin Parker, a neighbor to Wilson house, hearing an uncommon noise in the road near the house ran to the door and found that the raving proceeded from Wilson, who was traversing the road naked. At this the females were greatly alarmed, there being no man in the house, and fastening the doors placed themselves in an attitude to defend themselves. About 15 minutes after he was first seen in the street, shrieks from a female voice was heard and on looking through the window, he was seen in the act of throwing his wife on the ground; two or three more shrieks were heard after the fall, and he was seen to beat her with his fist as was supposed, for a stone wall intervening, they could only see his arm when raised to inflict the blows. After beating her about a minute with the fist he left her, stepped a few paces, and immediately returned to the spot where she fell, with a stone in his hand, and beat and mangled her head with it in the most shocking manner. The females saw his arm rise and fall and distinctly heard the sound of the blows inflicted, the distance from the house not being more than three or four rods.

When the work of death was completed, he left the corpse and with the fatal stone in his hand, went to the house of Parker. When approaching the house, he raved out that he had another to destroy! He first attacked the house at the door and split a panel in it, but finding it fastened securely he then went to a window, broke in the glass with his fist and threw into the house the bloody stone. A female placed herself at the window, and with an axe prevented his entering. The blood ran profusely from his hands and wrist, which were lacerated with deep gashes made by forcing them through the glass—for some time he employed himself in besmearing the house with the blood—saying, "I am sealing it with the blood of my wife."

Mr. William Haley, Jr., hearing the outcry hastened to the house where he found Wilson lying on the ground, near the door, smiting the door stone with his fist. As soon as Wilson saw Haley, he called out, "I have killed my wife," and pointing to the place where she laid, "there she lays under the wall dead." Haley immediately called two other men, and they seized and bound him—Wilson making little or no resistance.

After securing the maniac, the went to the spot where the fatal act was committed and found his wife a corpse, her cranium having been beat in and mangled in a most horrid manner—the appearance was truly frightful. During the following night and the next day, Wilson frequently declared that he had killed his wife. He was committed to prison to take his trial at Alfred, in September next.

York, June 14, 1835.

More Money of the Norfolk Bank Recovered. West and Thorn sentenced to the state prison for 15 years for robbing the Norfolk Bank at Roxbury, discovered a short time since to their counsel that they had buried a large portion of the stolen money in a hill at the rear of the city of Cincinnati where they were arrested. An accurate drawing and description of the place where the money was deposited were then obtained from them, and S. A. Moore, Esq., of this city, dispatched to recover the lost treasure. The Cincinnati Whig of May 29th, says: Mr. Moore brought a letter of introduction to one of our merchants who with Mr. Moore on Monday last went in search of the money. They discovered the place of deposit with but little difficulty, which proved to be in the large hill, back of the city, a short distance in the rear of the house of the late Luman Watson. After digging six or eight inches below the surface of the earth they found two stone jars, nearly sealed up, with the mouth downwards, in which were deposited $7, 898, in bills of the Norfolk Bank. The money being thus recovered, Mr. Moore set out for home rejoicing.

Singular Circumstance. Early in February last, a number of persons in Calais (Me.) were violently attacked by pains in the limbs, and in the bowels, alternate diarrhœas and costiveness, cramps, &c. The disease seemed to be of a character to baffle the skill of the physicians; it extended and in the course of some months, about one hundred persons of different conditions, sexes and ages were afflicted in this way. Many of these persons apparently recovered from their indisposition, and afterwards had a recurrence of the disease. Several of them died in great agony and as strong suspicions of *poison* were abroad, it is singular that no *post mortem* examination took place. An investigation however, was had by some of the inhabitants, and it was ascertained that there was only one article of food of which all the persons attacked with the disease had participated. This was some Muscovado sugar, which had been imported from the West Indies, and it was thought that this painful and lingering disease might have been occasioned by some deleterious matter contained in that article. A gentleman with his family, all of whom had been attacked with this singular complaint, but who are now convalescent, came to this city about a week since, and brought a quantity of the same sugar. It was analyzed by Dr. Charles T. Jackson, who ascertained that it contained *oxide of lead* in the proportion of one drachma to the pound! In what manner it became incorporated with the sugar is unknown. *Mer. Journal*

Piracy. We learn from the Louisiana Advertiser that a vessel called the Montezuma, commanded by a notorious pirate is now cruising off the coast of Texas, purporting to be a Mexican national vessel. The schooner Columbia, under Mexican colors, from New Orleans to Brassoria, and schooner Martha under American colors, have both been seized by this pirate and nominally ordered to Vera Cruz—but as the passengers were landed on the coast of Texas without their baggage, the vessels will, it is probable, be stranded there.

Fatal Accident On Sunday, May 24th, as Mr. Johnson Muzzey and Mr. George Woodbury of Weare, N. H., were returning from public worship in a one horse wagon, while descending a steep hill, the hold backs gave way, the horse took fright, ran, kicked badly, turned over the wagon, threw then both out and dashed Mr. Muzzey against the wall so furiously that his scull was fractured in a shocking manner; the bones in his right arm were also very badly broken. He lived till Monday morning, a little before 9 o'clock when he died. He was a young man of good and industrious habits and of unblemished character, in the 23rd year of his age. Mr. Woodbury narrowly escaped with the bones in his left arm dislocated and several other bruises. *Communicated.*

AWFUL ACCIDENT. About five o'clock yesterday evening a tornado passed through the town of New Brunswick, leveled part of the town, maimed and wounded a large number of people and killed three.

The accounts which have as yet reached town, vary somewhat as to the exact part of the town where the tornado entered, but all agree that the head of Schureman Street, about Dr. Janeway's residence was the place first injured to any extent. It passed through the entire length of Schureman Street which it literally leveled to the ground. More than fifty houses have been totally destroyed and the following persons killed.

Henry Booream; a boy 9 years old named Beard, and Mrs. Van Arsdale.

The town of Piscataway was almost entirely destroyed—nothing remained but the church and two or three buildings. The captain of the New Brunswick boat states that he was opposite Piscataway and nearly in the range of the tornado at the time but stopped his boat until it passed. The scene, he says was indescribably terrific; fragment of buildings were whirled into the air at a height of 5 or 600 feet and then dispersed in every direction.

A small lad, aged about 7 years, who was passing the streets was taken off the ground and carried thro' the air to the wharf a distance of nearly three hundred yards, and there deposited in safety.

From Staten Island we learn that great quantities of board and shingles fell there yesterday afternoon.

Killing a Cow for the Sake of the Hide. A man by the name of Long was recently tried at the Albany Mayor's Court, and convicted of one of the most diabolical acts of which we have lately read. He went to the farm of Mr. Isaiah Townsend a few miles from the city of Albany, killed and skinned a fine young cow, brought the skin to the city and sold it for two dollars. The Albany Evening Journal well says that his own cruel process should be applied to him, and that he should be made to taste the virtues and pleasures of a good *cow skinning*, till the hide was taken off his back. He was sentenced to three years imprisonment at Sing Sing.

Distressing Occurrence. On the 2nd inst., as the steamboat New Companion was on her way to St. Louis, a few miles above St. Genevieve, a young man named Silas M. Beemas about 18 years of age, while in the act of dipping a bucket of water, was drawn overboard and instantly disappeared under the wheel. The yawl was manned and sent in search of him. The boat rounded and came to and fell back near a mile; but all efforts were in vain. It is supposed that he received a blow from the wheel, which killed him instantly. The bucket was found floating below, staved to pieces. Aaron Beemas, the father of the deceased, his mother, brother and sisters were in company. Mr. Beemas was emigrating from Springfield, Mass., to Pike County, Illinois. At Cleveland, Ohio the afflicted family buried a little daughter about three years of age. She died of scarlet fever.

Two of the crew of the ship Mentor who were wrecked among the Pelew Islands in May 1832 and who, in attempting to find a place of safety, were captured by the natives of Lord North's Island, kept prisoner three years, and finally rescued by a barque from Liverpool, conveyed to Canton and from thence to the United States, are now in this city. Their sufferings from hunger and the cruelty of their captors have nearly destroyed their health—we are happy to learn that subscription papers for their aid will be opened at our insurance offices, and we trust they will present proud of the liberal humanity of our fellow citizens. *Boston Post.*

An Angel Caught. The Magazine and Advocate says that while the Mormon prophet Jo Smith was in Ohio engaged in proselytizing people to the faith of the "Golden Bible,'" he sought to give additional solemnity to the baptismal right by affirming that on each occasion an angel would appear on the opposite side of the stream, and there remain till the conclusion of the ceremony. The rites was administered in the evening in Grand River, near Painesville, not by the prophet in person but by his disciples. In agreement with the prediction of the prophet on each occasion a figure in white was seen on the opposite bank, and the faith of the faithful was thereby greatly increased.   Suspicion as to the incorporeal nature of the reputed angel at length induced a company of young men (unbelievers of course) to examine the quality of the ghost, and having secreted themselves they awaited its arrival.   Their expectations were soon realized by its appearance in its customary position, and rushing from their lair they succeeded in forcing it into the stream, and although its efforts to escape was powerful, they succeeded in bringing it in triumph to the opposite side of the stream when, who should this supposed inhabitant of the upper world be, but the Mormon prophet himself!   *Rochester Republican*

Arrival of the Constitution.   The U. S. frigate Constitution arrived at New York on Monday evening, from Plymouth, England, whence she sailed on the 16th May, having on board Mr. Livingston, late minister of Paris, and family.

To the Honorable the Justices of the Superior Court of
   Judicature holden at Exeter within and for the county
   Of Rockingham and state of New Hampshire on the
   First Tuesday of December, A. D. 1834
HUMBLY shew MARTHA PERKINS of Newington in the County of Rockingham aforesaid, that she has always resided in the state of New Hampshire.

That she was on the ninth day of April in the year of our Lord eighteen hundred and twenty-three, at Loudon, in the county of Merrimack, legally married to one Jonathan Perkins.

That from the time of her intermarriage with the said Jonathan Perkins to the present time, she has invariably conducted as a kind, obedient and faithful wife.

That said Jonathan Perkins however wholly regardless of his marriage covenant, vows and obligations, did at Newington aforesaid, on the twenty-seventh day of November, A. D. eighteen hundred and thirty-four commit the crime of adultery with one Ruth Adams and that he, the said Jonathan Perkins and the said Ruth Adams, did there afterwards on the same twenty-seventh day of November aforesaid, run away together and have both gone together into the parts wholly unknown.

Wherefore the said Martha Perkins prays that the bond of matrimony between her and the said Jonathan Perkins may be dissolved; and that she may have assigned her such part of the real and personal estate of the said Jonathan Perkins, as all circumstances duly considered may be just and reasonable.

MARTHA PERKINS

STATE OF NEW HAMPSHIRE
Rockingham, ss.
Superior Court of Judicature

Ordered that the foregoing petition be taken into consideration at the Superior Court of Judicature to be holden at Portsmouth within and for the said county of Rockingham, on the first Tuesday of December next; and that the said libellant cause the said Jonathan Perkins to be notified thereof by publishing the foregoing petition and this order of the court thereon in the New Hampshire Patriot and State Gazette, printed in Concord in said state three weeks successively, the last publication whereof to be thirty days at least prior to said first Tuesday on December next.

Dated at the office of the clerk of said Superior Court in Exeter of said county of Rockingham this 11th day of April, Anno Domini, 1835.

    Attest—P. CHADWICK, Clerk
Copy examined by
    P. CHADWICK

NOTICE

WHEREAS we the subscribers have made suitable provisions for the support of the following persons, viz; Sally Dow, Abigail Ladd, Sally Ladd, Mahala Monlton, Widow Mary Marsh, Widow Lois Allen, Widow Deborah Taylor, Emeline Walker, Ann Maria Hutchinson, Martha

Clough, Lucretta Barter, Caroline Barter, Jemima Barter, Elizabeth Sargent, Widow Jemima Barter, Henry Marsh, Mercy Elkins, Widow Mary Badger, Eunice B. Hutchinson, Benjamin Pervier, wife and child, Prince B. Cogswell, wife and three children, Betsy York, Clarissa York, Emeline York, Lydia York, Aaron Clough, Widow Hannah Garmon, Ruth Badger, Almira Gale and Cynthia Gale, paupers of Gilmanton; therefore this is to forbid all persons from harboring or trusting said paupers on the account of the said town, as we shall pay no debts of their contracting after this date.

JOHN HAM } Selectman
STEPHEN WEEKS } of
BRADSTREET GILMAN } Gilmanton
Gilmanton, March 20, 1835

MARRIAGES

In this town of the 24th last, Mr. Milton G. Boyes to Miss Sarah B. Smith both of Concord. On the 17th inst., Mr. William Gile to Miss Jane Smith both of Concord.

In Gilmanton, June 18, by Samuel Cate, Esq., Mr. Charles Minot of Franklin to Miss Rhoda A. Chapman of Gilmanton.

In Dover by Rev. Mr. Perkins, Mr. William Melcher to Miss Susan Brown of Dover.

In Alton, Dr. Jonathan Hill, of Gilmanton, to Miss Eliza, daughter of Mr. Miles Chesley, of New Durham.

In Orford, Mr. Joseph C. Broadhead, of Boston, to Miss Sarah W. Wheeler, daughter of J. B. Wheeler, Esq.

In Brattleborough, Vt., Mr. Abel Nutting to Miss Mary Ann Turner, both of Jaffrey.

In Gilman Village, June 9th, by the Rev. G. Beckley, Mr. William Smith to Miss Eliza Newman.

DEATHS

In Northwood, June 11th, JOHN J. DEMERITT, Esq., aged 29, the two last years a member of the Legislature. He was the only remaining son of Thomas Demeritt, Esq., being the third who has departed this life within the short period of three years. Jonathan, Sept. 8, 1832; aged 23, George W. March 10th, 1834 aged 22. Thus death hath blasted the fond hopes of affectionate parents and friends; for as the flower of the morning he hath faded away. Many can testify of his benevolence and deeply lament that he so early should wither and embrace his native dust. A solemn and impressive discourse was delivered on the occasion to a large assembly by Rev. George W. Ashley, from 2nd Samuel, 19th chapter 34th verse. "How long have I to Live." Printers in N. H. and Me. are &c.

In New Hampton, of consumption, Sumner Russell, artist of Boston, 27.

In Kentucky, Hon. Amos Davis, late Representative in Congress.

In Whitefield, Capt. Nathan Morrill, aged 78; Dr. Benjamin T. Sanborn.

In Boston, June 15, very suddenly, Mr. John Waite, aged 24 years, formerly of Lyme, N. H. Eastern papers, &c.

In Portsmouth, Mr. George Cate, aged 64 years.

At Rochester, Mrs. Mary D., wife of Mr. Anthony Pickering, aged 43.

In Gill, Mass., Mr. Amaziah Ballard, aged 59. He weighed at the time of his death 493 pounds.

In Royalton of the 6th inst., of inflammation in his head, George Davis, aged 28 years, son of Jacob Davis of Randolph.

NEW HAMPSHIRE PATRIOT & STATE GAZETTE
Concord, Monday, July 6, 1835

TORNADO. The Williamsport, Pa. Chronicle states that a destructive storm passed within a few miles of that borough on the afternoon of the 19th instant. The greatest injury sustained was by persons living on Lycoming Creek. The dwelling house of Mr. Alexander Crothers was unroofed, and otherwise injured; his barn was literally overthrown and his storehouse much injured. The barn of Mr. O. Watson was completely razed to the foundation; and out of a flourishing orchard of about sixty trees, but one is left standing, and that one stripped of all its branches. Mr. Wilhelm had his house unroofed. There was doubtless much other damage done. The Wilkesbarre (Luzerne County) Advocate of Wednesday, states that the proceeding Friday a hurricane passed in that neighborhood. A large number of orchards were completely leveled with the ground—one or two small houses were thrown down, and a number of houses and barns were unroofed. So violent was the storm at this point that a sound and flourishing hickory tree, from nine to ten inches in diameter, was twisted entirely off about ten feet from the ground. Five men were in the barn of Mr. M. at the time it fell; yet strange as it may seem, they were not materially injured.

We are sorry to learn that a fine young man (son of Dr. Cutter, corner of Barclay and Chapel Streets,) in a fit of derangement jumped out of a third story back window of his father's house yesterday morning, and was instantly killed. *Boston Post*

Dreadful Accident. About 11 o'clock yesterday a lamentable accident occurred in the city of Brooklyn. A scaffold had been swung in the rear of Mr. Titus' new building in Fulton Street, and opposite the third story, for the purpose of painting the back wall of the buildings, and two of the men, (there being three on the scaffolding) were engaged in their work when the support to the scaffold gave way and all were precipitated on the pavement below, and were awfully mangled and bruised by the fall. One of the three on the scaffolding had but a few moments before crossed from New York to see his brother and had both thighs broken. The others were so much injured as to leave but little hope of their recovery. Their names are Henry Dawson and Christopher Kenon. The other young man was the brother of Kenon.

N. Y. Cour. & Enq.

From the New York Daily Advertiser

Arrest of an English Magistrate. On the 10th May last, a publication appeared in the London Weekly Dispatch stating that a Mr. Robert Orris a magistrate of Norfolk England, and chairman of the Walsingham quarter sessions, had committed forgeries to the amount of £25,000 sterling; had defrauded T. W. Cole of £1000, and another neighbor of £3000, and leaving 12 motherless children, had absconded and gone to America. In consequence, a Bow Street police officer, named Henry Miller, shipped for this country, arriving here, with instructions to have Orris arrested, he applied to Mr. Bixley, a lawyer, for advice how best to proceed to effect his purpose when Orris should arrive. On Friday, Orris and his son who had been out traveling, arrived in town and took lodgings at Tammany Hall: and a writ having been issued from the Supreme Court at the suit of Cole for his arrest, in a civil suit, with a view to get him into custody, preliminary to criminal proceeding, Huntington, police officer, was deputized to find out and arrest him. This he succeeded in doing late at night, and the Walsingham magistrate slept in the prison. After his arrest the Bow Street officer went with some others to the lodgings of Orris and breaking open his trunks, without law or right, found in that of his son's upwards of $1000 which he took and had it secured. In the morning application was made by Orris to the British Consul, and it having been ascertained that he could not be held on the civil proceedings. He was discharged, and being taken to the police office, an affidavit was made out by the Bow Street officer Miller, against him. But, it was decided, that as no part of the money he was accused of having obtained by the forgery, was found upon him, and the evidence of his guilt not being presented before the police court in suit or form as to justify his intention, he was discharged from custody to range the country at pleasure.

Mr. M' Daniel, the present Warden of the State Prison, in his late report to the Legislature of the concerns of that institution, states that among other facts, that the Maine State Prison is an average annual expense to the state of *"four thousand five hundred dollars."* In this state where the facilities for the profitable management of an institution of this kind are not half as great as in Maine, many complain because our prison has not furnished a large revenue, rather than to have been a small expense to the state. We believe that no prison in the country has been of less expense to the state in which it is located, for the last few years, than has our prison. And those who have been the loudest in their complaints relative to the expense are now loudest in their denunciation of the executive, because they have made such arrangements, that for five years, it will be no expense at all. Consistency thou art a jewel.

Haverhill Republican

NOTICE

THIS certifies that I have given my son NATHANIEL WELLS his time and declare him free to act and trade for himself in all cases whatsoever, I shall claim none of his earnings nor consider myself liable to pay any debts of his contracting after this date. EDWARD WELL

            { Oliver B. Howe
Attest { Stephen Peabody
Shelburn, March 10, 1835.

DEATHS

In Beverly, Mass., widow Anna Corning, in the 96th year of her age. She had lived to see her offspring in children, grand-children, and great grand-children to the number of 128. Printers in Me., and Michigan are &c.

In Andover, Mass., Mary Elizabeth Morrison, eldest daughter of Charles G. Morrison, aged 4 years.

In Salisbury, Marinda, daughter of Mr. B. Fifield, of brain fever, aged 17.

In Bow, Mr. Jonathan Clough, aged 88 years and 10 months.

In this town on the 29th ult., at the residence of his father-in-law, Dr. Samuel Morrill, Mr. Charles T. Mixer of Saco, Me., aged 31. A little more than a month since, he left home thinking that a journey might prove beneficial to his health, but his disease was too firmly fixed; the hand of the destroyer was upon him, and the tender cord that bound him to the earth was soon cut asunder. He was a member of the Episcopal Church, and during the few "wearisome days and nights," of his confinement not a murmuring word escaped his lips. He bore his suffering with patience and his end was peaceful. Tranquilizing and consolatory to his bereaved companion and his friends must be the reflection that he has exchanged a world of suffering and sin, for a world of holiness and never ending pleasure. *Com.1*

NEW HAMPSHIRE PATRIOT & STATE GAZETTE
Concord, Monday, July 13, 1835

The Baltimore papers contain the melancholy intelligence of the death of Mr. Thomas Marshall, son of Chief Justice Marshall. His death was caused by a wound, which he received on his head from a brick, which the high wind of Saturday's storm forced from the Court house chimney. He was on his way to visit his father in Philadelphia. He was a gentleman of large landed estates, and a member of the Virginia Legislature. He has left a family of six children. His remains have been taken to Virginia for interment.

Fatal Affray. A rencontre took place on the 15th ult., at Courtland, Ala, between Alfred Gibson and Henry P. Joyner, in which the latter received a pistol shot, which almost instantly deprived him of life. The cause of the affray is not stated. The deceased was formerly a resident of Raleigh, N. C., but several years since removed to Alabama.

Mrs. Hemans. Of this sweet minstrel, recently deceased, the Athenæum gives the following biographical sketch.

Felicia Dorothea Browne was born in Liverpool, in a small, quaint looking house in St. Anne Street, now standing, old fashioned and desolate, in the midst of the newer buildings by which it is surrounded. Her father was a native of Ireland, her mother a German lady, Miss Wagner, was descended from or connected with some Venitian family, a circumstance which she would playfully mention, as accounting for the strong tinge of romance and poetry which pervaded her character from her earliest childhood. Our abstaining from any attempt minutely to trace her history requires no apology; it is enough to say that when she was very young her family removed from Liverpool to the neighborhood of St. Asaph in North Wales; that she married at a very early age; that her married life, after the birth of five sons, was clouded by the estrangement of her husband; that, on the death of her mother, with whom she resided she broke up her establishment in Wales and removed to Wavertree in the neighborhood of Liverpool, from whence, after a residence of about three years she again removed to Dublin, her last resting place.

Death of Chief Justice Marshall. The Philadelphia papers of Tuesday morning announce the death of Chief Justice Marshall. He departed this life at Philadelphia, about six o' clock on Monday evening.

The Rev. Mr. Cheever Convicted. The Boston Transcript states that:—"The trial of the Rev. Mr. Cheever, of Salem, for a malicious libel on Deacon John Stone, has terminated in a verdict of guilty upon the second count of the indictment to wit; that the defended had alluded in the article written by him, to Deacon Stone and had been guilty of a libel upon that individual. The defendant has appealed to the Supreme Court.

On Saturday, Elias Ham, foreman of Deacon Stone's distillery, Salem, received his sentence for an assault upon Rev. Mr. Cheever, with a cowhide of which he had pleaded guilty. It was a fine of $60 and cost of courts, the whole amounting to $141. 62.

MARY QUEEN OF SCOTS

The following lines cut from an old newspaper have been handed to us by a friend. They were composed by Mary Stuart, Queen of Scots during her imprisonment and just before her execution. Mary, the reader of history will remember, was arrested, imprisoned, and tried by order of Elizabeth, Queen of England, her sister and rival on the pretence of conspiring against her life. She was executed on the 8th of February 1587—about which time these lines were written. The unfortunate sufferer was distinguished by all those charms of persons, which command and secure admiration, and was possessed of high qualities of mind. She was well acquainted with Latin, French and Italian, in each of which she wrote with ease and no inconsiderable merit. The classical scholar will discover both beauty and simplicity in the annexed line.

> "O Dimine Deus! Speravi in tee,
> O care mi Jesu! nunc libera me!
> In dura catena
> In misera poena
> Desidero to!
> Languendo, Gemendo
> Aroro, imploro ut liberes me!"

We annex a translation not strictly literal, in which the sense and measure of the original are preserved.

> "O God my Creator! I've trusted in Thee.
> O Jesus my Savior! now liberate me.
> In fetters I languish—
> In sorrow and anguish,
> I still look to thee!
> In the depths of affliction
> I worship—and pray that I yet may be free!
> *Troy Budget.*

NOTICE

I the subscriber have given to each of my two sons James Taggard and David Taggard all their earnings from this time, until each of them shall be twenty-one years old.   JOHN TAGGARD
Hillsborough, July 9, 1835

CAUTION

THIS is to forbid any person purchasing a note of hand signed by me and running to Burnham Kimball of Derry. I do not recollect the exact date of said note, but it was between the 8th and 20th of September, 1834. Said note was obtained by fraud and without consideration, and will not be paid by me.   JOHN S. LIBBEE
Candia, July 8, 1835.

NOTICE

ALL persons are forbidden harboring or trusting STREETER HACKETT, an indented boy, on my account, as I shall pay no debts of his contracting.

SAMUEL MORRILL.

Gilford, July 1, 1835.

MARRIAGES

In Gilmanton, 28th June, by Rev. Peter Clark, Mr. Josiah Robinson to Miss Louisa Morrison both of Gilmanton.

In Pomfret, Vt., on Sunday evening, July 5, SAMUEL BUTTERFIELD, Esq., attorney at law, of Andover, N. H., to Miss MARY B. WARE, of the former place, and lately of this town.

In Bath, by Rev. D. Sutherland, Mr. David G. Goodall of Lisbon to Miss Martha D., daughter of Dr. John French of Bath.

In Acworth, Mr. Martin Spaulding, of Langdon to Miss Mary Silsby of Acworth.

In Windsor, Vt., Courtney Brigham of Lempster, N. H., to Miss Lovey Ann Lebourveau, of Keene.

In Kensinton by Elder E. Shaw, Mr. Elbridge G. Tappan of East Kingston to Miss. Sophia Sanborn.

DEATHS

In Alton, Deacon Ephraim Roberts, a Revolutionary soldier and pensioner, in the 79th year of his age. He joined the first Freewill Baptist Church in Alton, in 1805, and afterwards was ordained a deacon, which office he sustained till his death. His last sickness was long and severe, which he bore with uncommon Christian patience. He was well resigned and willing to depart and be with Christ, and could say with Paul, "there is a crown of life laid up for me above." A very affecting and appropriate discourse was preached at his funeral, by H. D. Buzzell, from Luke, 2nd 29—"Lord now lettest thou thy servant depart in peace." Printers in Mass., Vt., and Me., are &c.

In South Deerfield, where she had been for her health, Lucretia E., wife of Noah James of Boston, aged 29. Editors in Philadelphia, are &c.

In Canterbury, of consumption, Mrs. Rebecca, wife of John J. Bryant, Esq., and daughter of Benjamin Gale of Salisbury, aged 32.

The writer of this notice, from an intimate acquaintance with this excellent woman for several years, as from the observation of others concerning her, is induced to say that she approximated as near the standard of human perfection, as any individual within the circle of an extensive observation. With an education by no means inferior—the sweetness of her disposition and suavity of manners endeared her peculiarly to her immediate circle of friends. Through a Christian in faith and practice; in some respects her religious sentiments did not precisely accord with the most popular belief. Her aversion to religious controversy would seldom allow her to question the orthodoxy of the particular views of her friends, nor obtrude her own private opinion upon them. Her strength of mind held out to the last hour; she conversed with great composure on approaching dissolution; and having acted well her part in life, was happy in death. An interesting daughter about seven years old is left by Mrs. Bryant to sustain the loss of an affectionate mother.

On Friday, the 19th inst., at his farm in Peters-township, in Franklin Count, (Pa.) Capt. William McDowell. He was an officer in the Army of the Revolution, and one of the brave forlorn hope at Stony Point.

In East Kingston, of consumption, May 5, Mr. Jacob Rowell, 26.

In Rochester, Mrs. Mary D., wife of Mr. Anthony Pickering,, aged 43.

In Portsmouth, Mr. Thomas Moulton, aged 57.

In Dover, Enoch Page, son of Mr. John Nutter, Jr. of Rochester, aged 10 years. Mrs. Sarah Ann Jones, aged 24 years, wife of Mr. Ebenezer Jones, and daughter of Lieut. John Kenison of Wakefield.

In Rye, 10th inst., Mrs. Betsey Jenness, wife of Mr. Richard Jenness, Jr., in the 53rd year of her age. On the 11th inst., Mrs. Betsy Seavey, wife of Mr. Theodore Seavey.

In Newmarket, Mr. Simeon French, aged 22.

In Newcastle, Mr. Joseph T. Staples, aged 22, formerly of Portsmouth.

In Portsmouth, Mr. Thomas Moulton, aged 67.

In Baltimore, recently, Isaih Thomas, Esq., aged about 70, son of the late Isaih Thomas, who was known as the father of printing in the United States. The deceased was a native of Massachusetts, well known and highly respected.

In Saco, of consumption, June 29, Mrs. Mary S. Bean, wife of Mr. John Alexander, formerly of Salisbury, N. H., aged 27.

NEW HAMPSHIRE PATRIOT & STATE GAZETTE
Concord, Monday, July 20, 1835

A colored man named Shirley murdered another colored man named Boyer, with whom he had quarreled in Philadelphia on Saturday, by stabbing him in the street with a bayonet. Shirley was arrested when on his way to prison was taken from the custody of the officer and severely beaten by a number of blacks. The officer subsequently rescued him and he was taken to the hospital in the prison. He confessed the murder, and exhibited no regret for it.

Fatal Accident. We learn that a lad, the son of Mr. Billings of New Ipswich, was shot dead by another boy on Monday last. The gun was charged by Billings, the father of the unfortunate lad, and left in a situation exposed to the family. The two boys happened to be passing by it in the course of their play, when one of then took hold of it in a careless manner and supposing it unloaded, snapped it at his unsuspecting companion, who received the charge in his head, and died almost instantly. *Nashua Gazette*

Hangman Cheated. Theodore Wilson, who murdered his wife at Kittery, a few weeks since by blows on her head with a stone, died last week at the jail in Alfred. His death was occasioned it is stated, by wounds which he inflicted on himself on the day of the murder by broken glass in attempting to enter a window.

John Randolph's Will. It will be recollected by most of our readers, that Hon. John Randolph, at the time of his death, left two wills. By one he directed the emancipation of all his Negroes; in the other, he said not one word in relation to the subject. The act of emancipation was ordered by the first will; and it is now contended that it was revoked by making a second, although the second does not, as is usual in express terms, revoke the first. Gen. Walter Jones, of the city of Washington, is counsel advocate on the part of those who claim the abrogation of the original testament. The argument that will be thus brought up will be one of consequence and it is hoped that it will be decided in that way, which is now least expected. If the first testament should prevail upwards of five hundred Negroes will obtain their freedom. If it takes an opposite direction they must remain in bondage. There cannot be a doubt in the minds of those who watched and became familiar with the eccentric life of John Randolph that he did at one time intend the emancipation of his slaves; and as it would be a pity to have so good a design destroyed by accident or legal technicalities is hoped that the first will, will prevail. Those who were best acquainted with Mr. Randolph are of the opinion that he left his affairs in the state of vexation and uncertainty, for the sole purpose of preventing any settlement of his estates. A decision of the subject of the two wills will be had in a few days, in all probability, as the subject is now before the Supreme Court of Virginia.

Mr. Randolph filled so conspicuous a place in the annals of the country that the press may not be accused of illiberality or unkindness if it speaks freely of him now that he is dead. A man of varied and singular genius, and qualified by talent and education for the higher circles of life, he was an aristocrat by birth, education and principle, was disposed to hold the world at bay. His early reading and associations to say nothing about his native temperament, inclined him strongly in favor of the old baronial and feudal system, and to the last days of his existence, he is more resembled to the old English Baron than anything that is attached to the character of plain American gentleman. Yet, with all this inherent feeling of aristocracy around him he was professedly one of the strongest sticklers for democracy that the world has ever beheld. With those who joined hands with him, he was perpetually at war; and although he at all times commanded the almost unanimous vote of his district, he was not honored with the personal friendship or association of but very few of the whole number of his constituents. *Boston Gazette*

BREACH OF PROMISE. *Caution to Ladies.* The Circuit Court of New York says the Journal of Commerce has been occupied three days with the suit of George G. Barnard vs. John G. Gaul, and Mary H. Gaul, his wife. The lady whose maiden name was Powers resides in the city of Hudson and the plaintiff who is a journeyman painter resides in this city. During some seven or eight years the parties carried on an epistolary correspondence, in which they made the usual vows and professions of never ending love and affection, &c. &c., and agreed to be man and wife.

The lady, however, unfortunately changed her mind, broke off her engagements and married Mr. Gaul in the month of June 1833. The plaintiff of course became inconsolable and had recourse to the law to compensate him for his misfortune.

He accordingly brought an action against the lady and her husband, and obtained a verdict of one thousand dollars damages and costs. This case has excited great interest in New York. The Star observes a woman may have just cause of action against the perfidy of a man, because her sex exposes her to injuries of feeling and prospects from his infidelity, which leaves her no other redress than an appeal to the laws but this rule cannot work both ways. The sensibility and defenseless condition of a man thus jilted will not authorize him to seek damages out of the pockets of the successful suitor. Besides, jilting a man is an every day affair—he laughs it off and goes on with another and more successful suit. Not so a poor girl who has been cheated by a trifling fop she has no redress but in tears and privacy. When however, a lady asks a gentleman to release her from a *promise of marriage he should do it promptly and gracefully,* regret his own sad loss, and wish every happiness to the fickled fair one.

The Commercial Advertiser of Saturday evening says, we announce with absolute amazement, that the jury directly in the face of the charges and in our opinion, of the merits of the case have this morning rendered a verdict of ONE THOUSAND DOLLARS in favor of the plaintiff. We repeat every man of refinement and sensibility looks upon this verdict with amazement. Here is the case of a man wooing a young, well educated and interesting girl ultimately treating her in a manner that could not but break her heart if she loved him and then, because she did not love him, and could not marry him prosecuted her for a breach of promise and attempting to avenge himself by taking her money! And a New York jury has given him a *thousand dollars.*

MARRIAGES

In Keene by the Hon. S. Hale, Solomon Parsons, Esq. of Bangor, Me., to Miss Clara Sophia Johnson.

In Shewsbury, Mass., Mr. Abel Blake, Jr., of Keene to Miss Hannah T. Monroe.

In Nashua, Mr. Benjamin Kinsley, of Springfield, Mass., to Miss E. A. Parsons, of Nashua.

In Portsmouth by Rev. Mr. Cooke, Mr. John Charles Smith, to Mrs. Catharine Mary Morris. Mr. John H. Pinder to Mrs. Mary A. Bailey.

In Westmoreland, Barton Skinner, Esq., to Miss Elizabeth Works, both of Westmoreland.

DEATHS

At Canterbury, on the 10th inst., Mr. CHASE WIGGIN, aged 90 years and 15 days. He has been a member of the Society of Shakers in that town since its first establishment; owned the land on which the village is situated and contributed more than any other individual in its early stages to the prosperity of the Society.

In Campton, July 6, Mrs. Sarah, wife of Mr. Ebenezer Foss, aged 72. She was the mother of 13 children and lived to behold around her forty grand-children, and three great grand-children. About two and half years since she was seized with a paralytic fit which nearly deprived her of muscular motion for her the remainder of her days. This providence by which her companion is deprived of the wife of his youth, with whom he drank the mingled cup of life, is peculiarly afflictive. Her remains were interred on the 8th inst., and sermon preached from Matthew, XXV 6, by the Rev. J. R. Goodno'. In Mason on the 1st inst., after a short but distressing illness, Mrs. Eunice, wife of Mr. John Spaulding, and eldest daughter of Josiah Russell, Esq., aged 41 years. In her life she was beloved for her social virtues, and in her death she was lamented by all her acquaintances. She has left a fond husband and six children, most of them at a tender age, and many relatives to lament her sudden departure. Printers in N. Y., Maine, and Vt., are &c. In Garland, Me., July 3, Hon. Reuben Bartlett, formerly of Nottingham, N. H. He was killed by a log rolling over him at his saw mill. He has been for several years a member of the Maine Legislature. At Levant, Me., Ebenezer S. Piper, Esq., formerly of Stratham, N. H. He too has been a member of the Legislature of Maine. In Northfield, July 13, Mrs. Abigail Buswell, aged about 36. Printer in Maine are &c.

In Dunstable, Mr. Benjamin Wilson, aged 52. Mr. Jacob Blanchard, Jr. aged 21. In Londonderry, Mrs. Mary Glynn, wife of Mr. Moses Glynn, aged 39. In Hollis, Elisabeth Pool, daughter of Benjamin and Sarah Pool, age 39. In Keene, Mrs. Harriet W. Evans, wife of Mr. Mr. Nathaniel Evans, aged 36. Mrs. Rebecca Wilson, wife of Mr. James W. II, aged 45. Mrs. Sarah Seward, widow of the late Deacon Josiah Seward, of Sullivan, aged 85.

In Milford, N. Betsey, wife of Mr. Richard Jenness, Jr., in the 53rd year of her age. On the 11th inst., Mrs. Betsey Seavey, wife of Mr. Theodore Seavey.

In Portsmouth, Mr. Nathaniel Cotton, aged 74. Mrs. Elizabeth Moses, wife of Mr. Nehemiah Moses, aged 28.

In Rochester, Moses Young, Esq., aged about 69. He labored in his field as usual during the day, and ate his supper in the evening, when in a few minutes he was a lifeless corpse. Mr. Young was an enterprising and valuable citizen, a kind and affectionate husband and an honest man.

In Mobile, Mr. Enos Shattuck, formerly of this town.

NEW HAMPSHIRE PATRIOT & STATE GAZETTE
Concord, Monday, July 27, 1835

Col. Ethan Allen. We have heard one anecdote of Col. Ethan Allen, which we believe has yet been in print.

Mr. B., an attorney of Vermont, once received from some person in Boston a note of hand for £60, against Allen for collection. It being inconvenient for him at that time to pay the note it was sued. When the case came on for trial, Allen employed a lawyer to get the action continued until he could raise money to settle the demand, and accordingly the attorney, as the readiest means of accomplishing his object, determined to deny the genuineness of the signature. This would oblige the plaintiff to produce the witnesses to the note, who resided in Boston and could not be brought forward on the instant. The effect of the maneuver would be to cause the plaintiff to postpone the trial till the next court. When the cause was called it happened that Allen was in a remote part of the Court House and to his utter astonishment heard his lawyer gravely deny the signature of the note. With long and erect strides he rushed through the crowed and confronted the amazed "limb of the law," rebuking him in a voice of thunder.

"Mr. _____, I did not hire you to come here and lie—that is a true note—I signed it—I'll swear to it—and I'll pay it. I want no shuffling, I want time. What I employed you for was to get this business put over to the next court; not to lie and jiggle about it." The result was that the postponement of the claim was amicably arranged between the two lawyers.

Near Being Jonahized. We published a notice a short time since, from a Nantucket paper, of a narrow escape of a young man from the jaws of a whale in the Pacific Ocean. It turns out that the young man was from Portland. The following extract of a letter from him to his mother was published in the last Christian Mirror.

PACIFIC OCEAN }
Lat 5 N, S., Lon 109 W. }

Dear Mother—Having a good opportunity to write, I improve it and state that through the interposition of a kind Providence, my life has been miraculously spared and I am able to write to you. Four weeks ago I was very seriously hurt by a whale. The whale stove all three of our boats and got me in his jaw, knocked about half the scalp off my head, but did not affect my skull. He struck two teeth in my breast and one in each thigh—one wound was six inches long and two deep and he went off with four irons fastened to him. I suppose, dear mother this was one of the narrowest escapes from death ever known, and so little hurt!—not a bone broken! And I have so far recovered as to be about, and Captain Hussey thinks I shall be able to attend to duty and my boat again in two weeks. This, my dear mother, you may suppose will be a small satisfaction to me; but I assure you that I had rather be in a boat fastened to a whale, then any where else. My captain and mate have been father and brother to me since my injury, and I doubt whether there ever was a ship sailed the seas with such good officers as we have.

We have got sixteen hundred barrels of oil, and hope soon to get sixteen more, and be turning our faces homeward in the course of six or eight months. We have got fifteen whales to the waste boat, which I have had the pleasure of steering. I have killed seven whales with my irons. I should write you some more, my dear mother, at this time, but they have hoisted signals for whales at the masthead, and I am in hopes we shall get three.

              Your affectionate son,
                  AUGUSTUS HALE

Extract of a Letter from Capt. Low of ship Cabot, dated Canton, 28th Feb. 1835.—Feb. 10th, off the N W end of the Pelew Island, I took a man from a canoe who said his name was George Marsh, of Providence—that he was wrecked in the schooner Dash, of Boston, on the Matotes or Caroline Island, about 180 miles from Pelew, on the 14th March, 1834. He came on board naked, but in fine health—had been well treated by the natives. He is tall, light complexion, and about 21 years old. Marsh gave me the following information respecting other Americans left on the island adjoining those he was on:–Two men of the crew of the whale shop Mentor, lost there in 1832. There was three of the number left as hostages for forty muskets, which were promised the king by the captain of the ship. One had made his escape on board of a ship that was passing the island. There is an American boy about there also. When George got on board we were a long distance from the islands, and it was nearly dark and blowing very strong. If it had been otherwise I should have attempted to regain the island for the purpose of taking the rest of the men, although thirty or forty miles to windward. George says the inhabitants are very civil to them, and treated them well.

P. S. March 11th. George Marsh has gone in the Griffin, of Boston to the Sandwich Islands. He left the Cabot without my knowledge. However, I had no claim on him except as regards his deliverance from death, or a worse punishment, for I have heard by a vessel that has arrived here since that they fell in with the same canoe that brought him on board, four days after; the men lost their island and were in a very hungry condition. They were taken of board, fed and carried in sight of their island, to their great joy. They took their departure in good spirits. *Jour. Com.*

LIGHTNING

During the thundershower on Monday last, about 6 o'clock, p. m., lightning struck the house of Mr. Thomas Whitcher of this town. The family, consisting of eight persons was at tea. The fluid descended the chimney, crossing in its passage to the floor the leg of a stove and melting; it then followed the sleeper or beam, bursting up the floor, and passed out of the house. All the family, with the exception of Mr. Whitcher, were prostrated to the floor. A little girl was thrown quite across the tea table, while the chair in which she was sitting was left upon it. Another girl, about eleven years of age had her foot seriously injured—a piece of flesh about the size of a walnut being torn out and left hanging by the skin. A young lady sitting at the table had her shoes entirely torn to pieces and scattered about the room and her feet badly burnt. *Newport Spectator.*

Hurricane. The Illinois Register of the 19th June mentions that on the 18th ult., at about half past 8 o'clock, p.m., the town of Canton, in Fulton County, was visited by one of the most awful hurricane that has ever been witnessed in any port of the United States. Out of 50 or 60 houses or more in the village not more than 3 or 4 have been left standing, and those more or less injured. Mr. Swan and child and Col. Elias Foster's little daughter, 12 or 13 years of age, were killed upon the spot; Col. Foster himself and another gentleman were so much injured as to be beyond the hope of recovery—many others were badly bruised but not seriously injured—scarcely a person escaped without more or less injury. Horses, cattle and hogs in great numbers were instantly killed and lay scattered about the streets and fields. The streets, lots and fields were all around swept as the besom of destruction and this beautiful little village in now a heap of ruin.

Honorable and Horrible Murder. We find in the New Orleans papers an account of a duel recently fought in that city, the circumstances of which strike us as constituting as clear a case of murder as ever brought before a jury. The parties were a Mr. Dunn, clerk to a merchant named Minturn, and McMahon, clerk of one of the New Orleans Courts. The following are the particulars as stated in the New Orleans papers:

On Thursday night Dunn, (the deceased) had been drinking with McMahon and others at a cabaret in the vicinity our office; when McMahon in paying for the refreshments laid a picaillon (six piece) on the counter, which Dunn in the gayety of unsuspecting freedom took up and gave for two cigars offering then one of them to McMahon. The act passed unnoticed at the time. But McMahon having followed Dunn into the street demanded the picaillon. Dunn laughed at first but the other was in no merry mood. Dunn perceiving this offered his supposed friend a coin out of his pocket. "No," said McMahon, "give me my own picaillon." Back went Dunn to the cabaret but it was closed. This was expected perhaps by MaMahon who immediately commenced scurrilous reprobation's which attracted a crowd—Berry among others. Berry interfered and the dispute between him and Dunn proceeded to blows.

Then McMahon changed his mode of attack on Dunn; resumed the appearance of friendship and aware that Berry (who kept a shooting gallery for some time) was a shot, he drew Dunn aside, and instigated him to challenge his antagonist for the blow inflicted. Poor Dunn who was *Bacchi plenus* asked a respite till next morning, when he should have recovered and be more collected, but MaMahon would not wait. He himself wrote the challenge and having made Dunn sign it, he immediately brought it to Berry. The rendezvous was settled for the next morning.

MaMahon brought Dunn into the field in a state of drunken stupor or recklessness, scarcely knowing whither or why he went. But Dunn was a warm-hearted Irishman and neither cared for himself thought of the morrow nor suspected his friend. Berry is said to have deliberately taken his aim during the word of command on the first fire but Dunn escaped that. Matters were then sought to the amicably adjusted; but this McMahon imperiously refused; for his friend, forsooth must have satisfaction!—and this satisfaction poor Dunn had instantly.

Melancholy Accident. On Sunday last, (12th) seven young men and women started from Campobello for Casco Bay Island, in a boat for pleasure. Within a few rods of the last named island they were upset, and four drowned. The rest were saved by clinging to the boat, until relieved by assistance from Campobello. The names of those drowned were, George Wilson, Thankful Wilson, Hannah Parker, and _____Camplin; and those saved are, George Newman, Benjamin Parker, and Maria Wilson. The Eastern Democrat to which we are indebted for these particulars says that the young woman that was saved, supported herself and sister, however, unable to keep her in such a position as to prevent her drowning. When she found that her sister was dead she disengaged herself from her and saved herself by getting, with the assistance of the two young men already there, upon the bottom of the boat.

In Sterling's Trial for Bigamy in New York the other day, the indictment stated, says the Herald, "that on the 27th of January, 1831, the prisoner was married, by the Rev. H. Ballou to Miss Elizabeth Gale, of Boston, and afterwards, in the year 1834 while his former wife was still living, he had contracted matrimony with a Miss Hamilton, of New York, who has recently died in child birth." The witness for the prosecution proved to the satisfaction of the court that the facts stated in the indictment were true. The prisoner's counsel, Messrs. Brady and Wilson contended that the first marriage in Boston, the state of Massachusetts, was not valid. 1st, because the Rev. H. Ballou was not a regularly ordained minister in the place where the marriage was said to have taken place. 2nd, that admitting he was regularly ordained yet he belonged to the sect termed "Universalists," and was not considered by the law of the state of Massachusetts as qualified to act as a regular clergyman as that sect is not recognized nor its minister privileged as in other states. 3rd, the law imperatively requires that the banns of the marriage should invariably be published which was not the case in the marriage of the prisoner. These objection were, however, overruled by the court, as they considered the evidence brought forward quite sufficient to prove the validity of the prisoner's first marriage. The jury, after consulting for a short time, found the prisoner guilty. *Boston Post*

Remarkable Escape. The North River (N. Y.) Times states, that recently the crew of the sloop Henry passing down the river, saw something suspended down the side of the high range of mountains below Slaugher's Landing which resembled a female form. They immediately cast anchor and went ashore in the boat. On arriving at the foot of the mountain they found it to be a young girl aged about 16, *hanging by one foot in a cedar bush, about one hundred feet from the base and sixty feet from the top of the perpendicular rock.* To reach her from the bottom was impossible and providing themselves with a rope they hastened round to the top from which they lowered it. The unfortunate girl was yet able to fix it around her waist and by this means was drawn from her perilous situation. She proved to be Miss Phebe Wells, a niece of Mr. Benedict Wells, who had left his residence without the knowledge of his family with a view of going to New York to see her friends. Unacquainted with the passage of the mountains it is supposed she was unaware of the danger until she found herself descending the precipice and the rock being nearly perpendicular, her fall could only have been broken by the slight shrubbery which projects from the side of the cliff until materially injured and was conveyed to her friends in New York by the sloop.

MILLEDGEVILLLE, July 14. *More Indian Hostilities Below.* By later accounts from the counties between the Flint and Chattahoochee it appears that the situation of the unfortunate inhabitants is growing continually worse. We mention a few of the facts that have recently reached us. Three parties of Indians were lately discovered near Newton, a little village on the Flint and now the seat of justice of Baker County. The alarmed inhabitants sent an express twenty-five miles to Byron, the site of the former Court House of the same county for help and a party started to their assistance. On their way they discovered four Indians barbecuing a cow. These ran into the Co-lee-wa-Hee swamp. After reaching Newton and remaining all night there the party went out to reconnoiter, and found on the east side of the Co-lee-wa-Hee, a large Indian camp which had been hastily abandoned on their approach. They pursued them so closely that the Indians dropped a whole deer but were not overtaken. The next day they were seen on the waters of the Chick-a-sa-Hatchee, and guns were heard in that direction.

The country seems to be full of these murderous marauders. Several herdsmen driving up their stock came upon three or four Indians heavily loaded, probably with plunder. As the herdsmen approached them they laid down their packs apparently for a fight and the white men then seeing more Indians lying behind logs, with guns ready to fire and being unarmed themselves, they immediately retreated for safety.

Since then a reconnoitering party came upon another camp on an island in a pond in Early County. The whites forded the pond, killed three of the Indians and drove them from their camp where they found upwards of 500 pounds of dried beef.

In Baker not long since Mr. Holmes, the Sheriff of that county, with eight or ten men approached within about forty yards of a company apparently of six or seven Indians telling them they came as friends but thirty or forty suddenly rose up from their ambush and fired upon the whites. Three men were wounded, one in the leg, another more dangerously, being shot in the neck near the jugular, and the third it is thought mortally, the ball passing from hip to hip. Holmes' horse was wounded, and five balls were shot into that of old Mr. Johnson but the generous animal carried his master out of danger before he died.

If the inhabitants of those counties receive no more protection from the government for the next four years than they have for the last four it is thought and indeed, it is most evident they must evacuate the country.

Mr. Randolph's Will. *We are informed by a friend who left Richmond on Sunday morning; that the trial of the case of the late Mr. Randolph's will, which has occupied so much of the public attention, had terminated; but the judgment of the court was then unknown. Some* extraordinary development, it is said, have taken place in the course of the trial of a nature so prejudicial to the character of the testator as to make many of the most ardent friends and admirers desirous that the pleas of insanity should be confirmed by the court as a protection to his reputation. It is understood that if the will in question be set aside, a proceeding one which provides for the manumission of the testator's slaves, will take effect—unless it should it be invalidate by the same pleas of insanity, in which event the deceased would be considered as dying intestate. *Baltimore Patriot*

Lightning. Lightning on Tuesday night of last week killed a yoke of oxen belonging to Harrison Wilder of Sterling. They were lying under an apple tree, which showed but slight marks of the effect of the fluid.
Worcester Spy.

The report that Wilson, the man who murdered his wife in Kittery (Me.) a few weeks since—had died in jail is incorrect.

A Female Horse Thief. A person by the name of *Charles Stewart* was convicted in the Court of Sessions, New York City, on a charge of stealing a horse. After the conviction says the Mercantile Advertiser, the prisoner informed the counsel that she was a woman and on investigation it was found that her declaration was true. She stated that she was a native of the highlands of Scotland, and that she had resided on Long Island for the last four years in the garb of a man.
Providence Journal

DARING ROBBERY. Last week as Mr. Clendenning, of the town of Liberty, (Illinois) who came to our city (New Orleans) for the purpose of selling produce was walking on the levee near Poydras Street, he was accosted by a man who called him by name and told him that the captain of his flat had been attacked by the city guard, but had effected his retreat from them badly wounded;

he said that he was concealed in a remote part of the city, was most anxious to see him and offered to conduct Mr. Clendenning to the place. They had not proceeded far when he told Mr. Clendenning that it would be necessary for him to advance and see if any of the guards were in the neighborhood; if so, he would hoist his umbrella as a signal that he should pass carelessly by. After thus leading him through a number of streets till they arrived near an old house close to the French cemetery, he gave the signal, and requested Mr. Clendenning to go behind the wall of the burying ground as a place of safety. He had scarcely reached the place when two men issued from the house, advanced immediately towards him, presented two pistols and accused him of having counterfeit money to the amount of $4000, the sum he had received for the produce. Fortunately he had laid out most of his money and had only about $360 remaining, which they took. They threatened to shoot him if he did not go into the woods. One of the villains pointing to the canal observed that they had buried fifty persons there, that he was the only one they had suffered to escape as he was a brave man. Mr. Clendenning returned to town and applied to the police who we are happy to say rendered him every assistance in their power. The Mayor himself placed at his disposal many of the city guards as he thought would be sufficient and gave them directions to disguise themselves so as to enable them to better to succeed in their object. On Wednesday they arrested two of the villains, Anderson Murray and Benjamin Teterville in the Faubourg Lacourse. On Friday through the assistance of Mr. Thistle and Mr. Bennet, who deserve great praise for their activity, they arrested another in the upper Faubourg and the fourth at M'Carty Point. His name is Underwood. Three of these desperadoes are old convicts and are well known by the police. *Louisiana Adv., June 3*

Ex–President Adams reached his 69th years on Saturday last, the 11th of July.

The Wythe C. H. (Va.) Argus gives an account of the family of dwarfs residing in that country who are all remarkable for their handsome forms and fine proportions:—

"There are two males and two females—the height of the eldest, who is a male and in his 25th year, is 3 ft 6 in., and his weight is 34 pounds. The other male is in his 9th year, and 2 ft and 7 ¼ in height, and weighs 21 pounds. The eldest female is in her 11th year, and is 2 ft 2 in high and weighs 27 pounds. The other female is in her 7th year, is 2 ft 11 ¼ high, and weighs 27 pounds.

New Albany, (Indiana) July 3. We learn that Mr. Ladd, the editor and publisher of the Indianian at Corydon, Harrison County, Indiana, on Tuesday the 25th ult., attempted to kill his wife. After stabbing her several times, she fell and supposing her death immediate and certain he stabbed himself, the dirk passing through his heart. After he had fallen, he discovered his wife still alive and endeavoring to rise; he made another pass at her with the dirk, and exclaimed, "I believe I shall die first." The blow was warded off by throwing up her arm which received a severe wound. He survived but a few moments and his wife, from the last account was still alive though few hopes of her recovery were entertained.

Gazette

Sam Patch Outdone. On Wednesday last June 24, as Mr. Peter Cozzens was ascending a ladder reaching from the ridge of the roof of the Baptist Meeting House in Wickford, R. I. to the top of the tower, by a false step he fell from the ladder to roof a distance of about 6 feet. In sliding down the roof, with a presence of mind seldom equaled, he turned on his back (having fallen from the ladder to the roof face downward,) and from the eaves of the house he was precipitated to the ground a height of 25 feet alighting on his feet which made a deep impression on a coarse gravely soil. He immediately arose up, still retaining the saw in his hand which he had in falling from the ladder, and walked home, sustaining no further injury, than a trifling sprain of the ankles and one hand slightly wounded with a nail.

Providence Herald.

NOTICE

WHEREAS MOSES FELLOWS a town pauper of New Chester has absconded from my house, I hereby forbid all persons harboring or trusting him on my account him as I have made suitable provisions for his support.

DANIEL BARTLETT

New Chester, July 25, 1835

TO WHOM IT MAY CONCERN

THIS may certify that I have this day given to my son NATHANIEL CLARK, his time, that he is free to act and trade for himself, and that I shall neither in future claim any of his earnings nor consider myself responsible for any debts of his support.

JOSHUA CLARK

Attest { N. J. T. George
{ Ambrose Hill

Thornton, July 22, 1835.

NOTICE

I Do Hereby give to my son RANDOLPH GIBSON his time and authorize him to act and trade for himself. I shall not claim any of his earnings nor pay any debts of his contracting.   JACOB GIBSON

Bradford, July 4, 1835.

NOTICE

THIS is to forbid all persons harboring or trusting JONATHAN EATON, a town pauper on my account or on the account of the town, as I have made suitable provisions for the said Jonathan Easton.

Pittsfield, July 17, 1835   JOSEPH MARSTON.

NOTICE

I HEREBY relinquish to my son JOSEPH W. LEIGHTON his time and declare him free to act and trade for himself, and I will neither claim his earnings nor pay any debts of contracting after this date.

JONATHAN LEIGHTON.

Attest { David Follensbee
{ Jedediah Colley

Grafton, July 11, 1835.

MARRIAGES

In this town by Rev. Mr. Bouton, Mr. Joseph L. Jackson to Miss Cynthia M. Shute.

In Aulauga County, Ala., by Rev. James Tabor, James Colby, M. D. to Miss Sarah McLean, both of that county.

In Lowell, Mass., Rev. Mr. Waite of Waldron, Mass., to Miss Elouisia Peabody, formerly of Newport, N. H.

In Boston, Mr. William Clark, Amherst, N. H., to Miss Ellen M. Wagner.

In Northwood, Mr. Z. Dow Creighton, of New Market to Miss Susan E. Woodbury, daughter of Dr. Jonathan Woodbury.

In Bangor, Mr. Samuel B. Smith, to Miss Mary K. Reed, daughter of Robert Reed of Dover, N. H.

In Holderness, Mr. Jacob Weed, of Sandwich to Miss Emily, only daughter of John Cox, Jr.

In Boston, Mr. Charles S. Giles, formerly of Brookfield, N. H., to Miss Esther Ann Ober.

In Portsmouth, Mr. Silas Moody to Miss Mary Ann Wingate. Mr. John Pindar to Miss Mary A. Bailey.

DEATHS

In the town, an infant son of James and Mary McClaren. Printers in Boston are &c.

In Loudon, of consumption, Mrs. Mary Brown, consort of Samuel Brown, aged 63.

In Haverhill, Hon. Samuel C. Webster, Sheriff of Grafton County.

In Cincinnati, Ohio, Mrs. Harriet, consort of the Rev. Dr. Beecher.

In New Hampton, Mr. David Kelley, youngest son of Ebenezer and Sally Kelley, aged 25.

In Moultonborough, of consumption, Charles Bean, Esq, aged 29.

Drowned in Bangor, Me., Mr. Ephraim Butterfield, of Francistown, N. H.

In Portsmouth, Miss Ann Mary, daughter of Abraham Wendell, Esq., aged 24. Capt. Slyvester P. Lowe, aged 35. Mrs. Holmes, wife of Mr. Robert Holmes.

In Landaff, Samuel Noyes, Jr., 42.

In New York, Mr. Willoughby Lynde, one of the editors and proprietors of the New York Transcript, aged 27.

In Upper Gilmanton, July 7, of disease of the heart, Benjamin P. Morrill son of Benjamin Morrill II, Esq., in the 17th year of his age.

At Sterling, of apoplexy, Rev. Hosea Hildreth, Agent of the Massachusetts Society for Suppressing Intemperance. The subject of this notice possessed an unusual portion of intellectual discrimination and strength. His mind enlarged by liberal inquiry and assiduous application fitted him to be a useful and respectable instructor of youth and a Christian minister. He passed fourteen years in honorable employment as a teacher in Phillip's Academy Exeter, N. H. He is remembered by many with respect and gratitude, as rendering them important aid in their preparation for the public stage. The constitutional ardor and the strength of religious principle, which was manifest in the more retired scenes of life, animated and directed him in all his duty as a minister of Christ. In the moral reform of the day he felt a deep interest and to his active and laborious efforts, this community is vastly indebted for its progress.

NEW HAMPSHIRE PATRIOT & STATE GAZETTE
Concord, Monday, August 3, 1835

THE GRAVE OF JEFFERSON

The following is a description of the place where rest the remains of the sage of Monticello:—

"I ascended the winding road which leads from Charlottesville to Monticello. The path leads to a circuitous ascent of about two miles up the miniature mountain to the farm and the grave of Jefferson. On entering the gate, which opens into the enclosure, numerous paths diverge in various directions, winding through beautiful groves to the summit of the hill. From the peak on which the house stands a grand nearly, unlimited view opens upon the thick wooded hills and fertile valleys, which stretch out on either side. The university with its dome, porticos and colonnades looks like a fair city in the plain: Charlottsville seems to be directly beneath. No spot can be imagined as combining greater advantages of grandeur and seclusion. The house is noble in its appearance; two large columns support a portico, which extends from the wing, and into it the front door opens. The apartments are neatly furnished and embellished with statues, busts, portraits and natural curiosities. The grounds and outhouses have been neglected, Mr. Jefferson's attention being absorbed from such personal concerns by the care attendant on the superintendence of the university, which, when in health he visited daily since the erection commenced."

"At a short distance behind the mansion in a quiet, shaded spot, the visitor sees a square enclosed, surrounded by a low unmortared stone wall which he enters by a neat wooden gate. This is the family burial ground containing ten or fifteen graves, none of them marked by epitaphs and only a few distinguished by any memorial. On one side of this simple cemetery is the resting-place of the patriot and philosopher. When I saw it, the vault was just arched and in readiness for the plain stone which is to cover it. May it ever continue like Washington's without any adventitious attractions or conspicuousness, for when we or our posterity need any other memento of our debt of honor to those names than their simple inscription on paper, wood or stone, gorgeous tombs would be a mockery to their memories. When gratitude shall cease to concentrate their remembrance in the hearts of our patrons, no cenotaph will inspire the reverence we owe them.

MYSTERIOUS. We are informed that the body of an individual supposed to have died a natural death, was discovered on the 15th inst., in a hovel at a considerable distance from any habitation in the township called Dummer, (N. H.) near the Androscoggin River. When found he is thought to have been dead three or four weeks. There were found with him a valise, several articles of clothing, a memorandum and pocketbook, a small sum of money and some papers of value, among which were "The last Will and testament of Mehitable Simpson," &c.

He appeared to have been a man of about 60 years of age and from the fact of there having been found in his pocketbook a copy of a letter dated "Sandwich, May 24, 1835," addressed to "My Child," and signed "Joseph S. Simpson," it is supposed that his name was Simpson. The following is an extract from his memoranda:

"In the year 1835, on Monday the 27th of April, left Orford to seek my fortune, being driven from home through the interference of my mistress and her blessed neighbors, and the cursed selectmen who fleeced me out of two thousand dollars worth of property."

For the information of his friends if he has any, we are requested to say that his remains were decently interred. The articles found with him have left in the care of Mr. Benjamin Bean of Berlin, on whom they will call for them and settle the expenses incurred in his burial &c. Further particulars may be obtained by application to Mr. Bean, Col. S. H. King of Oxford, Mr.

John Lombard of Magalloway Mr. John Leighton of Berlin. *Portland Jeffersonian*

In January 1817, Mr. Harry Rockwell and Miss Esther Niles were united in the bands of matrimony by the Rev. Mr. West, of East Hampton. In October 1819, business called Mr. Rockwell to Savannah from which place he intended to return in about six months; but unforeseen circumstances prevented his return until the 4th of the present month—having been absent 16 years, 8 months and 27 days. During his absence Mrs. Rockwell obtained a bill of divorce, and was a second time married. With her second husband she lived until his death March 12, 1831, and from that to the present she remained a widow. On Saturday 4th inst. Mr. Rockwell arrived in Chatham, East Hampton Society, and found her that was once his wife in the same house in which he left her in 1819; and on Thursday afternoon the 9th inst. they were again united in the bands of matrimony by the Rev. Mr. Loper of Middle Haddam.
Middletown Sentinel

Lightning. Fourteen sheep and lambs were killed by a stroke of lightning in the pasture of Mr. Nathaniel Rowe of Gilmanton, on Saturday the 25th ult.

FATAL ACCIDENT. We learn by Mr. Tyler the mail carrier between this place and New Ipswich, that a Capt. Prichard, of the latter town, while on a journey with his wife through Wilton on Saturday last was thrown from his carriage and killed instantly! They were descending a hill when the horse stumbled and fell, throwing Mr. and Mrs. Prichard from the carriage. He was about 75 years of age. *Nashua Gazette*

FRIGHTFUL AFFAIR

The annexed frightful paragraphs are copied from the Louisiana Advertiser of the 11th instant. The facts detailed are circumstantial, and seem to carry an aspect of truth with them, which probably will be confirmed by subsequent accounts.

"We have just learned the particulars of the horrible affair reported by one of the steamboats yesterday. It appears that some persons had kept a gambling house at Vickburg for some time, and as usual in similar establishments had their pimps and decoys employed, inveigling inexperienced young men into the lion's den, where they were invariably fleeced of all they possessed, and frequently ill treated by the conductors. The inhabitants determined to abate the nuisance had held several meetings, and given notice repeatedly to the offenders to quit the city by a certain time or suffer the consequences of an outraged community. The day at length arrived when the committee waited on them and told them that their passage was paid for on board a steamboat and quit they must! They positively refused— the committee retired to deliberate and again, returned, but the house was closed, and whilst endeavoring to gain admittance, several shots were fired from the window, one of which struck Dr. Bodley, the chairman, and caused his immediate death. Another gentleman of respectability was severely wounded and the rest of the bullets passed through the hats of the other members of the committee.

The towns people immediately assembled, broke open the house, seized five men, the only inmates, dragged them out to the public square and HANGED them *instantly!!!* They posted sentries, and gave notice that any person who approached them for twenty-four hours would be served likewise. All the money, which was to a large amount, was piled upon a table before the suspended bodies, and the committee paid it away to all whom could prove they had lost money to the house. About twelve or fifteen persons in connection with the house started from the city in haste to avoid a similar fate. These are the particulars as we have heard them— we shall make no comment on so dreadful an occurrence, hoping the account has been exaggerated.

Since the above was in type, we have heard that Dr. Bodley was murdered in the gaming house, after having won a considerable sum of money at the table, which was the original cause of this execution of summary justice, or Lynch Law, as it is called.

The persons executed were Mr. North, who kept a tavern, Dutch Bill, his barkeeper, Mr. Samuel Smith, Mr. Cullum and Mr. McCall.

The True American gives another and we suspect a more correct version of the occurrence. We have no doubt that this is the same affair alluded to in the letter which we copied from the Philadelphia Gazette yesterday, and which represented it as connected with a Negro insurrection.

Insurrection of Slaves. In our paper of Monday, we copied from the Philadelphia Gazette an account of a projected insurrection among the slaves in Mississippi. The Nashville (Tenn.) Banner contains the following extract of a letter from Mississippi addressed to a gentleman in that city, which appears to confirm the story of the Gazette. We also give another extract of a letter, in reference to the same transaction received in Lynchburg, and published in the Virginian of that place.

"I take a few moments from that awful disease and confusion existing here, to inform you that his (Hinds) and several adjoining counties, have been under arms, day and night, in our defense, expecting every moment to be burned up or have our throats cut by the Negroes. A dreadful alarm exists, particularly among the females."

"An insurrection has, it appears, been on hand among the Negroes for the last six months, headed by white men. The massacre was to have commenced on the fourth of July. Their plans were well laid and no doubt but that thousands of the whites would have been murdered had we not been saved, only a week before the time, by a faithful Negro man who was in all the secrets, and was to have been high in command. He revealed to his master the whole plan; and to convince him of its reality, placed his master in a position were from his place of concealment, he could overhear one of their night meetings, at which the whole scheme was discussed."

"A great many Negroes were, in consequence, taken up in Madison Country, from whom the committee found out who the white leaders were. About 10 Negroes, and 5 or 6 white men have been hung without any form of law or trial except an examination before the examining committee. They are still going on trying and hanging. It appears from a confession that Dr. Cotton made that their route was to have commenced from some place above this and to proceed thence through the principal towns, to Natchez, and then on to New Orleans, murdering all the white men and ugly women—sparing the handsome ones and making wives of them—and plundering and burning as they went. Dr. Cotton, after being condemned upon a Negro testimony, made a confession and disclosed the whole plan. His accomplice is an old confederate of a man by the name of Murrell, now in the Nashville penitentiary.

BALTIMORE, July 23, 1835. [Correspondence of the Atlas.] There is a man in Baltimore by the name of Captain John S. Bassiere. He is perhaps thirty odd years of age—has a family—is tolerably well looking—is said to be fascinating in his manners—can spout French and Italian very fluently—has for some years past run a great rig in Baltimore, in the way of keeping a young ladies' riding school, running omnibuses, until he run them out of sight and himself out of funds—getting into private broils, quarrels, fighting, having duels, getting kicked out of lyceums and so forth. He has been almost the terror of the town. Every body almost despised him; and yet every body, almost, has been afraid of him. He has had a whipping at last, however, a severe one, almost as severe as it was just. Bassiere formerly boarded with a Mrs. S____, who has for a long time kept a respectable school for young misses. One of the young ladies attending this school is a Miss W.____, from Washington. Yesterday, her guardian, Mr. Baylies of Washington being in this city, called at the house of Mrs. _____, who has been for some time confined to her house with indisposition, to see his ward. He was told that she was not then in, but should be sent for. A person was sent; Baylies also took his hat and went out. He overtook the girl who was going after Miss W._____, and asked her where she was. The girl at first refused to tell him. This created suspicion and he soon prevailed upon her to show him to the house, which was none other than Capt. Bassiere's, who, although his family is staying in the country, still occupies or has occupied a house in town. Mr. Baylies rung, a servant came to the door, he asked for Capt. Bassiere. The servant said he was sick and could not be seen. Mr. Baylies said he would see him—pushed the servant aside and entered the house. He was proceeding up the stairs when he met Bassiere, words were exchanges, and so were blows! Magistrates and citizens attracted by the noise rushed in. Miss W_____ and daughter of Mrs. S_____ made *their* appearance in grand dishabille! The combatants were separated; Bassiere ran into his room, got his pistols, and aimed one at Baylies, which was no sooner done that the latter rushed upon him like a tiger, beat him down and smashed the life almost out of him. The spectators standing by and rejoicing to see the *"Devil get his due!"* Bassiere delivered himself into the hands of the law last night and went to jail for safe-keeping. Medical aid had to be sent for, and so severe was his beating that he had a number of fits last night. If he had not gone to jail he would have been killed by the enraged populace who assembled in multitudes round his house to demolish it, and to tar and feather Bassiere. The excitement today is very great. The wretch will surely be killed if he ever makes his appearance here again. His seduction of these two young girls has clapped the climax of his crimes. *Mrs. S_____'s school, upon which she depended for support is broken up*—but oh heavens, what must be the inevitable fate of her daughter and Miss W_____.

Dreadful Consequences of Fanaticism. Our readers will recollect an advertisement that appeared in the Transcript a few weeks since, describing the singular absence from home of a young lady named Reid, who had suddenly left her mother's house in this city and without saying where she was going to. One of her brothers, a respectable mechanic residing at New Haven, Conn., was apprised of the circumstances of his sister's being missing, and alarmed lest some accident might have befallen her, quitted his business, and instituted inquiries after her in different parts of the country. About a fortnight after he started in pursuit he succeeded in discovering the poor girl, who, but a few weeks ago, was glowing with health and vigor, and full of intelligence and sensibility, at a distance of nearly three hundred miles from New York, unconsciously wandering she knew not where, harassed, exhausted with hunger and fatigue, destitute of money and the means of procuring it, and a wretched miserable maniac.

It appears from the well attested documents that have been placed in our possession that the young lady above named, previous to abandoning her friends and home in the way we have described, had been persuaded by a member of Mr. Finney's chapel, to leave the church she had long been accustomed to attend and visit the place of worship, superintended by the former individual. On her so doing she was introduce to the pastor and he questioned her as to her habits, her disposition, her inclinations, and her religious feelings. To all these interrogation, she gave answers that would have satisfied any rational man, or any person whose motives were not impelled by an overwhelming, illiberal, and intolerant sectarian spirit. He, however, did not stop here. Madly zealous in promulgating the doctrine he had espoused—doctrines which, preadventure, properly inculcated may be pure and worthy—he denounced her former mode of living, in a wild and frightful anathema; pronounced her to be one of the accursed—without the possibility of redemption except through his means, and irretrievably lost unless restored by his intercessions and entreaties to the throne of grace.

To illustrate the course of argument pursued; to relate the various gross and impious expressions that were made use of; to expose the harsh and unfeeling language addressed to her; and to give the detail of the hideous and demonic pictures which they presented to her affrighted imagination, for the purpose of making her their proselyte, is a task for which we have no relish, and would impose upon the columns of our paper a stigma and a disgrace that we do not intend they shall ever merit. It may suffice to say that among the maneuvers, which they practiced, and the arts they exercised, they exhibited to her a Heaven and Hell Book in either of which they professed to have power to record the irrevocable decrees of eternal happiness or everlasting misery. So powerful were the effect of these repeated assaults upon the faith and representations to the excited mind of the deluded girl that she eventually was deprived of her reason, and added to the hapless crowd of the unfortunates that now tenant our lunatic asylums—victims to similar atrocities, and unsightly wrecks of poor humanity. *N. Y. Transcript.*

The Portsmouth, N. H. Gazette concludes an account of the recent robbery of the post office in that place.

A large part of the letter, papers, &c., were found Sunday last in Great Swamp, about two and a half miles from the Court House. They were broken open, much mutilated and otherwise injured. We believe that nearly all of them are recovered. The extent of the loss sustained by rifling them of their contents has not yet been ascertained—but from the general appearance of the letter, it is probably inconsiderable.

COLLEGE ANECDOTE

Many years since, when the late Lieutenant Governor Phillips, of Andover, Mass., was a student at the Harvard College, owing to some boyish freak he quit the university and went home. His father was a grave man of sound mind, strict judgment, and a few words. He inquired into the business, but deferred expressing any opinion until the next day. At breakfast he said, speaking to his wife,

"My dear, have you any tow cloth in the house, suitable to make Sam a frock and trowsers?"

She replied, "Yes."

"Well," said the old gentleman, "follow me, my son,"

Samuel kept pace with his father as he leisurely walked near the common and at length ventured to ask—

"What are you going to do with me father?"

"I am going to bind you an apprentice to that blacksmith," replied Mr. Phillips. "Take your choice—return to college or you must work."

"I had rather return," said the son.

He did return, confessed his fault, was a good scholar, and became a respectable man. If all parents were like Mr. Phillips the students at our colleges would prove better students, or the nation would have a plentiful supply of blacksmiths.

MARRIAGES

In Fryeburgh, Maine, by Rev. Amos J. Cook, Mr. Henry B. Brewster, of Boston, publisher and proprietor of the Independent messenger, to Miss Susan O. Eastman, daughter of Major John Langdon Eastman, of Fryeburgh.

In Sullivan by Rev. J. Wright, Capt. Ellsworth Hubbard, of Sullivan to Miss Nancy M. Hubbard, of Gilsum.

In Gilsum July 21st, by Rev. G. Beckley, Mr. Hezekiah Hoard, of Rowdon, Upper Canada, to Miss Arvilla Day, of Gilsum.

In Brattleboro', July 4th, by Hon. L. Whitney, Mr. Lemuel Bent, Jr., to Miss Susan R. Putnam, both of Winchester, N. H.

DEATHS

In Salem, on Monday last, ANDREW DUNLAP, Esq., late District Attorney of the United States for the District of Massachusetts. In the death of Mr. Dunlap society has met with a deep loss—his relatives and friends was an irreparable one. His health was exhausted in the service of his country—his strength and his brilliant talents were devoted to her service through a series of years with a zeal and fidelity to which he yielded up his existence—an existence which afforded all the happiness to be derived from the possession of rare intellectual gifts a highly cultivated mind, a generous and tender heart, numerous friends and affectionate connections. In the prime of life—of a period when he was just receiving the meed of fame honorably won—he was called upon to give up life and its vanities for eternity. He died as he had lived, and while he felt a strong and natural anxiety to recover his health, he met his fate with great fortitude—no repining, no murmur at its approach escaped his lips—he felt that he had performed his duty to man and to his Maker while he sojourned here, and finally bade the world farewell, leaving a bright and pure example for his fellow beings, and anticipating a glorious immortality hereafter. *Boston Post.*

In Haverhill, suddenly on the 21st inst., the Hon. Samuel C. Webster, Sheriff of Grafton County, aged 47 years. On Friday morning the 17th he was in his usual health—in the afternoon he was seized with inflammation of the bowels, which accompanied with mortification terminated his life on Tuesday following.

The funeral services were attended at the brick meeting house on Thursday at nine o'clock, a. m. The Superior Court being in session adjourned on Wednesday until Thursday at 2 o'clock, p. m., and the Justices of the Court and members of the bar were present during the religious services and united with the procession that followed the deceased to the place of his interment.

Mr. Webster graduated at Dartmouth College in 1808, and after completing his law studies, removed from this village to Plymouth in 1813, where with success he prosecuted his profession until his appointment to the office of the 1833, shortly after which he again returned to this place. Having previously to that period been a member of the House of Representatives of this state, in

1830 he was called to preside over the deliberations of that body. After leaving the popular branch he was to the council in which office and the several offices he has at different times held, he was uniformly sustained the reputation of an honorable man and an able and faithful public officer. As a politician he was firm and consistent in support of a democratic principles. Open, frank and confiding almost to a fault he was a firm friend, and a good neighbor and a valuable citizen.

By his sudden death his family are called to mourn the loss of one who was ever a most tender husband and an affectionate and indulgent father. Highly estimable in his private and domestic relations—firm in support of political principles and upright as a public servant, his loss will be severely felt by his party and the community as well as by his family and numerous circles of relatives and friends. *Haverhill Republican.*

In this town July 29, of consumption, Mr. Alfred K. Gould, a member of the Andover Theological Seminary.

In Bow, June 25, Mr. Samuel Alexander, aged 98 years, 8 months and 13 days. Printers in Vt., Me., and Md., are &c.

In Westmoreland, Mr. Caleb Livingston, 52.

In Stoddard on the 3rd inst., Mr. Samuel Dow, 79.

In Salisbury, July 20th, Mr. Noah West, aged 48.

In New Ipswich, Oraph M. Baldwin, wife of Mr. Edwin Baldwin, aged 25.

In Roxbury, Mass., Francis Gardner, Esq., Attorney at Law, formerly of Walpole, aged 63.

In Goffstown, July 21 Mr. John Dunlap, aged 51. His death was occasioned by a log rolling over his head, by which it was so crushed, that he died after an agonizing seventeen days. On the 23rd July, of Typhus fever after an illness of five weeks, David Barr, Esq., aged 52—in who were united an affectionate husband, tender parents and exemplary member of society. Printers in Maine and New York will please to notice both the above deaths. *Com.*

In Northwood, July 15, Miss Eliza Crockett, daughter of Samuel and Deborah Crockett, aged 35 years, a member of the Baptist Church in that place. A wise Providence has seen fit to call the afflicted parents, brothers and sister to follow a second daughter and sister to the grave within the short pace of seven weeks. They suffer an irreparable loss, but to her, we trust it is gain and that she has joined her sister, and is now around the throne of the Redeemer, whom she delighted to serve in life, praising him for the rich grace that was bestowed on her in this world of sorrow and temptation.

A few moments before her departure, she said to her friends, who were weeping around her, "weep not for me, but for your selves." Although very sudden to her was the approach of death she met it with calm resignation and willingly resigned her spirit to the care of that God who made it. *Com.*

In Stow on Saturday evening, 25th inst., Lyman F., only child of Forbes H. Oliver, of Boston, 13 months.

In Canandaigue, N. Y., of remittent fever, Mr. Asahel Harvey, Jr., aged 36, one of the proprietors and publishers of the Ontario Repository. Mr. Harvey was born in Surry, N. H. He was a printer by trade, and an uncommonly well instructed and skillful one; and his ingenious inventions for facilitating the business of book binding, which he also carried on, are decisive evidence of his mechanical talent. Industrious and upright in business, and amiable and estimable in his domestic and social relations, he had the good will and respect of all who knew him. He left a wife and one child.

NEW HAMPSHIRE PATRIOT & STATE GAZETTE
Concord, Monday, August 17, 1835

FROM ENGLAND
Explosion of a Coal Mine—One Hundred Lives Lost

In announcing the dreadful catastrophe in the Nun's Field in the last *Courant* it was not expected that a still more awful occurrence in this neighborhood, and one which it is feared has been tenfold more destructive to human life, would have to be recorded this week. Yesterday (Thursday) about half past 2 o'clock in the afternoon one of those dreadful explosions which have been so lamentably frequent in mining districts took place at one of Mr. Russells' collieries, at Wallsend, known by the name of Church Pit or Russell's Old Wallsend, by which is feared 25 men and 75 boys have lost their lives.

The number of work-people employed in this colliery is about 220. The hewers commenced working early in the morning and having finished getting the coal, it is left to be brought to the bottom of the shaft by the younger men and boys during the day, which is the reason why go great a proportion of boys were in the pit when the accident took place. As every individual who was down the shaft at the time of the explosion remains there still, it is not known, nor, as all have probably perished, is it likely to be explained by what means it was occasioned; similar accidents have generally been produced by incautiously removing the gauze from the safety lamps, and it is supposed in this instance to have originated in the same way, though every precaution was taken to prevent its removal. The colliery was viewed in the morning by Mr. Atkinson and his son, under-viewers, and it was by them considered perfectly safe and secure in every respect, there not being the least indication of any escape of gas and at the time of the explosion there were four over-men and deputies down who had been accustomed to work in the pits for upwards of 30 years. They are among the sufferers.

The catastrophe was made known to the banks–man by a considerable report which they speak of as being like an earthquake accompanied by a rushing of choke damp to the mouth of the shaft, bringing up with it some of the pit men's clothes, and other light articles from the bottom. There were two other shafts connected with this colliery, in one of which two men at work, who say they felt a slight shock at the time, and soon after a quantity of choke damp. They happily escaped by being drawn up immediately. In the third shaft no one was at work. On the alarm being given eight men volunteered to go down, in the hope of being able to save and bring up some of their companions. After descending to the bottom, however, in attempting to get to the workers, they instantly found themselves being suffocated by the foul air; they had the greatest difficulty in retaining the ropes, and were almost insensible before the could be drawn up again.

When our messenger left the place, between 10 and 11 o'clock last night, another effort was about to be made to descend the shaft and if possible to reach the suffers. We are sorry to say that but small hopes are entertained of being able to save any of their lives, as it is feared that either by being burnt at the moment of the explosion, or suffocated since, they are already the victims of this melancholy accident. It is barely possible, and that is all which can be said, that some of them may have been at the instant at a distance from the spot where the blast happened, and that the atmosphere may be such as to allow them to breathe until they can be got out and be rescued. The probabilities are so much against this that an escape would be little short of a miracle. The relatives and friends of the poor suffers are in a dreadful state of anxiety—almost of distraction.

Newcastle Courant.

In 1821 there was an explosion at the same colliery by which 75 lives were lost. We find that the number of persons in the mine on Thursday was 104. On Friday morning access was, with great difficulty, gained and in the course of the day the bodies of two men and 19 boys were brought up. In the afternoon S. Reed, Esq., the coroner, summoned a jury previous to meeting whom he went and viewed the bodies of the deceased. On his return to the colliery office the jury were sworn, Anthony Easterly, Esq., foreman, when the coroner briefly alluded to the painful nature of the duty. They would first view the bodies, he said, and afterwards meet him to receive the evidence of the witnesses on Monday, the 29th inst. The inquest was accordingly adjourned to that day. *Newcastle Chronicle*

Cost of Railroads. It is not generally known that by laying the iron rails on wooden piles (similar to the lines across the great marshes in the southern railroads) the cost does not exceed $5000 per mile, whereas the Boston and Providence rail road cost $50,000 per mile.

During the thunderstorm of Friday last, the schooner George Washington of St. George, Maine, while laying at anchor at Kittery Point, was struck with lightning and her Captain, Stephen Gardiner instantly killed. The George Washington was bound to Salem with a load of wood and bark, and had put in for a harbor. She was considerably injured. Capt. Gardiner has left a wife and four children. The meeting house at Kittery Point was also struck and we learn considerably damaged. The electric fluid descended the rod and would have passed into the earth, without doing much injury, if it had been complete; but some person having taking away the lower link of the rod, the fluid descended to the end and then passed into the body of the building.

Dr. Franklin, when on a visit to the town many year ago, remarked that Kittery Point was peculiarly liable to be struck with lightning, on account of some attractive properties in the ledges in its neighborhood. The correctness of the Doctor's observation has been fully verified since that time, for there is scarcely a place in the country that has been so often struck, as the neighborhood meeting house at Kittery Point. *N. H. Gaz.*

Suicide. Mr. Stephen Wright of this town, committed suicide by hanging on Sunday morning last. He had been deranged for several weeks, and had attempted several times to commit violence upon himself. His wife left him for a short time to call on one of her neighbors, and when she returned found him suspended by a clothesline in the shed adjoining the house.

Nashua Gazette

MARRIAGES

In Northfield on Sunday morning, July 25, at the Methodist Chapel, by the Rev. Charles R. Harding, Mr. Royal Blake of Lyme, to Miss Hannah S. Molony, daughter of the late John Molony, Esq.

In Greenland, Mr. William Coombs to Bangor to Miss Elizabeth A. B. Greenough of Greenland.

In Lyman, by Barron Moulton, Esq., Mr. James L. Blake, of Bridgton, Me., to Miss Ann, daughter of C. Emery, Esq., of the former place.

In Bath, Edmund B. Bedel to Miss Eliza Jane Smith.

In Lisbon, Mr. Ezra Foster, Jr., to Miss Milly C. Hibbard, daughter of Dyer Hibbard, Esq.

In Sharon, Vt., Mr. Leonard Worcester of Hanover, N. H. to Miss Minerva A. Carpenter of Sharon.

DEATHS

In Epping, Mr. Jonathan Rollins, aged 36. He was cut down in the midst of life leaving a wife and three children to mourn his loss. On his funeral occasion a discourse was delivered by Mr. Fullonton for Hebrew 9 27.

In Bath, Mrs. Betsey Towne, consort of Amos Towne, Esq., and daughter of the late Hon. William Tarleton of Piermont.

In Hollis, Mrs. Indiana, wife of Moses Proctor, Esq., 23.

In Hudson, Sarah Ann Burns, aged 15.

Drowned in the Piscataquog River in Goffstown, Alonzo S., only son of Moses Poor, Esq., aged 14. He was bathing in the river in company with another lad about the same age, when the attention of his companion was arrested by an unusual noise in the water. Looking around he discovered him at the distance of about 3 or 4 rods and where the water was only 3 feet deep, struggling and apparently in distress. He hastened towards him but before he could reach him the current had wafted him into deep water beyond his power to assist him. Neither of the boys could swim, and it was half an hour before assistance could be procured. By this sudden and distressing dispensation of Providence the parents have been bereft of a promising and intelligent child—the hope of their declining years, and society of the prospect of a virtuous and useful member. Editors in Mass., and Vt., are &c.

Drowned in Seabrook Lydia Smith, aged 15 and Emily Jane Heath, 11. They were on a point of land running into the sea, and unmindful of their danger till the tide came up to cut off their retreat, and washed them away. A couple of men were within sight of them but unable to afford them relief until it was too late.

At Salem, Indiana, Hon. Benjamin Parke, Judge of the United States District Court, in the 58th year of his age.

In Franklin, Widow Elizabeth Crane, wife of the late Mr. Henry Crane, formerly of Peterborough, aged 78. Printer in Boston and Me., are &c.

In Sherbrooke, L. C., Mrs. Eliza Jane, daughter of Mr. Asa Wheeler of Orford, N. H., and wife of Mr. Otis King, aged 27. Mrs. King was called from life in a very sudden manner. At evening she was in usual health and cheerfulness, and the next morning was no more. Her death is supposed to have been occasioned by the rupture of a blood vessel.

In Lowell, Mass., Mr. Henry Sanborn, aged 55 years, nine months, formerly of Sandbornton, N. H. Mrs. Sally Reed wife of Samuel Reed and daughter of James Saunders of Sanbornton.

In Wentworth, July 17, of consumption, Angeline, daughter of Moses Eaton, II. She commenced her bible in December last with an intention to have read it through before she arrived to the age of seven years, which would have been on the 25th. She had read to the last chapter of the 2nd Peter, when she was taken sick and died of the croup. At her funeral I. S. Davis delivered a discourse to a large audience from the last words she ever read—*Peace be with you all that are in Christ Jesus, Amen.*

In Hawke, July 24, Abigail Currier, aged 72. On the morning of the day on which she died she appeared as well as usual, remarked to her son, it is a pleasant morning—attended her work until 12 o'clock at noon. When the alarm was sounded the friends in the vicinity went in haste and found she had fallen from her chair, *and no signs of life appeared.* No persons were present when the summons came, but they soon assembled and apparently she died without a struggle. This woman was for a number of years a member of the Baptist church, and lived in the enjoyment of religion. She was favored with a retentive memory, enjoyed much consolation reading and repeating scripture, and her favorite hymns had a portion of glory similar to that which caused the face of the Lords prophet to shine. She would frequently say "blessed be the Lord, home looks good, I shall get home; our Lord and Savior said, blessed are the peace makers"—our departed sister belonged to this class. The portion of scripture to be used at her funeral was selected by herself sometime previous to her decease— "Blessed are the dead, &c." Elder Thomas Robie preached from the same; improvement and prayer by Rev. Mr. Nutter.

NEW HAMPSHIRE PATRIOT & STATE GAZETTE
Concord, Monday, August 17, 1835
ALARMING RIOTS

Riotous Proceedings in Baltimore. In consequence of some misunderstanding between the creditors and trustees of the Bank of Maryland a mob of several hundred persons last week near the residence of Revery Johnson, Esq., in Monument Square, Baltimore—who was in some manner connected with the affairs of the bank exhibited their disapprobation by breaking a few panes of glass. A general meeting of the citizens was called on Friday for the purpose of taking into consideration matters connected with the peace of the city. The meeting was very fully attended, and resolutions calculated to calm the public mind and prevent any farther acts of violence were adopted.

This meeting, instead of allaying, seemed to created more excitement and on Friday evening there was another assemblage in the square amounting to several thousand, of who says the Republican:—

"We do not think that more than 250 were of that class disposed to commit acts of violence. They began as on the preceding nights to shout and throw stones at the house, which they renewed at intervals for about two hours, and broke a large part of the glass in the front windows of the first story, and a few panes in the second. There were addressed by the Mayor of the City; and by Mr. Preston and Gen. Jones of Washington City, the two latter avowed themselves as the Council of the Creditors of the bank, and stated that they confidently expected in a day or two a decision from the Chancellor of the State favorable to their wishes, and which had only been delayed by his severe sickness. They implored the multitude to desist from all acts of violence and to retire to their homes, but the latter seemed not to heed this *appropriate and wholesome advice*, but continued through the whole time, in a much angrier mood than on the preceding evening.

A letter to the editor of the Atlas, published in an extra yesterday afternoon and dated 12 o'clock on Saturday night, furnished the following account of the doings of the mob on the night after that in which the preceding outrages took place: —

"About 7 o' clock tonight the Mayor placed citizens with clubs, turned for the occasion at the entrance of every avenue to Monument Square. As night came on the multitude began to assemble and grow more dense."

"The mob made several attempts to get at Johnson's house. They were repulsed by the citizens before alluded to and by some twenty or thirty mounted men. Stones, missiles, and pistols were fired, and voices and shouts raised. A number of men were severely wounded, among whom is a son of Doctor Baker, who was knocked from his horse, and as he fell his pistol went off and took effect on his own person. He is said to be dangerously wounded. At about 10 o' clock, the mob or a portion of it rushed up Charles Street, shouting "to Glenn's, to Glenn's!, to John Glenn's."

"They soon commenced an attack upon his house. They quickly broke all the glass in front, and commenced breaking in the front door which was strongly barricaded. About a dozen men were beating at the door with large stones, axes, and what not, for a full half-hour before it gave way, while thousands were looking on but none to molest the mob. They finally got into the house and now commenced the work of destruction anew. The window sashes were smashed out from top to bottom—then came out from the first, second, and third stories, chairs, tables, sideboards, pianos, mirrors, beds clothes, every kind of linen, carpets and in fine every kind of rich and costly furniture which can be imagined—the value of which cannot be less than six or eight thousand dollars."

"The beds of feathers and down were ripped open in the streets, and the ground was covered, and now is ankle deep, with their contents. Even the iron railing round the marble door-steps were all cut up. And while I am yet writing the sounds of the axes and stones of those who are cutting up the entire inside of Mr. Glenn's house, fall upon my ear like the wedging of a ship just before she is to be launched for the stocks. There go five or six guns in succession! A man comes into the room and says several men have been killed and more wounded! And yet almost every body looks on, if not with approbation certainly without any great manifestations of regret!"

"Several of the mob have been taken by the city authorities and carried to the watch-house. The mob will proceed there and release them. They are omnipotent now. It is generally believed they will next, after releasing their comrades, demolish the inside of Reverdy Johnson's house. If it is not done tonight, it will assuredly be done before they will be satisfied or appeased. It is said they will also destroy the house of Hugh McEldery before they finally quit.

The Steamboat Mail, which arrived after the above was prepared brings still further accounts of the doings of the mob on Saturday night, and the melancholy intelligence that seven lives were lost. Among the wounded were Mr. Findlay, Mr. Cheves and Mr. Adams. The Journal of Commerce says:—

"We have conversed with a gentleman who was in the midst of the scenes of violence, and has just arrived in the boat from Philadelphia. He says that the persons killed were not chiefly of the mob, and that the number was but seven, though forty or more were wounded."

"The horse guards were called out early but when they came upon the ground were driven off by the mob. The military fired repeated for an hour and a half, but it does not seem with any great affect. Our informant saw one surgeon who had extracted a handful of buckshot from various individuals.

The work of destruction was pursued on the buildings until 5 o'clock, a. m., when most of the rioters withdrew, but only to renew the war at the return evening. The persons to be attacked were all designated in anonymous letters. One or two houses were entirely destroyed except the walls."

"It was feared that the military force, assisted by the citizens generally would be unable to control the violence of the populace on Sunday night, and an express had been dispatched to the Present of the United States for help. The city was in a state of awful anxiety."

From the Philadelphia Sentinel

From Baltimore—More riot and destruction—The convicts set at Liberty. We take from the Philadelphia Exchange Books some further particulars in regard to the riots at Baltimore. They are of such a nature as to excite the fears of all.

The following are extracts of letters received at the Exchange, dated at half past 5 o'clock yesterday morning from a person whose statements may be relied on with perfect confidence.

"The Mayor's house has been attacked, and completely gutted of furniture—the mob are about to burn it, three other houses have been destroyed."

The letter ends by says, "God only knows where this may end."

The following is from very respectable authority, and may be relied on.

"The mob proceeded to the jail, and demanded the prisoners, 40 or 50 in number were given up without the least resistance."

The New Orleans papers states, that Hastur M. Childers, Esq., of the parish of Carroll, in Louisiana, who died on the 13th of December last, has directed that his Negroes (15 or 20 in number) be emancipated and sent at his expense, to Liberia. He give 500 to each of his favorites, and directs that all of them be provided with tools, provisions, and good common clothing sufficient for one year's use. After paying a donation of $10,000 to the Female Orphan Asylum at New Orleans, and several other legacies for his friends, he has bestowed the residue of his estate upon the Colonization Society.

ROBBERIES. Several robberies have recently taken place at the Springs, which seem to be infested by a gang of pick pockets. Mr. Richard Cobb of Boston, had his pocket book stolen from him last week at a ball, containing $600.

Riot. An attempt was made to tar and feather Thompson the renegade abolition incendiary, at Lynn, last week. He escaped the mob there as he did here, by getting out of the house under petticoats of certain she abolitionists.

Capt. Back. This gentleman who left Montreal in the spring of 1833 in search of Captain Ross has returned in good health and spirits. No accident happened to the expedition it its absence. Some valuable geographical discoveries were made. The greatest degree of cold experienced was 70 degrees below zero.

Great Fire in New York. On the 12th inst., a most destructive conflagration occurred in Fulton, Ann and Nassau Streets, in which about forty valuable stores and dwelling houses, and property estimated at over $2,000,000, were destroyed; and among the rest twenty-one printing offices. There had not been such a fire for thirty-five years. Five hundred men and an equal number of girls mostly employed in the printing offices and binderies were at once thrown out of employment. Insurance is stated at $215,000.

Pardon. *Bernardo de Soto,* Chief Mate of the Spanish schooner Pinda, which robbed the brig Mexican of Salem and for which robbery Capt. Gilbert and four of the Pinda' crew were executed at Boston in June last, has received a full pardon from the President and on Tuesday last was set at liberty. He was however, immediately arrested by his counsel *D. L. Child,* for his *fees,* and confined in the debtor's prison. De Soto was pardoned in consequence of the assistance he rendered to the crew and passengers of an American vessel wrecked on the

Bahamas in 1828. This D. L. Child, a roaring abolitionist, made up the modest bill of $877.66, and charged de Soto not only with his defense, but for defending the captain and crew, who were hung. Verily, it is a question whether the poor culprit gained much by slipping through the *hangman's* fingers to fall into the hands of the *lawyer*.

P. S. The Boston Post of Thursday says that *De Soto* was released from confinement at day light yesterday morning, having procured the requisite bail to be forth coming at the suit of Mr. Child.

SULLIVAN THE WHISPERER

James Sullivan who possessed the art of training the most furious horse by being permitted to be alone with him for a short apace of time, is thus recorded in the "Survey of the County of Cork," by Townsend, who justly remarks that, although the following facts appear almost incredible, yet they are nevertheless true, as he was an eye witness to them:

"James Sullivan was a native of the county of Cork, and an awkward ignorant rustic of the lower class, generally known as the appellation of the *Whisper*, and his profession was horse breaking. The credulity of the vulgar bestowed that epithet upon him, from an opinion that he communicated his wished to the animal by means of a whisper; and the singularity of his method gave some color to the superstitious belief. As far as the sphere of his control extended, the boast of *Veni, Vidi, Vici* was most justly claimed by James Sullivan, than by Cæsar, or even Buonaparte himself. How his art was acquired or in what it consisted is likely to remain forever unknown, as he has lately left the world without divulging it. His son, who follows the same occupation possess but a small portion of the art, having either never learned its true secret or being incapable of putting it in practice. The wonder of his skill in the short time requisite to accomplish his design, which was performed in private and without apparent means of *coercion*.

Every description of horses, or even mules, whether previously broke or unhandled, whatever their peculiar vices or ill habits might have been submitted without show of resistance, to the magical influence of his art, and in the short space of half an hour, became gentle and tractable. The effect though instantaneously produced him was generally durable. Though more submissive to him than to others, yet they seemed to have acquired a docility unknown before. When sent for to tame a vicious horse, he directed the stable in which he and the object of his experiment were placed, to be shut with orders not to open the door until a signal was given. After a *tete-a-tete* between him and the horse for about half an hour during which little or no bustle was heard, the signal was made; and upon opening the door the horse was seen lying down and the man by his side, playing familiarly with him like a child with a puppy dog. From that time he was found perfectly willing to submit to discipline, however repugnant to his nature before. Some saw his skill tried on a horse, which could never before be brought to stand from a smith to shoe. The day after Sullivan' half-hour lecture, I went, not without some incredulity, to the smith's shop, with many other curious spectators, where there were eye witnesses of the complete success of his art. This to have been a troop horse; and it was supposed, not without reason that, after regimental discipline had failed, no other would be found availing. I observed that the animal would seem afraid whenever Sullivan either spoke or looked at him. How that extraordinary ascendancy could have been obtained, it is difficult to conjecture. In common cases this mysterious preparation was unnecessary. He seemed to possess an instinctive power of inspiring awe, the results, perhaps of natural intrepidity, in which I believe a great part of his art consisted; though the circumstance of the *tete-a-tete* shows, that upon particular occasions something more must have been added to it. A faculty like this would in other hands have made a fortune, and great offers have been made to him from the exercise of his art abroad; but hunting, and attachment to his native soil were his ruling passions. He lived at home, in the style most agreeable to his disposition, and nothing could induce him to quit Dunhallow and the fox-hounds.

Chamber's Edinburgh Journal

DEATHS

In Franklin, Mr. Jonathan Whitcher, 79. Printers in Me., and Vt., are &c.

In Epping after a short sickness, Mrs. Ruth, wife of Mr. David Fogg, aged 26 years and 8 months, leaving three small children to mourn her early death.

In Cumberland, Mr., Mr. Robert S. Waldron, of Rye, N. H., aged 41.

In Nashua, Mr. Elbridge Gerry Roby, 24, son of Mr. William Roby. On Tuesday morning, Mr. Isaiah Davis, 66.

In Wentworth, Mrs. Perses Clifford, wife of Young S. Clifford, 35.

In Stoddard, Mrs. Nancy, wife of Mr. Marshall Messenger, was killed instantly by lightning on the 31st inst.

Andover, Mass., Miss Nancy, only daughter of Mr. Caleb Prince, of Salem, N. H., aged 28.

In Portsmouth, Isabella, 9 months, daughter of Abner Greenleaf, Esq.

In Boscawen on the 8th inst., Mr. Benjamin Couch, aged 50 years and 5 months, he was a believer in the heart cheering doctrine of a worlds' salvation. He has left behind a bereaved wife and eight children to mourn his sudden departure to the world of spirits.

NEW HAMPSHIRE PATRIOT & STATE GAZETTE
Concord, Monday, August 24, 1835

The Mar Claim. It will be recollected that two or three months ago it was published in the papers concerning the property of the Earl of Mar who died in England and left one son in Kittery, in the state of Maine. The heirs of his son, John Mar, have been making exertions to obtain the property which of right belonged to them; and last fall they sent an agent to New-Castle-Upon—Tyne, for the purpose of ascertaining whether there was any property belonging to the heirs in this country. The agent, Mr. James Mar has returned and notified all persons concerned, that he would report what he had been able to learn concerning the property and the prospect of obtaining it. He accordingly appointed a meeting at Gorham in the state of Maine, on the 15th of July, at which time and place, the agent reported that there was property in England, both real and personal to a very large amount belonging to the heirs in this country, nearly a yearly income of five hundred thousand pounds sterling, or two million four hundred thousand dollars, and there was no difficulty in obtaining the property. Since the report, speculations have run very high; in the short time of ten days, stock has risen from $1000 to $15,000. If the stockholders would hold the stock that is not already disposed of, it would undoubtedly be much more to their interest.

Dover Gazette

A Father and Mother Found—or the Clergyman in a Scrape. A droll case was arranged before the Police Magistrate yesterday afternoon. A Presbyterian clergyman of great respectability, of this city, whose name we withhold, [his name is Dunham,] has been discovered making too free with the flesh. Some time ago a foundling was picked up in the street. By some means or other the father and mother have been just discovered—the former the reverend gentleman in question, and the latter a tolerably good looking squibby woman of thirty. The reverend gentleman was duly examined yesterday afternoon, entered into engagement for the support of the child, and dismissed with the benediction of the magistrate. "For God's sake," said the magistrate, "don't tell the names." "Be sure of that," said we, "the mother is rich enough without the name."

N. Y. Morning Herald

Daring Villainy. A mare and wagon belonging to Mr. Gideon Chase of Hiram, were stolen from Mr. Daniel Ross' in this city, between 8 and 9 o'clock in the evening, (29th,) in the most audacious manner. Mr. Chase had gone into Ross' for a moment; on coming out, his beast and wagon were missing. The villain, who took them, was then so near the Mr. Chase could hear the rumbling of the wheels. He pursued but the thief with dexterity in keeping with his profession succeeded by turning into a number of streets in escaping. The mare was valuable— worth $100. *Eastern Argus*

Singular Fatality by Lightning. Two men were killed by lightning in Woolwich, Conn., on the 27th June. They had retired to bed in the garret containing two beds, the head of each standing against the chimney, together with two others; the lightning struck the chimney and killed one man in each bed; the other two escaped unhurt! The lightning passed into the chamber below where an old lady was reading her bible with her hands on the leaves and her fingers spread open. It passed through her fingers burning two of them, and the corners of half a dozen leaves of the Bible; thence it descended to the lower room, where a man was sleeping on a iron bound chest, it stove the chest to pieces, the man receiving no material injury. There were 28 people in the house.

Most Shocking Accident. Edwin Rand of Amesbury, a young man about 25 years of age employed in the dye house of the Amesbury Flannel Manufactoring Company, returned on Tuesday morning last from his breakfast and commenced work before the usual time, and before the other men had returned to their labor. The kettle in which he was preparing goods for coloring was at a full boil, and it is supposed that he got on or near the top of it, in order to push the goods under the preparation, and lost his balance was precipitated into the boiling liquor. By some means or other he succeeded in getting out and reached an upright aqueduct, and raised the clapper by which means cold water poured on him, affording him momentary relief. His cries of distress reached the ears of the workmen who were returning from breakfast, and they repaired to the dye house and found the poor young man in the most pitiable condition. Medical aid was immediately called but he was scalded so severely it was of no avail, and he survived but a few hours. He was a very faithful and industrious young man, and the only support of a widowed mother. *Courier*

A sailboat containing 18 persons, was upset by a flaw of wind, near Smithfield, N. C., on the 8th inst. Twelve persons were drowned, as follows; Mr. James Dozier, lady and 7 children, Rev. Hankins, Miss Potter, and one black man. The bodies of 6 of the children of Mr. Dozier were all that had yet been found.

Messrs. Hiram Dixon, of Elliot, Me., and Samuel Bullard, of Barnstead, N. H., left Portsmouth, 3rd inst., in a sailboat on a fishing excursion, intending to return the same evening. The masts and sails have been picked up 15 miles S of Isle of Shoals, and the oars and boat went on Hog Island. They were undoubtedly drowned.

The Committee of Vigilance for the parish of Prince William have offered a reward of *one thousand dollars* for the detection and delivery into their custody of any person who shall be proved to have been acting agent in this state of any Northern Abolition Society.
Charleston paper.

Remarkable Cure. A young man in this village had a finger cut off by the blade of a hay cutter a few days since. It was divided between the first and second joints. Dr. Deane was called in about fifteen minutes afterwards; the severed portion had fallen among the hay, and was then pale and cold; it was taken up, washed in warm water, secured on the stump by sewing and bandages, and is now entirely reunited. This fact should serve as a lesson in all similar cases, to 'save the pieces.' *Franklin Merc*

Mr. Reverdy Johnson has returned to Baltimore and issued a short address to his fellow citizens. He says his property is all destroyed—that he is an innocent man; that he was absent when the riot took place but has now returned with his family to resume his profession, and will not leave the city with life. He does not value, he says, the loss of his property, if his fellow citizens will but believe, as he trust they will, that he is utterly incapable of committing the fraudulent acts attributed to him.

The ex-mayor Mr. Hunt has also published what purports to be the reasons why he resigned his office—the amount of which is that the citizens did not respect him sufficiently to sustain him in the exercise of his official powers.

Abduction of a Child. Great excitement has been created in Mobile by the abduction of a child of Dr. Gesnard. He was seized and carried off by the doctor's own brother, who refused to deliver him up, unless he was paid the sum of $300,000. A negotiation was carried on through the medium of another brother, who was supposed to be implicated in the transaction and the doctor was about to comply with the demand, when the people arose in their might seized the negotiator, conveyed him to a place of confinement, and finally by threats and promises, prevailed on him to confess that he knew where was secreted his brother and child, and undertake to restore the child to his much afflicted parents. Accordingly at nightfall a steamboat was charted, and the party with the guide proceeded up the river for the place designated about 15 or 20 miles off, and the next morning returned with the stolen child in safety to the great joy of the parents. The brothers were permitted to go at large, on condition of their leaving the country never to return.

INSANITY

A physician was once called to see a man laboring under the fancy that he was converted into a teapot. And when the physician endeavored to ridicule him out of the idea, he indignantly replied, 'I am a teapot,' and forming a semi-circle with one arm by placing his hand upon his hip, he said 'there is the handle,' and thrusting out the other arm, 'there is the spout. Men have believed themselves converted into barrels rolled along the street. One case is recorded of a man who believed himself a clock and would stand for hours at the head of the stairs clicking with his tongue. A respectable tradesman in England even fancied himself metamorphosed into a seven piece, and took the precaution of requesting as a particular favor of his friends that if his wife should present him in payment, they would not give change for him. Some have supposed that many armed knights were engaged in battle with them. A sea captain in Philadelphia believed for many years that he had a wolf in his liver. A madman in Pennsylvania hospital believed that he was once a calf, and mentioned the name of the butcher whom killed him and the stall in Philadelphia market, on which his flesh was sold, previously to his animating his present body. One man believes his legs to be made of butter and with the greatest caution avoids the fire; another imagines them to be made of glass, and with extreme care wraps them up, and guards them in wooden boxes when he goes out to ride. A prince of Bourbon often supposed himself to be a plant, and taking his stand in the garden would insist upon being watered in common with the plants around him. A

French gentleman imagined himself to be dead, and refused to eat. To prevent his dying of starvation two persons were introduced him in the character of illustrious dead like himself, and they invited him after some conversation respecting the world of shades to dine with another distinguished but deceased person, Marshal Turenne. The lunatic accepted this polite invitation and made a very hearty dinner. Every day while his fancy prevailed, it was necessary to invite him to the table of some ghost of rank and reputation. Yet in the other common affairs of life the gentleman was not incapacitated from attending to his own interest.

GENERAL DANIEL MORGAN

General Morgan of Virginia was a distinguished officer of the American Army, in the war of the Revolution. He was a native of New Jersey, but must have removed into Virginia when quite young; for he had been residing there about twenty years when the war began. Little has been recorded of his family or education, but it is said he was destitute of property and drove a wagon some time for a living. In the expedition of General Braddock against the French and Indians on the Ohio, which was undertaken soon after, he served as a private at the age of twenty-two or three and was wounded. On a charge of contumacy to a British officer in this campaign he is said to have received five hundred lashes! One can hardy conceive of his surviving such a severe punishment; and perhaps there was some favor shown by the men who gave them. It is mentioned to his honor that in the war of the Revolution he was humane and generous in his treatment of the British officers who fell into his hands. After Braddock's unfortunate expedition, he resumed his former occupation; and soon acquired property to purchase a small farm. For some years after he was twenty he was much addicted to boxing and gambling; but soon became frugal as well as industrious, and lamented the excesses of his early years; yet his boldness and courage were retained.

lamented the excesses of his early years; yet his boldness and courage were retained.

When the war began he was early appointed to command a troop of horses in Virginia. And with this company he marched to the American Army at Cambridge in the summer of 1775. General Washington who knew him well, had great confidence in his bravery and patriotism; and detached him to join the expedition against Canada the following autumn. No officer was more distinguished then Morgan on that memorable occasion: and when Arnold was wounded in the first assault, the command fell on him. Soon afterwards, when General Montgomery was slain, Morgan, with others was taken prisoner. While in the hands of the British he was offered the rank and pay of a colonel of that service, which he indignantly rejected. The following year Morgan was exchanged and immediately joined the American Army. Washington gave him command of a rifle corps, with which he was detached to the assistance of Gates, then opposing the British Army in its advance from Canada. He bore a distinguished part in the battle, which preceded the surrender of Burgoyne near Saratoga in October 1777. When he joined the main army after the glorious event he was employed by the Commander-in-Chief in several perilous enterprises, which he conducted with equal courage and judgement. In 1780 he found his health declining, and retired from the army; but was again inducted to join the army in the south, where the British were making depredations on the inhabitants. He now received a commission as a Brigadier General, and followed Gates into South Carolina. But Gates was obliged to retire, without accomplishing anything for the British were far the most numerous. Yet, this did not discourage Morgan. He commanded in the attack on Colonel Tarlton at the Cowpens, who was defeated, and Morgan, Colonel Howard, Colonel Washington and General Pickens, were honorably noticed by Congress, for their brave conduct on that occasion. When General Greene was afterwards appointed to the command of the Southern army,

Morgan continued some time with him. The army was obliged to retreat for want of men and provisions. And it was said Greene and Morgan did not agree as to the route best to be taken and soon after he retired from the army; some said in disgust, but others with more probability of truth, (for on a former occasion he had yielded to General Greene's opinion, and that the latter had nothing arbitrary in his deportment,) that his state of health made it necessary for him to return to his family. General Morgan served one term in Congress, from Frederic County; and he appeared in the field once more, having command of the Virginia militia against the *whiskey* insurrection in Pennsylvania in 1794. He died in 1799, the same year in which the death of Washington occurred.

MARRIAGES

In Acworth on Sunday evening last by the Rev. Mr. Gilman, Mr. John W. Morse, merchant of Weare to Miss Lucy Anna Gove, daughter of the Hon. Jonathan Gove.

In this town, by Rev. Mr. Bouton, Mr. Thomas Wells to Miss Lucy H. Currier, of Goffstown.

In Warren, Mr. Jonathan H. Cross of Piermont to Miss Joanna M. Webber.

In Acworth by the Rev. Mr. Merrill, Mr. John P. Davis to Miss Caroline Wallace, daughter of Capt. Adam Wallace.

In Lisbon, Mr. Silas Parker to Miss Eliza Stevens.

In Bethelehem, Mr. Levi Whipple of Lisbon, to Miss Hannah Hadley of Bethlehem.

In Grafton, Capt. Joseph Chase of New London to Miss Nancy Powell.

DEATHS

In this town, Mrs. Lamprey, aged 68. Charles Tarleton, infant son of Col. Horatio Hill, 4 weeks. A child of Widow Flanders.

In Chester, Miss Jane G. Bell, daughter of Hon. John Bell 21.

At Perry, Ohio, Joseph Kimball, Esq., of Plymouth, N. H., aged 52. Mr. Kimball was on his return from Illinois.

In Weare, of consumption, Miss Hulda, daughter of the late David Gove, in the 46th year of her age. During her sickness, which was long, she manifested great resignation to the will of her heavenly father, desiring that she might have patience to wait all the day of her appointed time. Printers in Vermont are &c.

In Haverhill, Mrs. Ruth Ames, widow of the late Solomon Ames, aged 70.

In Sandbornton, Captain James Wadleigh, 53.

In Gilmanton, Mr. Benjamin Morrill, 70.

In Hollis, Mrs. Mary, wife of Mr. Abram Putnam, 26.

In Pittsfield on the 18th inst., Brackett L., only son of Moses Norris, Jr., Esq., a remarkably promising child, 18 months.

> Away from time his spirit's flown,
> To that God who gave it birth,
> Tis gone, the beauteous bud is gone;
> T'was too pure to dwell on earth.
>
> Too fair that bud below to bloom,
> Where trouble and sorrow reign,
> It's gone to a happier home,
> That's free from sorrow, sin and pain.

Near Little Rock, Arkansas, after an illness of five days, Colonel Bernard Smith, Register of the Land office at that place, aged 59 years and 11 days.

In Tuftonborough, of consumption, Mr. Isaiah W. Horne, aged 25. He left a wife and one child to mourn his loss, a father and mother who leaned on him for support in the decline of life.

He was tender and affectionate as a husband and father, a dutiful son, a generous brother, a kind neighbor, a good citizen and Christian.

> Sweet is the scene when virtue dies,
> When sinks a righteous soul to rest,
> How mildly beam the closing eyes,
> How quiet heaves the dying breast;

>A holy quiet reigns around,
>A calm which nothing can destroy,
>Naught can disturb that peace profound
>Which such unfettered souls enjoy,
>Its duty done as sinks the clay,
>Light from it load the spirit flies,
>While heaven and earth combine to say,
>Sweet is the scene when virtue dies.

Printers in Mass., and Me., are requested &c. *Com*

At Eden Bower, near Georgetown, in the 48th year of his age, Dr. Robert French, Assistant Surgeon in the Army of the United States. Dr. French was a native of Georgetown in which place he commenced the practice of medicine, and continued to reside, until his appointment in the medical staff of the army in 1819. The deceased had many friends—for he was generous, affectionate and warmhearted, of great purity of purpose and with the kindness feelings toward all men. But he was more than this—he was a Christian—for many years a zealous and active Christian, engaging with ardor in all the benevolent institutions of the day, which have for all their object the temporal and eternal welfare of man. It has fallen to the lot of but few persons to suffer so much from sickness as did the deceased—having for more than three years past been afflicted with the painful disease of which he died—but he suffered with meekness and with submission and without a murmur. It must be a great consolation to his bereaved widow and relatives to know that as he lived the life of a Christian so he died the death of a Christian—having hope in death—exchanging for him a life of pain and suffering in this world for one of peace and happiness in the eternal world. *Globe*

In Hopkinton, Elizabeth Cleave, only child of Mr. Robert W., and Mrs. Molineaux of Boston, aged 22.

>"She died to sin, she died to care,
>But for a moment felt the rod,
>O mourner!, such the Lord declares,
>Such are the children of our God!"

NEW HAMPSHIRE PATRIOT & STATE GAZETTE 1835

ABEEL, Mr. 23
ABERCROMBIE, Doctor 96
ADAMS, 176 J. G. 120
  John Quincy 137
  Mr. 202 Ruth 149
  Soloman 60
AIKEN, Andrew 51
ALEXANDER, John 161
ALLARD, Charity H. 11
ALLEN, Ethan 167
  George W. 141
  Jason 102 Lois 149
  Susan 141
ALSTON, Governor 128
  Mrs. 128
AMES, Jason H. 69
  Nathan W. 59 Ruth 216 Samuel 9
  Stephen 59 Solomon 216 Thomas Spafford 59
ANDERSON, 176
ANDREWS, W. 1
ANGIER'S Tavern 44
ARBUCKLE, General 135
ARMOUR, Margaret 132
ARMSTRONG, F. S. 135
ARNOLD, 133 214
  Benedict 4 67 Mrs. 67
  Rev. Mr. 49
ASHLEY, George 69
  George W. 151
ATKINS, Samuel 119
ATKINSON, Mr. 194
ATWOOD, David 127
  J. 103 John 127
AUSTIN, Miss 79
  Stoten 11
AVERY, E. K. 98

AVERY (continued)
  Edward 57 Harriet Osgood 100
  Richard 140 Samuel 100 Sarah Newman 100
AYERS, Samuel 43
BACK, Captain 204
BADGER, Mary 150
  Ruth 150 S. C. 74
BAGLEY, Moses 59
  Rachel 32 Sarah 59
BAILEY, Isaiah 59
  Mary A. 165 179
BAILY, Emery 32 Mr. 43
BAKER, Doctor 201
  Ruth 59
BALCH, Nathaniel 72
BALDWIN, Edwin 132
  Oraph M. 192
BALLARD, Amaziah 151
BALLOU, Adin 120
  H. 172
BANFIELD, Durcella 31
BARBER, Robert 126
BARBOUR, P. N. 118
BARNARD, Emily M. 39
  George G. 164 Moses 39 Polly 39
BARR, David 192
BARRETT, Rev. Mr. 132
BARRON, William 19
BARTER, Caroline 150
  Jemima (2) 150
  Lucretta 150
BARTLETT, 36 Daniel 178 David 48 Ezra 103
  Mr. 56 Nehemiah 101
  R. 11 Reuben 166
  Robert 72

NEW HAMPSHIRE PATRIOT & STATE GAZETTE 1835

BARTON, Anne 71
  Benjamin 71
BASSETT, Dr. 28
BASSIERE, John S. 186
  187
BATCHELDER,
  Benjamin 132
  Ebenezer 120
  Ebenezer III 8
  Mary 132 Nathaniel
  100 Nathaniel, Jr. 100
BATES, Reuben 37
BAYLIES, Mr. 186 187
BEALE, George 72
BEAN, Betsey 104
  Charles 104 180
  Benjamin 182 Elizabeth
  19 Jesse 19 Mary S.
  161 Mr. 25
BEARD, 146
BECKLEY, G. 150
BEDEL, Edmund B. 197
BEECHER, Harriet 180
  Rev. Dr. 180
BEEMAS, Aaron 147
  Silas M. 146 147
BELL, Jane G. 215
  John 215
BENNET, Mr. 176
BENT, Lemuel, Jr. 190
BERNARD, Emily M. 39
BERRY, 171 Nathaniel
  75 Samuel 11
BILLINGS, Mr. 162
BIXLEY, Mr. 153
BLACK Coat, 93
BLAISDELLL, William 19
BLAKE, Abel, Jr. 165
  James L. 197 Royal
  197

BLANCHARD, A. G. 118
  Jacob, Jr. 166
  Nahum 49
BLISS, Henry 109
BLODGETT, Alice 99
BLUNDEN, Joseph 123
  124
BOBB, 124
BODLEY, Dr. 184 185
BODWELL, John 114
BONNELL, J. 118
BOOREAM, Henry 146
BOSWELL, Rev. Mr. 70
BOUTON, Rev. Mr. 31
  59 120 179 215
BOUTWELL, C. C. 102
BOWLES, Charles 27
  James 26 Lydia 27
BOYER, 162
BOYES, Milton G. 150
BRADDOCK, General
  213
BRADLEY, Richard 100
BRADY, Mr. 172
BRATLY, Mr. 125
BREED, Stephen P. 99
BREWSTER, Henry B.
  190
BRIDGES, James 39
  Mary 39
BRIGGS, Mr. 4
BRIGHAM, Courtney 159
  Levi 140 Nancy Hazen
  140 141
BROAD, 22 Joseph C.
  150
BROADHEAD, Jonathan
  C. 150
BROCKWAY, Freeman
  32

NEW HAMPSHIRE PATRIOT & STATE GAZETTE 1835

BROTON, Benjamin S 100
BROWN, 81 Benjamin 23 Dr. 28 Edward 111 Edward C. 101 Eliza 70 Hannah 32 Jeremiah F. 68 John 57 John L. 61 Joseph 59 83 Mary 179 Nancy 32 Nathan 32 Obadiah 37 Samuel 179 Sarah 140 Stephen 111 Susan 37 150
BRYANT, Ithiel W. 19 John H. 160 Rebecca 160
BUCHANAN, Judge 98
BUCK, H. 4
BUCKMAN, John 50 Susan A. W. 50
BUGBEE, Peter 51
BULLARD, Samuel 210 Silas 121
BUMFORD, Charles 31
BUNKER, Betsey 126
BUONPARTE, 205
BURGOYNE, 4 112 121 214
BURKE, 4
BURLEY, Elizabeth G. 19
BURNHAM, Jacob 19
BURNS, Robert 34 Sarah Ann 197
BURPEE, Nathaniel 60
BURR, Aaron 128 Col. 67
BUSWELL, Abigail 166
BUTLER, Ebenezer 47

BUTLER (continued) Enoch 47
BUTMAN, John 126
BUTTERFIELD, Ephraim 180 Samuel 159
BUZZELL, Edward 111 H. D. 140 159
BYRON, 108
CADY, Joseph C. 26
CAESAR, 205
CALIF, Josiah 103 103
CALVERT, John 83 84
CAMLIN, 171
CANFIELD, Capt. 108
CAPEN, Valara Ann 100
CARPENTER, Eliza 19 Joseph 11 Minerva A. 197
CARR, John 38 Joseph 19 Sarah Elizabeth 38 Sarah M. 1000
CARTER, B. F. 13 Benjamin F. 59 Captain 130 131 Charles D. 11 Joseph 99 Olive Ann 11
CARY, Charles 76
CASCO, Jacob 44
CASWELL, Abraham 17 Samuel B. 17
CATE, Samuel 150 George 151
CAVERNO, Rev. Mr. 120
CHADWICK, P. 149
CHAMBERLAIN, Levi 99
CHANDLER, General 81 Samuel, Jr. 111 Walter S. 2 3
CHAPMAN, Rhoda A.

NEW HAMPSHIRE PATRIOT & STATE GAZETTE 1835

CHAPMAN, (continued) 150
CHASE, Charles 31 Elbridge 100 Elbridge G. 92 Gideon 209 Jeremiah 33 50 Joseph 215 Moses 126
CHEEVER, Rev. Mr. 157
CHENEY, Prentice 76
CHESLEY, Eliza 140 150 John 126 Miles 126 150
CHEVER, Mr. 202
CHILD, D. L. 204 205
CHILDERS, Hastur M. 203
CHRISTIE, Mr. 56
CHURCHILL, D. C. 16
CILLEY, Daniel P. 101
CLARK, Jeremiah, Jr. 57 70 Joshua 178 Nathaniel 178 Peter 159 Rev. Mr. 103 Susan 111 William 179
CLARKE, 3 Mr. 122
CLARY, Joseph W. 93
CLAY, John Randolph 132
CLAYTON, Mr. 119
CLEAVES, Elizabeth 217 George 27
CLENDENNING, Mr. 175 176
CLIFFORD, Isreal 101 Joseph 19 Perses 207 Young S. 207
CLOUGH, Aaron 150 Betsey 32 Jonathan 155 Lydia 104 Martha 150

CLOUGH, (continued) Phinehas 58 Susan 32 Thomas 58 104 William 12
CLUFF, Ezekiel 9 30 Sally 9 30
COBB, Richard 204
COBURN, J. L. 118 Robert 37
COCHRAN, Jeremiah 31 Joseph B. 103
COFFEE, Washington 13 14
COFFIN, Enoch 71
COGSWELL, Prince B. 150
COLBATH, Charles 111
COLBY, James 179 Maria 26 Samuel 31 Sarah 32
COLE, T. W. 153
COLLEY, Jedeiah 179
CONNELL, George 100
CONNER, Benjamin 104 Francis C. 104
CONVERSE, G. & N. 118
COOK, Amos J. 190 Isaac 19
COOKE, Rev. Mr. 165
COOMBS, William 197
COOPER, 83
COPP, Dearborn 19
CORBIN, Louisa L. 132
CORLIS, Ransom 31
CORLISS, Kimball 11 Roxana 59
CORNING, Anna 155
COTTON, Dr. 186 Nathaniel 166
COUCH, Benjamin 207

NEW HAMPSHIRE PATRIOT & STATE GAZETTE 1835

COUCH, (continued)
  John III, 126
COWAN, James 44
COX, Emily 179
  John, Jr. 179
COZZENS, Peter 177
CRANE, Elizabeth 198
  Henry 198
CRAWCOUR, 41 42
CREIGHTON, Z. Dow 179
CRESSY, Daniel 69
  Edward 69
CROCKETT, Deborah 192 193 Eliza 192 Samuel 132 192
CROELL, Jonathan P. 37
CROSBY, Hudlah R. 93 J. 93 Thomas R. 103
CROSS, Jonathan H. 215 Martha 38 50
CROTHERS, Alexander 152
CULLUM, Mr. 185
CUMMINGS, Charlotte 92 David 141 Fanny 141 Rev. Mr. 70 111
CURRIER, Abigail 199 Benjamin 50 Jane 11 John 50 Lucy H. 215 Mary Ann 50 Mary D. 50
CUSHING, Jonathan F. 103
CUTLER, Judith 71 72 Zarah 71
CUTTER, Ammi R. 92 Benonia G. 27 Captain 57 Dr. 152 Paulina 11 Phebe 27

DALTON, Mr. 107
DANFORTH, Sophronia 92
DANIELS, Lydia 104
DAUSSATT, Mr. 15
DAVIDSON, Robert 100
DAVIS, Amos 151 Aquillia 27 Benjamin 111 George 151 I. S. 199 Isaiah 207 Jacob 151 John P. 215 Lucinda 11 Nathaniel Grout 59
DAWSON, Henry 153
DAY, Arvilla 190 Jane 92 Jehiel 49
DE LAYETTE, Gilbert Mortier 137
DE SOTO, Bernardo 204 205
DEAN, David 133 Harriet S. 59 James 140
DEANE, Dr. 211
DEARBORN, Abraham 103 Charles C. 103 Joseph 100 Winthrop 18
DEMERITT, George 151 John J. 151 Jonathan 151 Thomas 150
DENNETT, Benning 11
DENNISON, Isaac 85
DINSMOOR, Mrs. 35 Samuel 34 35 36 Robert 133
DIXON, 129 130 Hiram 210
DODGE, Elizabeth 103 J. C. 27

NEW HAMPSHIRE PATRIOT & STATE GAZETTE 1835

DOLLAFF, Francis 8
DON Quixote, 77
DOW, Benjamin 132
   Joseph B. 68 Josiah,
   Jr. 99 Mr. 90 Sally 149
   Samuel 68 192
   Samuel, Jr. 126
   William 68
DOWNING, Julia M. 111
DOZIER, James 210
DRAPER, Hannah R. 132
DREW, William 56
DROWNE, Felicia
   Dorothea 156
DUDLEY, Franklin 48
DUNHAM, 208 209
DUNLAP, Andrew 14 190
   John 192
DUNN, Mr. 170 171
DURGAN, John 51 Sally
   51 52 53
DUTCH Bill, 185
DUTTON, Elizabeth 12
   John 12
DYER, Elder 76
EASTERLY, Anthony 96
EASTMAN, Betsey 11
   John Langdon 190
   Susan O. 190
EASTON, Caroline Maria
   92 Jonathan 178
EATON, Angeline 198
   Benjamin 60 Moses, II
   198 William 140
EDGERLY Samuel 57 70
ELIZABETH, 157
ELKINS, Daniel 99
   Mercy 150
ELLIOT, Com. 16 28
   Elizabeth 60

ELLIOT, (continued)
   Julia Ann 92
EMERSON, Brown 60
   Mary Hopkins 60
EMERY, Ann 197 C. 197
EMMONS, Benjamin 111
   Sarah 111
EMPEROR of Austria 55
ENTMAN, John 111
EPPS, Mary 111
EUSTICE, John William
   50
EVANS, Harriet W. 166
   Mary 31 Nathaniel 166
   Rev. Mr. 49 Sarah Ann
   B. 126 William 83
EVERETT, Edward 81
EWES, Sarah 59
FAIRIFELD, W. S. 104
FARRINGTON, Meriam
   104
FAVOR, David 38
FELD, John 114
FELT, Captain 87
FELLOWS, Moses 178
FERDINAND, 55
FERRIN, Enos 104
   Otis 104
FIELD, George P. 118
FIFIELD, B. 155
   Mirinda 155
FINDLAY, Mr. 202
FING, Thomas F. 32
FINN, 3
FINNEY, Mr. 188
FISK, Samuel 59
FLAGG, George W. 111
FLANDERS, Widow 215
FOGG, David 207 Josiah

NEW HAMPSHIRE PATRIOT & STATE GAZETTE 1835

FOGG, (continued) 127 Mary 127 Mary Ann 127 Ruth 207
FOLLENSBEE, David 179
FOLSOM, Elizabeth D. 11 John 31 John O. 10 Levi 11 Lucy 31 Phebe 31
FORT Arbuckle, 138
FORT Edward 4 5 7
FORT Gibson, 136
FORT Morgan 2
FORT Smith 13 14
FOSS, Ebenezer 165 Isaac 9 Jeremaih 11 Sarah 165
FOSTER, Elias 70 Ezra, Jr. 197 Misses. 85
FOWLER, William 109
FRANKLIN, Dr. 196
FRANSWORTH, T. B. 70
FRASER, General 6
FREEMAN, S. 40 41
FRENCH, Eli 132 John 159 Martha D. 159 Rev. Mr. 19 Robert 217 Simeon 161
FROST, W. R. 85
FULLERTON, Hannah 133 134 Jeremaih 133
FULLONTON, Joseph 19 Mr. 197
FURBER, Luke 50 Betsey 50
GALE, Almira 150 Benjamin 160 Elizabeth 172 Cynthia 150

GALLUP, William 111
GARDINER, Stephen 196 Francis 192
GARLAND, Enoch O. 59
GARMON, Hannah 150
GATES, 214 General 4 Horatio 49
GAUL, John G. 164 165 Mary H. 164 165
GAY, Ann 37
GEORGE, David 92
GEORGE Ezra 141 Ezra, Jr. 141 Hannah 92 N. J. T. 178 Sally 49 59
GERRISH, Samuel 32
GESNARD, Dr. 211 212
GIBBS, Frances Ann Sophia 132 Harry Leake 132
GIBSON, Alfred 156 Jacob 178 William 99 Randolph 178
GIDDINGS, Hannah 11 Joseph 11
GILBERT, Captain 204 Harriet 1 T. 1
GILE, William 150
GILES, Charles S. 179
GILMAN, Hiram 37 Judith 19 Mary A. 92 Martha 141 Mary Jane 139 Rev. Mr. 215
GILMORE, Gawin 59 Sally Anne 59
GILPATRICK, Samuel 111
GLENN, John 201
GLYNN, Mary 166

NEW HAMPSHIRE PATRIOT & STATE GAZETTE 1835

GLYNN, (continued)
  Moses 166
GOODALL, David G. 159
GOODHUE, Harriet A.
  99 Samuel G. 104 105
  106
GOODNO', J. R. 165
GOODNOUGH, J. R. 53
GOODWIN, James 120
  Mary Ann 104
GORDON, William 11
GORSHORN, Isabel 32
GORSHORN
  John 32
GOULD, Alfred K. 192
  Edward 70
GOVE, David 216 Hulda
  216 Jonathan 215
  Lucy Anna 215
GRAFTON, Elizabeth 50
GRANT, Joseph P. 80
  Sergeant 3
GREELEY, Almeda 126
GREELY, Joseph 59
GREEN, Benjamin 131
  Jeremiah 132 Judge
  56 Nancy 132
GREENE, Gardiner 125
  General 214 215
  Mary A. 103
GREENLEAF, Abner 207
  David 60 Isabella 207
GREENOUGH, Elizabeth
  A. B. 197
GREER, John 85 86
GREGG, John 104
  Mrs. 104
GREY, John 3
GRIDLEY, F. 64
GRIFFIN, Joshua 70

GRINNELL, George 63
GRISWOLD, Capt. 1
GROSS, Marolin 26
GRYMES, John R. 15 16
GUNNISON, Olivia 51
  Samuel 51
GUTMANN, Simon 21 2
HACKETT, Streeter 159
HADLEY, 81 Hannah
  215
HAINES, Abigail P. 9
  Elizabeth W. 9
HAINES
  Hannibal 58 Josiah
  9 Martha P. 9
  Stephen 9
HALE, Augustus 168
  S. 165 William, Jr.
  143
HALL, James F. 43
HAM, Elisa 157
  Eliza 100 John 150
  Solomon 100
HAMILTON, Miss 172
HANKINS, Rev. 210
HANSON, Sophia S. 120
HARDING, Charles R.
  197
HARDY, Jeremiah 58
  Reuben 58 Silas 58
HARPER, J. M. 92
  Mr. 25
HARRINGTON, 81
  T. J. 118
HART, Lydia 60
HARTHAN, Elizabeth
  100 Ezra 100
HARTWELL, Betsey 32
  Isaac 32 Joseph 99
  William 32 D

NEW HAMPSHIRE PATRIOT & STATE GAZETTE 1835

HARVEY, Asahel 193
  David 59
HASCALL, 90
HASELTON, Charles 126
  Daniel 126
HASTINGS, Charles 38
  Mary 38
HAZARD & Carter 85
HAZELTINE, Life A. 92
HAZELTIRE, Eliphalet 70
HEAD, Abel B. 33
HEALY, Samuel 71
HEATH, Emily Jane 198
  Harriet Maria 70
HEDGE, Anna F. 92
HEMANS, Mrs. 156
HEMENWAY, Cynthia 49
HENLEY, John D. 130
HERREN, 43 44 John 29
HERSEY, Peter 18
  Samuel 18
HEYWOOD, William 60
  William, Jr. 60 61
HIBBARD, Dyer 197
  Milly C. 197
HILDREATH, Hosea 180
HILL, Ambrose 178
  Edward 8 Horatio 215
  Jonathan C. 150
  Jonathan, Jr. 140 Mr.
  25 42 William 8
HIMES, Rev. Mr. 26
HOARD, Hezekiah 190
HOBSON, Jonathan 49
  Lucy 60
HODGDON, C. C. 31
  Patience 111
HOIT, J. S. 141
  Louisa Ann 141
HOLMES, Mr. 174

HOLMES, (continued)
  Mrs. 180 Robert
  180
HOMES, John 59
HOOK and Eye
  Manufactory 84
HOOK, 125 Gustavus
  124 Isaac 124 Jacob,
  Jr. 124 John 124
  Josiah 124 Nelson
  124 Richard 124
  Rudolph 124 Samuel
  124 Solomon 124
  Thomas 124
HOOKER, Dr. 4
HORACE, Hon, 57
HORNE, Dorcas 19
  Isaiah W. 216 217
  Tristram 19
HOWARD, Colonel 214
  Henry 37 38
HOWE, George W. 100
  Oliver 154
HOYT, Caroline 72
  Celana 94 Joseph G.
  49 Joshua F. 94
  Lydia R. 11 Olive 94
  Tristram 38 William
  27
HUBBARD, Ellsworth
HUBBARD, (continued)
  190 Nancy M. 190
HUES, Sybel 49
HUGGINS, Mr. 32
HULL, Commodore 16
HUNT, Hiram K. 1
  Martha 1 Mr. 211
HUNTINGTON, 153
HURD, Anna 104
HUSSEY, Captain 168

NEW HAMPSHIRE PATRIOT & STATE GAZETTE 1835

HUTCHINSON, Ann Maria 150 Eunice B. 149 Mehitable 32
HYDE, Benjamin T., 11
ILSELY, Peabody 103
IVES, Mr. 16
JACKSON, 137 Charles T. 145 General 77 78 Joseph L. 179 President 28 75
JACOBS, Alfred C. 70 Andrew 70 Sarah 70
JAMES, Lucretia E. 160 Noah 160
JANEWAY, Dr. 146
JEFFERSON, 137 181 Thomas 102
JEFFTS, Ester 92
JENKINS, Mark 10
JENNESS, Anna Y. 19 Betsey 161 166 Richard 161 Richard, Jr. 161
JEWELL, James 111 Sarah 111
JEWETT, Sally 126 Sally 140
JOHNSON, Clara Sophia 165 Col.136 137 John 26 M. R. 93 Moses 26 Mr. 174 Reverdy 200
JOHNSON, (continued) 201 202 211 William 92
JONES, A. D. 37 Daniel 50 David 4 7 Ebenezer 160 Enos 112 General 200 Mr. 118 S. 111 Sarah Ann 160 Walter

JONES, (continued) 163 William Gwynn 115 116
JORDAN, Henry & Co. 25
JOY, E. C. 91
JOYNER, Henry P. 156
KARKA, Amanda 21
KAVANAGH, Edward 25
KEAHAN, Hector S. L. 56
KELLEY, David 180
KELLEY Ebenezer 180 Sally 180
KELLY, Benjamin 31
KENDALL, Amos 72 Andrew Jackson 72
KENDRICK, Georgiana 100 James 100
KENISON, John 160
KENISTON, John 148
KENNEDY, Daniel 65 John 111
KENON, Christopher 153
KENT, 116
KEYES, John 141 Lucy 141 Ruth 99
KIDDER, John 120
KIMBALL, Betsey B. 93 Burnham 158 Caleb W. 120 Elizabeth 101 Horace 119 Increase S. 114 John 134 Joseph 11 216 Nehemiah 101 Ruth Maria 121 Samuel 93 Susan F. 120
KING, Otis 198 S. H. 182

NEW HAMPSHIRE PATRIOT & STATE GAZETTE 1835

KINSLEY, Benjamin 165
KNAPP, Dr. 129
KNIGHT, Aaron 70
  B. 92 Rev. Mr. 11
  William 94 111
  KNOWLES, Josiah 49
  Mr. 79
  KNOWLTON, Mary 37
  William 17
KNOX, Samuel 15
LA FAYETTE, 137
LABRANCHE, Mr. 14 15 16
LADD, Abigail 149
  John 141 Mr. 177
  Sally 149
LAISDELL, Isabella 82
LAMPREY, Mrs. 215
LANGDON, 36 Abigail 76 John 34 Josiah 72 Josiah, Jr. 72 Sarah 72 Seth 76
LAVEILLE, Mr. 83 84
LAVERGUE, Mr. 15
LAW, Edward 132
LAWS, Thomas 102
LAWTON, Mr. 124
LEARNED, Sally 141
LEAVENWORTH,
  General 128 129
  Henry 117
LEAVETT, John 20
LEAVITT, Josiah 57
  Greenleaf 57
LEBOURVEAU, Lovey Ann 159
LEFAVOR, Elizabeth 11 Robert 11 19
LEIGHTON, Jonathan

LEIGHTON, (continued)
  179 Joseph 183
  Joseph K. 179
  Martha Ann 92
LEIPER, Biddy 113
LEWIS, A. 118 Mr. 15
  Seth W. 26
LIBBEE, John S. 158
LIBBEY, Miriam 100
LINSKY, 62 Madame 62
LITTLE, Eliza 20
  Samuel N. 126
LIVINGSTON, Caleb 192 Capt. 65 Mr. 28 45 148
LOCKE, Ariadne 71
  Ethan 33 Hall J. 33
LOMBARD, John 183
LONG, 146 B. F. 111
LOPER, Rev. Mr. 183
LORING, H. H. 118
LOTHERS, Sarah 140
LOUGEE, Joseph 48
LOUIS Phillippe 98
LOVEJOY, Julia Ann 26
LOVEJOY'S Hotel, 45
LOW, Capt. 168
LOWE, Chauncy 45
LUSK, Mr. 74
LYNDE, Willoughby 180
MACCREA, N. C. 118
MACMURPHY, B. H. 104
MACNISH, Doctor 96
MANSION House, 14
MANSON, B. S. 59

NEW HAMPSHIRE PATRIOT & STATE GAZETTE 1835

MANY, James B. 117
MAR, Earl of 91 208
   James 208 John 208
MARCH, George W.
   150 Henry 12
MARKET House, 21
MARCY, Nancy Ann
   66 67 Marvin, Jr. 3 4
   Mr. 66 Mrs. 66
MARSH, George 168
   169 Henry 150
   Hepzibah 72 John
   72 Mary 150
MARSHALL, Chief
   Justice 156 157
   Thomas 156
MARSTON, Abigail 111
   Jonathan 111
   Joseph 178 Mary
   C. 59
MARTIN, Francis 87
   Lucy 111 Samuel 99
MARY Stuart 157
MASON, 129 130
MATTHAIS 81 82
MCCALL, Mr. 185
MCCLAREN, James
   179 Mary 179
MCCLURE, David 126
MCDEARMID, William
   141
MCDONALD, Samuel 47
MCDOWELL, William
   160
MCELDERY, Hugh 202
MCENALLY, James 87
   88 89
MCINTIRE, Lydia 19
MCKEEN, Albert 120
MCLAUGHLIN, E. B. 84

MCLEAN, Sarah 179
MCMAHON, 170 171
M'CREA, Jane 4 5 6 7 8
M'DANIEL, Mr. 154
MEANS, Robert 36
MELCHER, William 150
MELVIN, Nathaniel P. 59
MELVIN (continued)
   Reuben 133
MERRILL, A. 57 George
   Anson 104 George C.
   72 Hiram K. 31 Joseph
   59 104 Moses 20
   Rev. Mr. 215 Thomas
   72
MESERVE, Daniel 126
   Joanna 126
MESSENGER, Marshall
   207 Nancy 207
METCALF, Betsey 120
METTERNICH, Prince 55
MILLER, 154 Henry 153
   Mr. 130
MILLS, Harriet Maria
   139
MINARD, Samuel 10
MINOT, Charles 150
MINTURN, 170
MITCHELL, Moses 48
MIXER, Charles T. 155
M'NEIL, Mrs. 5 6 7 8
MOLINEAUX, Pauline
   217 Robert W. 217
MOLONEY, John 197
   Hannah S. 197
MONLTON, Mahala 149
MONUMENT House, 81
MONROE, Hannah T.
   165

NEW HAMPSHIRE PATRIOT & STATE GAZETTE 1835

MONTGOMERY,
    General 214
MOODY, Bradstreet 38
    Silas 179
MOONEY, 107
MOONEY, Patience 11
MOORE, 45 Eliza Ann
    59 Jacob B. 2 S. A.
    144
MOREY, Rev. Mr. 92
MORGAN, Morgan 62
    General 213 214
    215 James 48
    Smith 32
MORRILL, Aspah 48
    Benjamin 216
    Benjamin II, 180
MORRILL
    Benjamin P. 180
    Lovilia 27 Nathan
    151 Paul 27 Phebe
    S. 31 Samuel 155
    159 Sarah B. 50
MORRIS, Catherine
    Mary 165
MORRISON, Charles G.
    155 Henry 10 Isaac
    Henry 10 Lieut. 42
    Louisa 159 Lucy 126
    140 Mary Elizabeth
    155
MORSE, Charles A. (2)
    58 Elizabeth 111
    Gideon 57 John S.
    58 John W. 215
    Peter 99 Stephen 99
MORTON, Mr. 83 84
MOSELEY, Franklin 11
MOSES, Elizabeth 166
    Nehemiah 166

MOSES, (continued)
    William T. 12
MOULTON, Eunice 99
    Thomas 160 161
MOYLE, Dr. 23
MUNROE, 81 John 111
MURPHY, 54
MURRAY, 176
MURRELL, 186
MUSSEY, William 93
MUZZEY, 81 Johnson
    145
NAPIER, Mrs. 113
NELSON, J. S. 117
    Major 117
NETTLETON, Aaron, Jr.
    133
NEWELL, Rev. Mr. 11
NEWHALL, George P.
    101 Thankful 101
NEWMAN, Eliza 150
    George 172
NEW Market
Manufactory Co. 39
NICHOLS, William B.
    126 140
NICKILS, Richard 43
NILES, Esther 183
NOAH, 42
NORRIS, Brackett L.
    17 216 Moses, Jr.
    131 216
NORTH, Mr. 185
NOYES, Clement 94
    Naome A. 101
    Naomi 94 Samuel,
    Jr. 180
NUDD, 9
NUGENT, James 83
NUTE, Ezra 101

NEW HAMPSHIRE PATRIOT & STATE GAZETTE 1835

NUTE, (continued)
  Ezra D. 101 Isreal
  19 Nancy 101 John,
  Jr,. 160 Rev. Mr. 199
NUTTING, Abel 150
OBER, Esther Ann 179
OLCOTT, Mary 120
  Milles 120
OLIVER, Forbes H. 193)
  Lyman F. 193
ORDWAY, David 103
  Joseph 103
ORR, John, Jr. 60
ORRIS, Robert 153 154
OSBORN, Dr. 130
PAGE, Enoch 92 102
  160 John G. 139
  Reuben 92
PAINE, John R. 131
  Sarah 131 Vienna
  120
PALFREY, Damaris 101
  John S. 101 Mr. 84
  Mrs. 101
PALMER, 124 D. S. 49
  Mr. 87 88 89
PARKE, Benjamin 198
PARKER, 81 Benjamin
  142 143 172 Bradley
  47 Hannah 171 Louis
  B. 47 Silas 215
PARKS, Mr. 84
PARMELEE, Catherine
  C. 49
PARSHLEY, Druzilla W.
  103
PARSONS, E. A. 165
  Solomon 165
PATRICK, W. 49
PATTEN, David 75

PATTEN, (continued)
  Melinda 70
PATTERSON, Captain 45
  Daniel 59 John 123
PEABODY, Elouisia 179
  Stephen 154
PEASLEE, Abigail 18
  Isreal 18 Moses 18
PEAVEY, Elizabeth 19
PECK, Samuel F. 64
PEEL, Robert 26
PERKINS, Harriet 140
  Jacob 100 140 John
  141 John, Jr. 141
  Jonathan 148 149
  Martha 148 149 Mary)
  102 Peter 103 Rev. Mr.
  150
PERLEY, J. G. 132
PERRY, Dr. 28 Mrs. 84
PERSON, Ira 100
PERVIER, Benjamin 150
PETTERSON, John 120
PHILADELPHIA, 88
PHILBRICK, Betsey 20
  33 Daniel 75 76
  Josiah 27 Peter 20
  33 Peter H. 20 33
  Sarah 27
PHILLIPS, Lieutenant
  Governor 189 190 Mr.
  190 Samuel 190
PHILLY, 88 89
PHINNEY, Elias 81
PICKENS, General 214
PICKERING, Anthony
  50 151 160 Levina
  70 Mary Ann 50
  Mary D. 50 151 160
PIERCE, Benjamin 36

NEW HAMPSHIRE PATRIOT & STATE GAZETTE 1835

PIERCE, (continued)
  Joshua D. 132
  Squire 64 Elijah 81
PILLSBURY, Benjamin
  38 Moses 59
PINDER, John H. 165
PINGREY, Jeremiah 50
PINGRY, Jeremiah 38
PINKNEY, Charles 60
  William 60
PIPER, Ebenezer 166
PITMAN, Abigail 72
PLACE, Amos 12
  Joshua 12
PLATH, 19
POND, 3
POOL, 46 Benjamin
  166 Elizabeth 166
  Sarah 166
POOR, Alonzo S. 197
  198 Moses 197
PORTER, 81 Reuben 74
PORTER'S Ferry, 54
POTTER, Isabella 24
  Miss 210 Robert 24
POWELL, Nancy 215
POWERS, 164 Abijah
  50 Olive 50 52
PRATT, Rev. Mr. 132
PRAY, Jenett 50
PRENTIS, Lydia Jane 70
PRESSEY, Ebenezer G.
  70
PRESSY, John S. 126
PRESTON, Mr. 200
PRICHARD, Capt. 183
  Mrs. 183 Sarah
  Elizabeth 37
PRINCE, Caleb 207
  Nancy 207

PRIOR, Capt. 3
PROCTOR, Indiana 197
  Moses 197
PROVOST, Mrs. 67
PURINGTON, Lydia 32
PUTNAM, Abrah 216
  Mary 216 Susan R.
  190
QUEEN of England 157
QUIMBY, Henry 58
  Jeremiah 58
  Timothy 70
QUINCY, Charles 71
  James 121
QUINN, John 111
RAND, Edwin 209 210
  Obed 19
RANDOLPH, John 162
  163 Mr. 174 175
RATHBURNE, J. P. 122
  123
RAY, P. P. 94 95
  Susan 94
RAYNOE, Esther 98
READ, Nancy 20
  Thomas 20
REED, Aaron K. 132
  General 35 Joseph
  132 Mary K. 179
  Robert 179 Sally
  198 S. 196 Samuel
  198
REID, 188 189
REMICK, James K. 119
REYNOLDS, Joseph 55
  56 Mrs. 55 56
  William 55 56
RICE, Mr. 84
RICHARDS, William 85
RICHARDSON, Deborah

NEW HAMPSHIRE PATRIOT & STATE GAZETTE 1835

RICHARDSON, (continued) 104 Elder 19 S. Q. 14
RICHELIUE, Cardinal 110
RIDDLE, Mary 101
RIPLEY, Hannah 37 James W. 133
RISING Sun Tavern, 85
ROBERTS, E. 89 Edmund 65 Ephraim 159 William S. 92
ROBEY, William H. H. N. 111
ROBIE, Thomas 199
ROBINSON, Abigail D. 19 Belinda R. 126 Drusilla 90 Josiah 159
ROBY, Elbridge Gerry 207 Ichabod 132 Lyman 132 William 207
ROCKWELL, Harry 183 Mr. 24
ROGERS, George S. 100 104 John 82 83 Nathaniel P. 100 104
ROLLING, Jonathan 197
ROMARINO, General 21
ROOT, General 129
ROSS, Captain 204 Daniel 209
ROWE, Daniel 126 140 Nathaniel 183
ROWELL, Jacob 160
ROWELL, Cyrus 31
RUGGLES, Judge 82
RUSSELL, Benjamin 126 Betsey 126 Dorcas 26

RUSSELL, (continued) Josiah 166 Moses 60 Mr. 194 Sumner 151
SAGE, Sylvester 83
SANBORN, Benjamin T. 151 Henry 198 Moses 31 Smith 9 Sophia 159
SARGENT, Betsey 76 Charles 43 Elizabeth 150 G. L. 8 120 Joseph 76 Martha 141 Samuel 33 Samuel, Jr. 8 William W. 58 William T. 8
SATINETT Factory, 24
SAUNDERS, Jacob 57 70 James 198
SAWYER, Moody U. 140
SCALES, Joseph W. 92
SEAVEY, Betsey 161 166 Nathaniel 103 Theodore 161 166
SENTER, Caroline 92 Caroline S. 71
SEVERANCE, Joanna 20
SEWARD, Josiah S. 166 Sarah 166
SEWELL, Alice S. 37
SHATTUCK, Enos 166
SHAW, E. 159 Micajah M. 98 Oliver 71 Sarah N. 92
SHED, Rebecca A. 111
SHELDON, Sylvester W. 124
SHEPARD, Elizabeth Emeline 23 Hannah S. 33
SHERBURNE, James

NEW HAMPSHIRE PATRIOT & STATE GAZETTE 1835

SHERBURNE,
  (continued)
  138
SHERIDAN, Joseph 82 83
SHIBBLES, Capt. 44 45
SHIRLEY, 162
SHUTE, Cynthia M. 179
SILSBY, Mary 159
SILVER, Mr. 73 Mrs. 73
SIMONDS, Abigail 31
SIMPSON, Captain 122
  Joseph S. 182
  Mehitable 182
  Reuben 92
SISE, E. F. 36
SKINNER, Barton 165
SLATER, Samuel 96 97 120
SLEEPER, Henry 120
  Moses 120
SMALL, Benjamin 49
  John III, 49
SMITH, Benjamin 49
  Bernard 216 C. 57
  Colonel 87 Eliza 71
  Eliza Jane 197
SMITH Hannah 19 J. J Jr., 80 Jane 150
  Jo 147 148 Joel B. 139 John Charles 165 Lydia 198 Mr. 24 Noah G. 103 Reuben 51 Rev. Mr. 19 Samuel 185 Samuel B. 179 Sarah 32 Sarah B. 150 William 150
SNOW, William 43
SONDERHAUSER S. Prince 62

SPARHAWK, Samuel 120
SPARKS, Jared 4
SPAULDING, Eunice 166
  John 166 Martin 159
SPENCER, David 45 46
SPOFFORD, Hiram 11
SPRINGER, Henry 126
ST. CLAIR, Ira 47
STANDISH, Samuel 5 6
STANIELS, John 48
STANLEY, Nehemiah, Jr. 11
STANNARD, Henry W. 90
STANWOOD, Jane 70
STAPLES, Joseph 161
STARK, Mary 132
STEELE, Caroline Matilda 132 Gurdon 132
STERLING, 172
STEVENS, 3 Eliza 215
  John M. 112 Moses, Jr. 9 Peter 93 Rachel 98 Rhoda 126 Samuel C. 141 Sarah H. 112 Smith N. 26
STEWARD, Agnes 112
  Charles 174 Oliver Sparhawk 120
STICKNEY, Hannah H. 70
STINSON, Cyrus 116
STOCKER, Kneeland 26
STOCKES, Gov. 135
STONE, John 157
  Phinehas 26 Sarah 26
STORRS, Rev. Mr. 126
STRONG, H. W. 104
SULLIVAN, 36 James 205 206 207

NEW HAMPSHIRE PATRIOT & STATE GAZETTE 1835

SUTHERLAND, D. 159
   David 59
SWAN, Mr. 170
SWARTWOUT, H. 118
SWEAT, Judith 141
   Paul 141
SWETT, Thomas 17
TABOR, James 179
TAGGANT, Thomas R. 103
TAGGARD, James 158
   John 158
TALLANT, Mary W. 49
TAPPAN, Elbridge G. 159
TARLETON, Charles 215
   Colonel 214 William 197
TASKER, Sophronia 104
TAYLOR, 124 Deborah 124 Mary 104 113
TENNY, Ruth Merriam 141
TETERVILLE, Benjamin 176
THATCHER, Rev. Mr. 111
THAYER, Ephraim 20 George 20 Maria 20
THEAKER, Capt. 46
THING, Dudley 99
THISTLE, Mr. 176
THOMAS, Isaih (2) 161
THOMPSON, 204
   Charles E. 120
   George Gilbert 100
   Hannah 99 James M. 132 Joseph II, 38 39
THORN, 143
THURSTON, Hannah 26

THURSTON, (continued)
   Stephen 26
TIBETS, Joel P. 111
TITUS, Mr. 152
TODD, 36 Amos 197
   Betsey 197
TOWNSEND, Charles 33
   Isaiah 146 John 33
TRACY, O. 103
TUCKER, Elizabeth M. 71 Levi 98 Levi, Jr. 98
TURENNE, Marshal 213
TURNER, Mary Ann 150
   William 59
TUTTLE, Charles 37
TUXBURY, Joseph, Jr. 13 Lualla 13
TYLER, 63 Mr. 183
   Mrs. 16 17 62 63 64
TYRON, Mrs. 107
UNDERHILL, 176
   Charles W. 120
UPHAM, Nathaniel G. 137 138
VAN ARSDALE, Mrs. 146
VAN BUREN, 115
VAN SANTFORD, Anthony 30 Mrs. 30
VAN VECHTEN, Lieutenant 5
VARNEY, Sarah 111
VARNUM, Peter 48
VENNARD, Andrew B. 71
WADLEIGH, James 216
WADSWORTH, Samuel 11

NEW HAMPSHIRE PATRIOT & STATE GAZETTE 1835

WAGNER, Ellen M. 179
  Miss 156
WAITE, John 151
  Rev. Mr. 179
WALDO, 18
WALDRON, Daniel B. 103
WALKER, B. 118
  Captain 117
  Emeline 149 John 19 Mrs. 113 Rachel 103
WALLACE, Adam 215
  Caroline 215
WALLIS, Edmund R. 31
  William 31
WALTON, 43
WARD, Charles H. S. 12 Elliot 135
  Samuel 109
WARE, Mary B. 159
WARING, John U. 14
WARREN, 47
WASHINGTON, 67 182
  Colonel 214 General 214 215 Mrs. 186
WASHINGTON House, 90
WATSON, Luman 144 O. 152 R. D. 84
WAY, Asa 38
WEARE, 36
WEATHERBY, Nathaniel 133
WEAVER, Mr. 124
WEBBER, Joanna M. 215
WEBSTER, Daniel 114 137 Joseph 92
  Samuel C. 179 191
WEED, Henry R. 31

WEED, (continued)
  Jacob 179
WEEKS, Stephen 150
WELLINGTON, Rev. Mr. 26
WELLS, Benedict 173
  Edward 154 Elmira 39 Nathaniel 154
  Peter 39 Phebe 173
  Thomas 215
WENDELL, Abraham 180 Ann Mary 180
WEST, 143 Noah 192
  Rev. Mr. 183
WESTGATE, N. W. 70
WETHERBEE, Luther 92
WETMORE, Nathaniel D. 19
WHEELER, A. 126 Asa 198 Eliza Jane 198)
  J. B. 150 M. B. 150 O. 118 Rufus 33 Sarah 150 Sarah W. 150
WHELLER, Joel 92
WHICHER, David 60
WHIPPLE, Commodore 122 123 John 58 Levi 215
WHITAKER, James 112
WHITCHER, Jonathan 207 Thomas 169
  William 32
WHITCOMB, John 60
WHITE, Josiah W. 131
  Judge 124
WHITEHOUSE, Enos 101 John C. 101 Mary 101
WHITING, Samuel 38
WHITNEY, Joshua 12

NEW HAMPSHIRE PATRIOT & STATE GAZETTE 1835

WHITNEY, (continued)
  L. 190 Mary 93
WHITTAKER, Mr. 120
WHITTIER, Isaac, Jr. 10
WIGGIN, Chase 165
WILCOMB, Capt. 56
WILDER, Harrison 175
  Henry S. 91 92 Martin
  91 Samuel L. 111
WILHELM, Mr. 152
WILLARD, Cyrus 59
WILLEY, Elizabeth
  111 Hannah 74
  Joseph 74
WILLIAMS, 26 Rev. Mr.
  26 Ruel 23
WILLIAMSON, John
  Allen 113 114
WILMARTH, Mr. 24
WILSON, 175 Benjamin
  166 George 171 James
  166 John 92 John
  Jay 92 Maria 172
  Mr. 172 Parna 92
  Rebecca 166 Thankful
  171 Theodore 142 143
WILSON, 175 Benjamin
  166 George 171
WILSON
  James W., II, 16
  John 92 John Jay
  92 Maria 172 Mr.
  172 Parna 92
  Rebecca 266
  Thankful 171
  Theodore 142 143
WINGATE, Mary Ann
  179
WINN, Cyrena L. 104
WINTER, Rev. Mr. 140

WISE, 3
WOOD, Henry 120
  Joseph 118
WOODBURY, George
  145 Jonathan 179
  Joshua E. 103 Susan
  E. 179
WOODMAN, Sally 70 71
  Samuel 59 70 71
WOODS, David 90
  J. 49 100
WOODWARD, Rosalind
  103
WORCESTER, Leonard
  197
WORKS, Elizabeth 165
WRIGHT, G. 118 George
  117 J. 190 Lieut. 117
  Stephen 197
WYMAN, Joseph 36
YORK, Betsy 150
  Clarissa 150
  Emeline 150 Lydia
  150
YOUNG, Belinda 11
  John Henry 33 50
  Joseph III, 12 Moses
  166 Mr. 44 63

www.ingramcontent.com/pod-product-compliance
Lightning Source LLC
Chambersburg PA
CBHW070311230426
43663CB00011B/2083